S0-CBI-617

SYNDROMES OF PSYCHOSIS

Syndromes of Psychosis

MAURICE LORR
Chief, Outpatient Psychiatric Research Laboratory,
Veterans Administration, Washington, D.C.

C. JAMES KLETT
Chief, Central Neuropsychiatric Research Laboratory,
Veterans Administration Hospital,
Perry Point, Maryland

DOUGLAS M. McNAIR
Research Psychologist and Assistant Chief,
Outpatient Psychiatric Research Laboratory,
Veterans Administration, Washington, D.C.

A Pergamon Press Book

THE MACMILLAN COMPANY
NEW YORK
1963

THE MACMILLAN COMPANY
60 Fifth Avenue
New York 11, N.Y.

This book is distributed by
THE MACMILLAN COMPANY
pursuant to a special arrangement with
PERGAMON PRESS INCORPORATED
New York, N.Y.

Library of Congress Catalog Card Number 63-19266

*Set in 11 on 12 Imprint by Santype Ltd, Salisbury, Wilts
and printed in Great Britain by Barnicotts Ltd, Taunton, Somerset*

CONTENTS

PREFACE

THIS monograph had its dual beginning in the pioneering studies of T.V. Moore on the fundamental psychotic syndromes and in the methodological developments of multiple factor analysis by L.L. Thurstone about the same time. More immediately the studies reported here arose out of the need for more precise and objective ways of assessing the effects of the newer drugs on hospitalized psychotics. The construction and development of the *Inpatient Multidimensional Psychiatric Scale* was in part motivated by such needs. Much of the data reported here was collected in connection with studies designed to evaluate the newer treatment modalities. While the need for adequate criteria of change provided the initial impetus for these studies there were other, broader motivations. The hope of establishing a more objective taxonomy for the so-called behavior disorders through the isolation of the major psychotic syndromes and psychotic types was the over-riding goal.

The book is written primarily for the researcher in the mental health field. The need for an objective and quantitative system for describing and classifying abnormal behavior is certainly patent. The book should prove useful as a supplementary text for graduate courses in advanced abnormal psychology or psychopathology. It is hoped that the practicing clinician, be he psychiatrist or psychologist, will find here much of interest and of use. The findings, we believe, will also prove to be provocative and of value to the personality theorist.

For the opportunity to conduct our research program and for an unhampered freedom for inquiry rarely equalled even in a University, we are especially grateful to the Research Service of the Veterans Administration. We are also appreciative of the continued and warm support of members of the Central Office Psychiatry, Neurology, and Psychology Service. They have provided encouragement and made available a broad range of professional support and patient data.

At various stages of the research, many of the findings and

techniques have been reported to the Executive Committee on Cooperative Studies in Psychiatry. We are indebted to these individuals for their critical comments and discussion. Clyde Lindley, formerly secretary of the Committee, was particularly helpful on administrative matters.

We are especially grateful to the following for their sage comments, advice on style, and their fortitude in reading the entire first draft of the manuscript: Thomas G. Andrews, Ph.D., Jacob Cohen, Ph.D., Eugene M. Caffey, Jr., M.D., Henry A. Davidson, M.D., Arnold P. Goldstein, Ph.D., Wayne H. Holtzman, Ph.D., Richard L. Jenkins, M.D., and Alex D. Pokorny, M.D., Gilbert Honigfeld, Ph.D., Paul McReynolds, Ph.D., and David Pearl, Ph.D., were also kind enough to read much of the manuscript. The manuscript was typed in several drafts by Mrs. Bertha D. Carter who was also helpful in tabling data, proofreading, and all of the little chores that are involved in writing a book.

M.L., C.J.K., D.M.McN.

CHAPTER 1

INTRODUCTION

THE MAJOR goals of this monograph are to present evidence for a set of ten psychotic syndromes and preliminary findings concerning six syndrome-based patient types. In addition hierarchical and circular orderings of the syndromes are proposed as two possible conceptual models for linking the syndromes together. A critique of current psychiatric classification explicates the need for and importance of research in this area. The methods and findings of recent investigations seeking to identify the psychotic syndromes are critically reviewed. Next presented is a description of the experiments leading to the measurement, isolation, and confirmation of ten psychotic syndromes. The last half of the book deals with the problem of type identification. Following a discussion of conceptual and methodological issues in typing, a report is given of a series of studies out of which six psychotic types emerged. The monograph concludes with a description of certain type difference dimensions.

The present chapter deals with the basic orientation and the guiding presuppositions of the investigators. The major concepts used in the report are defined. The principle approaches used for data collection and data analysis are also briefly described.

GUIDING PRESUPPOSITIONS

The experiments and the report as a whole are guided by certain assumptions and beliefs. An explicit statement of the investigators' orientation and philosophy is nearly always helpful to an understanding of why certain concepts and methods are chosen rather than others. A major presupposition is that an objective taxonomy is an important, if not necessary, first step for the study of the behavior disorders. A disorder must be recognized before it can be studied or its antecedents or causal determinants identified. Objective and accurate syndrome description is also essential to the establishment of diagnostic and treatment procedures adequate for dealing with such disorders. It is equally important for the proper evaluation of the effectiveness of the various therapeutic modalities. Cattell's (1940) dictum that nosology necessarily precedes etiology represents a similar assumption. Eysenck's (1953) equally strong assertion concerning the logical priority of classificatory knowledge to the identification of causes is well known.

In this connection it is interesting to note that in physical medicine recognition of a syndrome has often preceded discovery of its cause (Jenkins, 1953; Eysenck, 1960). Malaria, first distinguished by Hippocrates, was not only diagnosed but treated with a specific therapeutic agent for several hundred years before its origin was fully understood. Tuberculosis was described in the time of Christ but the tubercle bacillus was not identified until the nineteenth century. General paresis is another example of the recognition of a syndrome prior to the determination of its cause. Initially accepted as a psychiatric disorder it was later shown to be associated with central nervous system syphilis. These examples also illustrate that, in the absence of known etiology, syndrome description may constitute the only directly available knowledge of a disorder. Hence the importance of definitive syndrome description and measurement.

A neutral position is taken relative to the origin or nature of the psychoses or of "mental illness". Mental illness may be a "myth" (Szasz, 1961), a disease process, an interpersonal problem, the end product of a hereditary defect, or the resultant of a biochemical substance. It seemed best to proceed in a disinterested fashion towards examination and analysis of available facts. A broad spectrum of deviant behaviors are generally recognized and classed as indicators of the "psychoses". It is possible to isolate and measure the psychotic syndromes through an analysis of the deviant behaviors characterizing the group of disorders without resort to hypotheses as to their bases or antecedents. Once a set of diagnostic categories is established any particular explanatory hypotheses can be tested for fruitfulness and degree of fit.

THE BASIC CONCEPTS

The concepts of symptom, syndrome, and type are central to the investigation and thus require careful definition and some discussion of their meaning and use in the monograph.

A symptom is defined in an ordinary dictionary as any condition accompanying or resulting from a disease. Medical dictionaries refer to it as "a sign of any change either subjective or objective occurring during disease and serving to point out its nature and location". The term *symptom will hereafter be used to refer to any deviant behavior, posture, attitude, or verbalization accepted in ordinary usage by clinicians as an indicant of a functional psychosis.* The term will not be used as a sign or token of a disease. An alternative term for symptom was not used because no satisfactory substitute could be found and also because in actual practice psychiatrists and psychologists use the word much as it is defined above.

The medical dictionary defines a syndrome as "a set of symptoms which occur together; the sum of signs of any morbid state or disease." As used here the term will carry no implications of a morbid physical condition or disease. By a *syndrome is meant a group or complex of symptoms or deviant behaviors that tend with high frequency to occur together.* Consider the following descriptive signs: manifests taut, strained body musculature; moves or shifts about restlessly; fingers clothing; drums fingers or fiddles with objects; startled by noises; face or neck muscles twitch; palms are sweaty. Here is a group of behaviors that occur together, and thus represent a functional unity. The common element appears to be motor tension. Furthermore, the syndrome can be conceived of as present in all persons from a zero to a maximum degree; a continuous quantitative variable. A syndrome is analogous to the physical dimensions of a person like his height or weight and thus implies relative independence from other dimensions. The syndromes of psychosis, so considered, are thus the independent dimensions of these disorders. Collectively they constitute a description of what is meant by "psychosis".

Another implication of considerable importance to the dimensional conception of the syndromes is that they are not necessarily mutually exclusive or incompatible. At any given time an individual exhibits to some degree all of the syndromes simultaneously. One person is primarily depressed, withdrawn, and retarded motorically. Another individual is mainly suspicious, hostile, and hallucinating. But every individual can be measured and described in terms of all of the existing syndromes. This is comparable to a quantitative description of a person's basic abilities. Each person can be measured and assigned a score to represent his ability to reason, handle visual materials, comprehend word meanings, or deal with numerical processes. Just as the scores considered together constitute a profile of a person's abilities, so also can syndrome measures be used to represent a patient's behavior disorder.

The third concept of a patient type may now be considered. A syndrome is a group of symptoms that covary and are distinguished by some common characteristic. In contrast *a type is a class or group of persons having distinguishing characteristics in common that clearly set it apart from other groups.* The distinguishing attributes in the case of say, a character type such as hysteric, would be a range of scores on a set of defining personality profile elements. Analogously a psychotic type consists of a group of patients distinguished by a range of scores on all of the syndromes that define the psychotic disorders. For example, a Hostile Paranoid type (see Chapter 12) is a class of patients all of whom are distinguished by high scores on the syndromes of Paranoid Projection and Hostile Belligerence, and by relatively low scores on all remaining eight syndromes. The current psychiatric notion of a diagnostic category is similar to the concept of type as defined here.

METHODS OF INVESTIGATION AND ANALYSIS

A number of very different approaches to the differentiation and identification of the psychotic syndromes might have been taken. Basic data could have been collected by means of cognitive and perceptual tests, projective devices, self-report questionnaires, and biographical inventories. The basic procedure chosen instead was systematic observation of behaviors exhibited in a psychiatric interview. Observations were recorded in the form of judgments of degree recorded on a standardized rating schedule. There were several reasons why this approach was taken. First and most importantly, clinical observation provided the basis of currently recognized syndromes. Hence its use is most likely to yield data comparable to that on which the syndromes and categories are based. Second, tests and questionnaires are more appropriate when clinical groups and entities are already established. It is here assumed that the psychotic syndromes have not been established adequately. A further reason relates to the present status of psychological measurement in the behavior disorder field. Available measures are of doubtful value for they also depend on the current diagnostic schemas for validity and these are being questioned.

The rating schedule which comprised the date collection instrument was not an arbitrary or random assembly of rating scales. Ten carefully formulated hypotheses provided the basis for the construction of seventy-eight scales that led to a standardized instrument called the Inpatient Multidimensional Psychiatric Scale (IMPS). The hypotheses were framed on the bases of (a) careful study of *Mental Disorders* (Committee on Nomenclature, 1952); (b) a review of the literature on factor analytic studies of the syndromes; and (c) an examination of a broad sample of texts concerned with the psychotic disorders. The approach thus took into account current, clinically derived descriptions of the psychotic syndromes as well as the findings of factor analytic experiments.

To test for the existence of the postulated syndromes, the statistical method of factor analysis was applied. This procedure has as its specific object the isolation of functional unities or the confirmation of hypothesized dimensions (Harmon, 1960). Factor analysis is not unlike what a clinician does when he interviews a cross-section of psychiatric patients, notes that certain symptoms and behaviors tend to go together, attaches a label to the symptom complex, and says it's a syndrome. The major differences are that in factor analysis a specific mathematical model is applied, a larger number of symptoms are examined simultaneously for syndromes, the search is more rigorous and systematic, and finally the findings are more easily checked by other investigators.

SUMMARY

The objectives of the monograph are (1) to present evidence for ten statistically derived psychiatric syndromes; (2) to offer a preliminary definition of six psychotic types or classes; and (3) to present supporting data for two theoretical models of the organization of the syndromes.

The major guiding presupposition is that an objective taxonomy and nomenclature is an important step in the study of the behavior disorders.

Three basic concepts are defined without reference to a disease process. A symptom is regarded as a deviant behavior. A syndrome is defined as a group of symptoms that occur together and is conceptualized as a dimension present in all patients to some degree. A psychotic type is a class of patients all of whom are characterized by a range of scores on the psychiatric syndromes.

The method of data collection is systematic interview observation. Ten syndromes postulated on the basis of the best clinical and statistical evidence available are tested by the statistical method of factor analysis.

In the chapter to follow a critique of the status of current psychiatric nomenclature and nosology is presented.

CHAPTER 2

A CRITIQUE OF CURRENT PSYCHIATRIC CLASSIFICATION

THE FIRST chapter was concerned with the principal aims of the investigations reported. Several crucial concepts were defined and illustrated. In addition, some discussion was presented relative to the need and importance of an adequate nomenclature and taxonomic system. In the present chapter the current psychiatric diagnostic system is critically examined. Each of the claimed defects of the system is considered in turn. The major sources of difficulty in the official diagnostic and statistical manual are then broadly sketched.

CURRENT ATTITUDES

American psychiatry is currently dynamic in emphasis and its descriptive functions are regarded as sterile, outmoded, and unimportant. Consequently, the study of symptoms or manifest behaviors is apt to be disparaged as "undynamic" to the detriment of sound clinical observation and diagnosis (Grinker, Miller, Sabshin, Nunn, and Nunnally, 1961). Yet consider what happens to a patient just admitted to a hospital. His behavior and symptoms are noted or recorded. Then the psychiatrist or resident, following an interview, or the psychologist subsequent to projective test administration, formulates the patient's problem in psychodynamic terms. Usually these formulations are fixed and conventionalized, and derived from the literature (Grinker *et al.*). Although originally heuristic and imaginative, an explanatory hypothesis has become a cul-de-sac. Unless alternative explanatory hypotheses are developed, further advance is blocked. Thus an undynamic descriptive category is replaced by a stereotyped dynamic formulation.

Current attitudes towards formal diagnosis are based in part on the argument that the diagnostic categories do not really tell us anything about what is wrong with the patient. The same argument could, of course, be brought against any disorder prior to clarification of its origin and development. Additionally, as Meehl (1959) has cogently argued, there is no inconsistency between classifying a patient to a diagnostic group and also formulating an explanation of his motivations and defenses. However, "the demonstration that patients have psychodynamics, that they suffer with them . . . does *not* necessarily tell us what is the matter with them, that is, why they are patients" (Meehl, 1959; p. 107). Patients like other people have concerns about dependency, sex, hostility, and authority. The question is in what respects do the psychodynamics of patients differ from those of healthy populations?

The shift during the past forty years in the role and importance of descriptive diagnoses is very likely the resultant of two processes, one being the advent of Freudian dynamic psychiatry, and another being the change in the role of psychiatry in the hospital. When custodial and institutional care was the primary concern of the physician, major emphasis was placed on the classification of patients with respect to their symptoms and behavior. Diagnosis was considered to have certain implications for ward assignment as well as for duration and course within the hospital. Treatment being primarily custodial, the psychiatrist could exhibit his professional skills only in diagnosis. Stimulated by the newer theories concerning psychodynamics and defense mechanisms, by the introduction of the shock therapies, by prefrontal lobotomy, and by the tranquilizers, psychiatric interest shifted from diagnosis to therapy. It would seem that there is now a need for a fresh look and a reappraisal of formal diagnosis. There is need for a closer linking of diagnosis to psychodynamics on the one hand, and to constitutional, physiologic, and biochemical bases on the other.

THE USES OF PSYCHIATRIC DIAGNOSIS

Descriptive diagnosis has been disparaged as undynamic, criticized as unreliable, and inveighed against as lacking in predictive utility. Despite these criticisms, psychiatric diagnosis has a wide variety of administrative uses (Caveny, Wittson, Hunt, and

Herrman, 1955). The legal use of diagnosis for insanity determinations, for ascertaining criminal responsibility, and for declarations of incompetence is well known. Diagnosis is involved in commitment of patients to institutions, affords a basis for ward assignment, and is needed for institutional record keeping. Despite its fallibility, diagnosis furnishes a basis of rejection for military service and grounds for discharge from service following the appearance of deviant behavior. A veteran's eligibility for compensation and the extent of his compensation is also ascertained from his diagnostic label. Diagnoses are used to study rates of occurrence of disorders over time and from one culture to the next.

The use of diagnosis in therapy is equally widespread. Acceptance or rejection for psychotherapy and selection of the therapist is in part determined on the basis of whether the individual is diagnosed neurotic, psychotic, or a character disorder. In the hospital electric shock may be given the agitated and depressed patient, a tranquilizer administered to the tense schizophrenic, and an energizer prescribed for the retarded and depressed individual. Diagnosis even has a role in prevention. Individuals on the verge of psychosis may be aided by early diagnosis and preventive treatment. Diagnosis may also be important to a patient's family if it provides a reliable prognosis.

Also, despite its reputed unreliability, the diagnostic class is widely used in psychiatric and psychological research. Evaluations of new treatment modalities depend partly on diagnostic class information. Groups compared for treatment effects must be homogeneous in diagnosis. After all, neurotics do not behave like schizophrenics or psychopaths. Anyone engaged in test validation or test standardization recognizes the need to know what types of patients are being tested. Investigations concerned with defense mechanisms, personality structure, and motivation often utilize specified diagnostic groupings for comparative purposes.

In view of the expressed dissatisfaction with and claimed defects of the present nomenclature and diagnostic system, what accounts for such broad uses? For Meehl (1959), a basic argument for the utility of formal diagnosis as presently conceived is that there is sufficient etiological and prognostic homogeneity among patients belonging to a given diagnostic class that assignment of a patient to the class has implications which it is clinically unsound to ignore.

CLAIMED DEFECTS OF THE CURRENT NOMENCLATURE

Dissatisfaction with the current schema for classifying the behavior disorders has been widely expressed. Criticism ranges from Menninger's (1959) call for elimination of all "labeling" and Rotter's (1954) condemnation of the entire process to mild suggestions concerning the need for further refinement of the present system. The major claimed defects may be grouped as being concerned with (a) unreliability or disagreement among diagnosticians; (b) number of unclassifiable cases; and (c) lack of prognostic utility. A fourth claimed defect is that the system lends itself to abuse.

An important complaint is that diagnosticians disagree too much as to how a patient should be classified. Since the issue of reliability will be discussed in greater detail later only a brief summary is given here. Experiments indicate that reliability of classification, as judged by the extent of simple agreement, varies with the diagnostic group. Agreement among judges is highest for the broader more inclusive generic classes such as the organic disorders, the functional psychoses, and the neuroses. Agreement is much less for specific diagnoses. Also higher agreement levels are attained for the psychotic and organic disorders than for the psychoneuroses and the character disorders (Kreitman, 1961).

A closely related complaint is that the number of cases of a given diagnosis per 1000 admissions varies from hospital to hospital and may indeed vary markedly from one ward to the next (Pasamanick, Dinitz, and Lefton, 1959). Rates differ from one decade to the next, and from one culture to the next. Rates also vary enormously from admission to discharge (Jenkins, Bemiss, and Lorr, 1953). Perhaps it will suffice to say at this point that agreement, particularly for specific functional disorders, is typically below acceptable levels.

Other sources of dissatisfaction are the number of unclassifiable cases and the comparative rarity of typical cases. Consider for a moment what this means. Each diagnostic class is defined by several symptoms and a varying number of other criteria such as previous history, duration of illness, and type of onset. Inclusion or exclusion of a patient from a category is on an all-or-none basis.

For example, a patient is either classed as a Schizophrenic reaction, simple type, or he is not. He cannot be categorized into two classes at the same time. Inability to classify may result from the presence of the same symptoms in two categories (Freudenberg and Robertson, 1956). Involutional psychotic reaction, Psychotic depressive reaction, and Manic depressive reaction, depressed type, illustrate three such overlapping classes. Unclear or ambiguous definition of a category, would also make for difficulty in classification.

Perhaps the most important criticism is that the nosological system lacks predictive value or validity. This problem is discussed more extensively in a later section. Lack of validity means that psychiatrists often complain that the diagnostic classes convey little of value. They charge that diagnoses do not aid in treatment choice or that it fails to indicate duration and course of illness. A partial rebuttal to this criticism is that practical-use-criteria are unlimited. A scheme predictive for one purpose should not be expected to work for a different purpose. A set of categories predictive of response to tranquilizers may have no relation or relevance to response to psychotherapy. On the other hand it is expected that a classification scheme should at least be broadly predictive of future behavior and capable of suggesting important common psychological processes.

The fact of abuse of a method is, of course, no criticism but it is a matter of interest. Pokorny (1961) points out how practical needs creep into a diagnostic system and result in its abuse or misuse. Patients judged to require commitment are likely to be called psychotic. Clients selected for individual psychotherapy are labelled neurotic. At one time a majority of prisoners were automatically labelled psychopathic. Since schizophrenia implies a chronic illness of long duration, some psychiatrists avoid use of the label because of its implications. A diagnostic label often makes a person eligible to take a sick role in our society just as the witch-doctor label permits an individual certain freedoms not shared by his neighbors in another culture. The complaint that diagnoses evoke counter-behaviors in others may also be classed with abuses of the system and do not represent valid criticisms. For example, released psychotics are perceived as "mental patients" and are treated differently from ordinary individuals by neighbors, employers, and former friends. Destructive and combative patients are apt to be locked up, and conversely, "locked patients" are likely to be viewed as dangerous. The Menninger protest against labeling, while important therapeutically, is not logically relevant as an argument against diagnosis. The solution lies not in the elimination of the method but of the abuses.

BASIC CONCEPTUAL AMBIGUITIES

There are several confusions and ambiguities in the current nomenclature and classification system that account for many of the problems described. These confusions also reduce the system's practical utility and scientific value. Basically the problem is that the concepts of type, disease syndrome, and trait syndrome are confused. To fix ideas, it is first necessary to examine these three concepts.

A class in the generic sense consists of a group of entities (i.e., symptoms, objects, persons) that belong to it and are called members of the class. There are one or more defining criteria that must be satisfied for an entity to be a member; otherwise it is not a member.

Now consider a syndrome. In physical medicine the concept refers to a group of symptoms that occur together and indicate a disease. Take a disease like pneumonia. You either have or do not have the disease. You don't have a touch of pneumonia. Further, all or nearly all symptoms and signs of pneumonia must be present before the physician says the syndrome is present. Thus a syndrome in medicine is a special case of a class and is comprised of symptoms.

Next consider a "type" in the ordinary sense of the word. It also is a special case of a class and consists of persons manifesting a common set of characteristics. All members of the type "Schizoid Personality" (assuming such exists) have the same set of traits in common that differentiate them as a group from other types.

In psychiatry the concept of a syndrome is very different from that in medicine. It is much more like the notion of a personality trait. Both traits and syndromes are defined by a group of indicators that go together and have in common a tendency to behave in a particular way. Concepts like anxiety, depression, hostility, and paranoid tendency exemplify the kinds of syndromes that characterize the "disorders of psychogenic origin". It is not difficult to conceive of such syndromes as being present in all patients but manifested in different degrees in a particular patient. Given a means of measurement, each person can be described in terms of the degree to which he was excited, retarded, anxious, disoriented, or paranoid during an interview. The syndromes of the "behavior disorders" are thus like distinctive dimensions or measurable magnitudes. Each patient can have a position on each dimension. In short, it is believed that in psychiatry, the syndrome is not a class concept or qualitative category but should represent instead a continuous quantitative variable measurable in terms of degree.

Examination of *Mental Disorders* reveals that the diagnostic categories are regarded as classes. Psychiatric diagnosis consists essentially in assigning a patient to a single category although mixed diagnoses are recognized. Assignment is all-or-none, i.e., a patient either belongs or does not belong to a category. In light of the preceding discussion, which disorders appear to represent true disease syndromes? Which disorders might be regarded as "types" and which would more validly be conceptualized as trait syndromes?

A careful reading of the section on Psychotic Disorders supports the hypothesis that the psychoses are conceived as types or classes of patients even though some like Psychotic depression are trait syndromes. When the reader encounters the Psychophysiologic Autonomic and Visceral Disorders and the Psychoneurotic Disorders, he observes a change. Here the language clearly refers to symptom-groupings or syndromes, and not to patient groupings. For example, a Psychophysiologic skin reaction includes neurodermatosis, pruritis, atopic dermatitis, hyperhydrosis, and so forth. These are symptom complexes and not people. Anxiety reaction, conversion reaction, phobic reaction, and obsessive compulsive reaction represent trait syndromes. There is no difficulty in conceptualizing the Psychoneurotic Disorders as varying in degree. The Psychophysiologic reactions are more like disease syndromes. In the Personality Trait Disturbance there is a return to the type concept. The categories are said to apply to individuals or cases.

The disorders caused by or associated with impairment of brain tissue function, that is, the Acute and the Chronic Brain Disorders, resemble true disease categories. A "Chronic Brain syndrome associated with central nervous system syphilis" is analogous to pneumonia. Either you have this syndrome or you do not. No one thinks of these conditions as "types" for the emphasis is on the physical signs and symptoms and not on the individual.

In summary it can be said that the diagnostic manual has applied the concept of a class, borrowed from physical medicine, indifferently to three kinds of "mental disorders". Three distinguishable conceptualizations are actually involved. One is the class concept of a syndrome of disease which is properly applied to the acute and chronic brain disorders. The second concept, that of a type or group of patients, is applicable mainly to the Psychotic Disorders and to the Personality Disorders. The third concept, that of a trait syndrome, a continuous and quantitative variable, is relatively new. The Psychoneurotic Disorders are best considered in terms of the latter. The Psychophysiologic Disorders seem best categorized as disease syndromes as it is difficult to regard them as being present simultaneously like traits.

It is the present investigators' assumption that the Psychotic Disorders can be described both in terms of measurable syndromes as far as symptoms and deviant behaviors are concerned, and as types. The two approaches are both needed and are complementary. As far as the co-called Personality Disorders and the Psychoneuroses are concerned, it would appear worthwhile to establish the major syndromes experimentally. A typology, however, would require additional measures of interpersonal behavior and ego maturity (Sullivan, Grant, and Grant, 1957) to be successful. Whether there are "neurotic types" as well as "personality types" is a question to be explored clinically and experimentally.

THE PROBLEMS OF RELIABILITY AND OBJECTIVITY

What conditions must a procedure of observation, measurement, or classification satisfy to be regarded as objective and reliable? In what respects does the manual as represented in *Mental Disorders* fail to satisfy these requirements? To clarify the meaning of terms the concept of reliability is elaborated.

Any psychological measurement may be regarded as one observation among many that might be made. Analogously, an observer's rating is representative of similar observers' ratings. If there is sufficient agreement or consistency among observers then it is possible to generalize from the set of available judgments to a broader class of similar judgments. A coefficient of reliability is thus an index of the degree of generalizability from one or two observers' ratings to a universe of similar observers. It follows that the participating observers or diagnosticians should be representative of the universe of observers to which it is desired to generalize.

Anyone who has conducted investigations involving judgment in this area knows that it is unsafe to assume that all observers are skilled in their assigned tasks. Diagnosticians do not automatically recognize and differentiate among patient classes nor among behaviors characterizing the disorders presumably covered in training. For example, apathy is easily confused with depressive mood, and manneristic movement may be called a compulsive act. Many observers despite training forget about the dangers of overall impressions, use leading questions, and make unfounded higher order inferences from dynamic formulations. It may be argued that much of the supposed lack of agreement in allocating patients to classes is due to diagnostic error. In brief, lack of skill and experience on the part of the judges is no basis for inferring that a nosological class does not exist. Perhaps the proper inference is that observers make diagnostic mistakes.

Ideally the interview itself should be standardized as to aims, scope, length, and degree of structure. Psychiatric interviews may vary markedly in the behaviors evoked and in the reports elicited as a function of goals, the degree of non-directiveness or structure, and even the order of the questions asked. An interview that is primarily therapeutic in purpose may elicit markedly different kinds of information than a conventional diagnostic interview involving direct probing questions.

Of greatest importance to reliability is a set of standardized and behaviorally defined terms and concepts. It is in this respect especially that the present nomenclature is lacking. None of the symptoms descriptive of the various reactions are defined. Apparently it is assumed that all users can and will resort to psychiatric texts as needed or that clinicians are well informed on such terms. The specific classes are defined by adjectives and occasionally by technical terms (e.g., regressive behavior). The number of symptoms or other criteria required before a patient is properly allocated to a class is left unspecified. The weights to be assigned individual criteria for membership in a class, or the method of combination is left to the clinician's judgment. There should be no surprise that there is so little agreement but rather that there is so much! The definitions may be adequate for clinical practice but certainly they lack the precision required of a scientific instrument.

Studies of diagnosis have been reported by Boisen (1938), Ash (1949), Mehlman (1952), Hunt, Wittson, and Hunt (1953), Foulds (1955), Schmidt and Fonda (1956), and by Norris (1959). Recently Kreitman (1961) reviewed all available studies. Further research is being conducted by Beck (1962) and his colleagues which includes a study by Beck, Ward, Mendelson, Mock and Erbaugh (1962), and another by Ward, Beck, Mendelson, Mock, and Erbaugh (1962). In view of the recent summary by Kreitman only a short review need be presented here.

Concordance of diagnostic judgment has been found to vary according to the diagnostic group. Greater agreement is achieved when using broad generic categories of psychotic, neurotic, character disorder, and organic. High agreement levels are also attained for the more severely disturbed patient.

Kreitman's summary shows that concordance for broad groups over the studies reviewed is as follows:

Functional Psychoses	89–59%
Psychoneuroses	46–24%
Character Disorders	74–44%

Concordance of diagnosticians for specific diagnostic categories within major grouping is lower and ranges as follows:

Functional Psychoses	66–31%
Psychoneuroses	24–12%
Character Disorders	46%
Organic Disorders	74–53%

Ward *et al.* (1962) made a study of the reasons for diagnostic disagreement which is illuminating. Variation in the patient's behavior from interviewer to interviewer represents one small source of error. Variation in behavior of the interviewers was a major source of disagreement. Different interviewer techniques led to elicitation of different patient material. Interviewers also varied in their interpretation of the observed data and in the weights assigned to such data. The greatest source of disagreement lay in the inadequacies of the nosology. Excessively fine distinctions were required to categorize ambiguous clinical pictures. Forced choices were required when several entities appeared present. Finally, unclear criteria for specific diagnoses were a source of difficulty.

THE PROBLEM OF VALIDITY

How valid is the present nosological scheme? This is a basic question that has many answers. Earlier, it was indicated that the present diagnostic system is in fact widely used for administrative, therapeutic, and research purposes. However, nothing was said about its actual established value, although broad usage suggests that the users find the scheme has some merits.

To discuss the problem, it is first necessary to distinguish between several kinds of validity which are further discussed in Chapter 7. The first kind may be called construct validity. A construct is a supposed unitary trait or a syndrome, like an anxiety reaction, and is assumed to be reflected in behavior or test performance. It is a concept formally proposed with definition and limits explicitly related to empirical data. Types are also constructs and need to be established through scientific observation and comparison.

From the viewpoint of psychological measurement, as was argued earlier, the syndromes are in need of more precise definition and determination. The clinician typically collects observations on accidental samples from unspecified clinical populations. These observations are weighted subjectively in unknown ways to arrive at a judgment which is qualitative in nature and open to theoretical and other bias. The validity of the clinician's syndromes is checked qualitatively in terms of agreement between proposed symptom complexes and the anecdotal reports of other clinicians. As Cameron (1948) observes, changes in standard nomenclature are periodically modified by group decisions. Imagine a group of chemists assembling together to determine the number of elements

and their position in the periodic table by similar democratic processes.

Patient types can also be determined more rigorously than at present and checked on comparable samples for reproducibility. The defining variables for the psychotic types could consist of the major psychotic syndromes. A diagnostic type would then be defined as a class of persons distinguished by a certain range of syndrome scores. An Excited-Grandiose type, for instance, would be defined by specified high scores on syndromes measuring Excitement and Grandiosity, and low scores on all other syndromes (see Chapter 12).

A second type of validity may be described as external validity. Suppose relevant external criteria like therapeutic response, length of hospital stay, duration of illness, or Wechsler–Bellevue score are collected at the same time the patient's syndromes are assessed. A syndrome or a type will have external validity to the extent it is predictive or informative of the criteria just described. To what extent is the classification system in present use externally valid or useful for making the varied predictions desired? No effort will be made here to provide an answer. However, it should be pointed out that the success or failure of a classification scheme should not be based solely on its utility for decision-making or other practical ends. A more important basis for judging the validity of a system is its contribution to an understanding of the behavior disorders, and its fruitfulness in leading to antecedent or causal processes.

NEED FOR UNIFORM CRITERIA

Considering the state of knowledge in psychiatry, it would seem preferable to differentiate the functional disorders on the basis of observed behavior alone. Once the syndromes or types have been established experimentally and on a uniform basis, then additional principles of classification can be considered. Thus syndromes (or types), presently labeled differently on the basis of secondary criteria, would be recognized as identical. For example, it is likely that the categories of Manic depressive reaction, depressive type and Psychotic depressive reaction have a common profile of symptoms. Paranoia and Schizophrenic reaction, paranoid type could probably be combined.

At present, multiple criteria of classification are employed. In addition to current symptoms, premorbid personality, duration and course of illness, type of onset, and precipitating events are introduced as qualifying conditions for membership in a diagnostic category. The incomplete use of the defining criteria can be illustrated with the Psychotic Disorders. A previous history of symptoms defines Involutional psychotic reaction, the Manic depressive reactions, and Psychotic depression. Duration and course of illness contribute to the definition of all of the psychotic reactions except Psychotic depressive reaction, and the Schizophrenic reactions called paranoid type, chronic undifferentiated type, and schizo-affective type. Premorbid personality is mentioned only in connection with Involutional psychotic reaction. Type of onset is mentioned in connection with only two categories.

A related issue concerns the definitions of the major functional disorders. A psychotic disorder is said to be characterized by (a) personality disintegration; (b) failure to test and evaluate correctly external reality in various spheres; (c) failure to relate effectively to other people or to their work. No measures of disintegration, ability to evaluate external reality or to relate "effectively" to people are suggested, nor are these concepts defined. A Psychotic reaction is described as one in which "the personality in its struggle for adjustment to internal or external stresses utilizes severe affective disturbances, profound autism and withdrawal from reality, and formation of delusions and hallucinations" (*Mental Disorders*, 1952; p. 12). Similar explanatory definitions couched in terms of dynamic defense mechanisms are provided for the psychoneurotic and the other types of reactions. Granted that such definitions provide a plausible and provocative framework for the symptom descriptions that follow, they are nevertheless hypothetical in nature and as yet unproved. It would seem preferable to have a set of objective descriptive categories that are presented without a pseudo-support in theory. As presented in the manual, the general definitions of the reactions tend, if anything, to obscure the primary task of allocating individuals to specific categories on the basis of manifest behaviors, symptoms, and self-report data.

Following a searching examination of current research on the biochemical and physiological aspects of behavior, Chodoff (1960) concludes that definitive help on the classification of psychiatric conditions is not at present emerging from the laboratory. Even if other methods were available, behavior must still play an important role in psychiatric nosology. The establishment of criteria that have universal application among psychiatrists "will have an importance for psychiatry that can hardly be overstated" (Chodoff, 1960; p. 191).

SUMMARY

The current attitude of American Psychiatry is that formal diagnosis is sterile, undynamic, and unimportant. It is argued that diagnosis is not in conflict with psychodynamics and has an important role. The uses of psychiatric diagnoses for administrative, therapeutic, and research purposes is shown to be widespread. The claimed defects of the present nomenclature are reviewed. These are unreliability, number of unclassifiable cases, lack of predictive utility, and abuses. Several important conceptual confusions in the nomenclature are critically examined. It is argued that disease syndromes, psychiatric syndromes, and types are confused and should be differentiated. Various sources of unreliability are reviewed and the problem of validity is discussed.

CHAPTER 3

ISOLATION AND MEASUREMENT OF TEN PSYCHOTIC SYNDROMES

DEVELOPMENT of an objective standard measuring device was a necessary first step in the establishment of the major syndromes observable in psychotics and in the evolution of a plausible classificatory scheme. This chapter describes the construction and development of such a measuring instrument and the isolation of ten psychotic syndromes. None of the available rating schedules and behavior inventories appeared adequate as judged by criteria shortly to be made explicit.

BACKGROUND

Rating scales and behavior inventories for use with psychiatric patients have proliferated concurrently with the increased interest in research on mental health problems and with the consequent need for measuring devices. One of the earliest reported forms, still in use, is the Phipps Psychiatric Clinic Behavior Chart developed at the turn of the century (Kempf, 1915). Another is Plant's (1922) scheme for rating patient ward conduct. The Moore (1933) scales were perhaps the first set designed with some understanding of psychometric principles.

Soon after World War II a number of forms appeared. They were stimulated by a need for evaluating patient change, by the advent of prefrontal lobotomy as a treatment modality, and by the advances made in psychometric techniques such as factor analysis. The Psychiatric Rating Scale (Wittenborn, 1951) and the Multidimensional Scale for Rating Psychiatric Patients (Lorr, 1953) are two representatives of standardized rating schedules. Both are designed for use by professional personnel and both draw on interview and ward observations. Most other devices as, for example, the MACC Behavioral Adjustment Scale (Ellsworth, 1957) and the L-M Fergus Falls Behavior Rating Sheet (Lucero and Meyer, 1951), are concerned with ward and hospital behavior and are designed for completion by psychiatric aides and nurses. A different approach is taken in the pioneering Hospital Adjustment Scale (McReynolds, Ballachey, and Ferguson, 1952). To simplify the rating task for aides and nurses, McReynolds assembled a list of behavioral statements descriptive of hospital adjustment. The rater simply indicates whether the behavior was or was not characteristic of the patient. Since then there have appeared such behavioral inventories as the Psychotic Reaction Profile (Lorr, O'Connor and Stafford, 1960) and the Palo Alto Group Psychotherapy Scale (Finney, 1957).

The use of adjectives to describe patient behavior and symptoms has been less common than the use of scales or inventories. The reason undoubtedly lies in the tremendous variation in meanings connoted by an adjective and the consequent reduction in interrater agreement. Typically the various adjectives are left undefined and accordingly are ambiguous. An example is the Phipps Clinic Behavior Chart which is simply a set of adjectives to be checked as present or absent. The psychiatric rating scale developed by Malamud and Sands (1947) consists of sets of scaled adjectives. For example one scale runs as follows: Despondent, Woeful, Unhappy, and None of the above. Single terms are defined in detail. A difficulty is that appropriate adjectives to define a particular step in a scale are often not available in the language. It would appear more effective to eliminate the adjectives and to use the definitional descriptions instead.

A recent review (Lorr, 1960) listed nineteen published rating schedules. Although only the more carefully developed devices are described, fewer than half of these provided manuals for scoring or normative information. The nine behavior inventories listed are designed to measure such concepts as hospital adjustment, mental status, and ward behavior. Most are relatively primitive devices from the standpoint of both psychological and measurement theory.

It seems clear that the most fruitful direction for the development of scales is toward the construction of instruments that can advance psychological understanding of an area. Tools that assist in administrative decision-making are useful but usually are of little scientific value. The need is for measurement devices that possess some degree of generality beyond the specific uses of the moment. As Marschack (1954) and Loevinger (1957) have argued, devices designed to effect immediate decisions contribute no more to a field like psychology than rules for boiling an egg contribute to the science of chemistry.

THE RESEARCH PLAN

As indicated earlier our aims were twofold. The principal goal was to identify the syndromes (dimensions) of psychotic behavior. In order to achieve this objective it was first necessary to construct an adequate set of measures. The clinical and factor analysis literature was searched and ten psychotic syndromes were postulated. A preliminary rating schedule, the Inpatient Multidimensional Psychiatric Scale (IMPS) was devised. Descriptive data were collected on a substantial sample. The scales were then examined for reliability, correlated, factored, and tested for the existence of the ten syndromes. Next the preliminary form of IMPS was revised, and data were collected from a second norm sample. Once again the correlations among the scales were analyzed to test for the postulated syndromes. These in brief were the procedures followed. The remainder of the chapter will be devoted to the details of the two experiments.

THE HYPOTHESIZED SYNDROMES

Ten syndromes were hypothesized as major guides in the construction of scale variables included in IMPS. Most were derived from prior factor analyses reported by Degan (1952), Wittenborn (1951), Guertin (1952), and Lorr (1955). However, all of the symptom complexes appraised here were restricted to those determinable within the limits and framework of an interview. The names given the syndromes are somewhat arbitrary, but the intent is to convey the underlying response pattern. For convenience the syndromes are also identified by three letters. Use was made either of the first three letters of a name or of three consonants in the name. Each syndrome postulated is described below.

A. *Excitement* (*EXC*). The defining characteristics are excess and acceleration of speech and motor activity. Mood level and self-esteem are high. Restraint in expression of emotion and feeling is lacking.

B. *Hostile Belligerence* (*HOS*). Manifest and verbal hostility, expressions of resentment, and an attitude of suspicion of others' intentions are characteristic of the syndrome. There is much complaining and irritability and a tendency to blame others for their difficulties.

C. *Paranoid Projection* (*PAR*). This syndrome is defined by morbid beliefs that attribute hostility, persecution, and even a controlling influence to others.

D. *Grandiose Expansiveness* (*GRN*). This syndrome is marked by delusions of grandeur, an attitude of self-importance, and at times, a conviction of having a divine mission.

E. *Perceptual Distortion* (*PCP*). This grouping is characterized by hallucinations that threaten, accuse, demand, or extol.

F. *Anxious Intropunitiveness* (*INP*). This syndrome is marked by anxiety, fears, lowered mood level, and self-depreciation. Guilt, remorse, and self-blame for real or imagined faults are equally prominent.

G. *Retardation and Apathy* (*RTD*). The defining behaviors are slowed and reduced motor activity, ideation, and speech. Apathy and disinterest are also characteristic.

H. *Disorientation* (*DIS*). This symptom cluster represents a measure of disorientation for time, place, and person.

I. *Motor Disturbance* (*MTR*). Rigid bizarre postures, grimacing, and repetitive movements are the main behaviors defining this syndrome.

J. *Conceptual Disorganization* (*CNP*). Irrelevant, incoherent, and rambling speech as well as neologisms and stereotyped use of words and phrases characterize this syndrome.

In constructing the syndromes reference was made to the Diagnostic and Statistical Manual of the *Mental Disorders*. However, actual formulation was based primarily on empirical analyses. The goal was to evolve a set of symptom clusters operationally defined and unhampered by theoretical and nosological biases.

THE KINDS OF VARIABLES MEASURED

The variables selected to define each of the various symptom complexes were restricted to (a) behaviors manifested and observable in the interview; (b) ratable verbalizations concerning current feelings, thoughts, and beliefs; (c) answers given in response to orientation questions. The manifest behaviors rated are exemplified in such activities as rate and quantity of speech, emotional expression, and body posture. Expressions of guilt, self-blame, and suspicion are illustrative of verbalizations regarded as ratable. Included among self-reports recorded were statements concerning voices heard and beliefs such as being persecuted or talked about.

Since the objective here was to measure currently discernible behavior, feeling, and attitudes, information based on prior ward and interview data was specifically excluded. In other words the period of observation was restricted to the interview. The major advantages are first, better experimental control of what is being measured and second, a sounder basis for measuring change. If observations are not so restricted it is not possible to say what behaviors have changed over a specified period. It is certainly true that there are consequent losses. A patient may have admitted hearing voices in an earlier interview but does not do so in the test interview. On the other hand there is a greater gain in precision. Scales based on social history were also excluded. This exclusion in no way denies nor minimizes the importance of social history. Biographical inventories and social histories have been and are useful devices and possibly one could be constructed as a base for a diagnostic system. However, in view of the present purpose social history items have no role.

Also excluded were inferences based on dynamic interpretations. If, for instance, a patient is overly polite and deferent, some judges conclude that the patient is "really" hostile. This inference may be correct but it does not describe the phenotypic or manifest characteristics of the individual which are desired. Sound accurate phenotypic description was the goal and not dynamics. As in the case of social history, the exclusion (as much as feasible) of inference and dynamics implies no derogation. The view taken here is that dynamic inferences are most valid when based on accurate description. As ordinarily made, inferential judgments are distinctly less reliable than those based on manifest behaviors.

THE STANDARD OF REFERENCE

A rater must be provided a reference or standard if he is to make a judgment of the degree to which a trait is manifested. Suppose a rater is asked whether a patient's speech is slowed, deliberate, or labored. His ratings will depend upon whether the reference group consists of other hospitalized patients or normal individuals out of a hospital. The standard of comparison chosen was the typical behavior of a normal individual of comparable age, sex, and social class. The inter-rater reliabilities later obtained tend to justify this choice. Use of the hospital population as a standard was rejected because such populations vary markedly; also individual raters may be confined in their daily observations to very select portions of these populations. A normal reference group was for these reasons judged most likely to yield uniformly comparable judgments.

GUIDING CRITERIA IN SCALE WRITING

In preparation for the construction of IMPS a group of forty clinical psychologists were sent a brief questionnaire concerned with the Multidimensional Scale for Rating Psychiatric Patients (MSRPP), the predecessor of IMPS. Inquiry was made about ambiguities in wording, difficulties in rating, possible omissions of symptoms, and similar matters. This information, with other available scales, and certain psychometric principles, led to the development of a guiding set of criteria for constructing the scales.

(1) Each scale should, as far as possible, describe a single variable or unidimensional continuum of behavior. One of the more common defects in scale writing is the inadvertent inclusion of two or more variables for appraisal. A scale designed to measure dejection should not make reference to anxiousness unless there is evidence that the two are the same variable. Adequate continua can be constructed by stripping down modifiers to a minimum and providing concise behavioral definitions. The practice of hypothesizing a set of constructs in advance is especially helpful. Scale writing can then be organized around these constructs.

(2) Related but nonequivalent scales should be included. The need for some redundancy seems not to be recognized by many who work in this field. How many clinicians would think of testing a child's ability to do arithmetic by administering one problem? Surely, since chance plays so great a role in such an operation, several problems are needed. Yet clinicians often seek to measure

major concepts with single scales. Every measurement includes random error as well as factors peculiar to its form or style. Thus it is ordinary practice in psychological measurement to include a range of items all designed to tap the same basic variables. This procedure is especially important in describing individual behavior where relatively little is known concerning the construct postulated. To illustrate, Anxious Intropunitiveness includes not only self-depreciation but also lowered mood, guilt and remorse, and obsessive thinking. A single scale approach to concepts cannot duplicate this variation in behaviors.

(3) The scales should be unipolar continua. A unipolar variable extends from a value of zero to a maximum value. In contrast a bipolar variable extends from an extreme value through zero to an extreme opposite. A scale of depression is an example of the first while a depression versus elation scale is an illustration of a bipolar continuum. Logical and verbal opposites unhappily are not necessarily psychological opposites. A behavioral opposition must exist and not merely an opposition in meaning. Since true behavior opposites will have high negative correlations, it is best to establish bipolarity by means of empirical data. A trait may have no opposite or it may have several alternatives. For example, the opposite of exhibitionism need not be self-effacement; it may be indifference to attention. The absence of dominance need not mean submission; rebellion and autonomy may be the alternative behaviors exhibited.

(4) The scale variables and dichotomous (e.g., Yes or No) items should possess discriminatory validity. A useful measure must differentiate among individuals. This implies that the distribution of ratings should cover all scale values. In the case of a dichotomous item the percentage in the larger category should not be more than 90 and the percentage in the smaller category should not be less than 10. In general, dichotomous items that split the population in half afford the maximum discrimination. If all patients or no patients are characterized by a given trait there is no differentiation. A common misconception is that an item with high rater agreement is necessarily a good item. Suppose that within a study all patients are rated as being "nonsoilers". The item is nevertheless useless since it fails to separate one patient from the next.

(5) Scales should be independent of, or relatively impervious to, such rater biases as theoretical persuasion, value scheme, or moral code. One effective way of avoiding this problem is to eschew technical terminlology. Illustrative are words such as regression, superego strength, primary process, introjection, narcissism, and acting-out. Even psychiatric terms such as compulsion, hallucination, mannerisms, blocking, systematized delusion, and withdrawal require careful definition if used. Psychologists and psychiatrists may differ markedly in their use of such concepts. To reduce bias the language of the scale must be kept clear and simple.

ANCHORING THE SCALE

Another problem faced in developing a rating instrument is establishing a suitable scale of measurement. Measurement is used here to refer to the process by which the scale or yardstick is developed and not to its application once it has been constructed. This distinction should be kept in mind in order not to confuse the two processes. Use of a scale to "measure" an attribute of a person involves a fairly simple process of comparing the quantity to be measured with the scale steps. Let us define measurement of an attribute as an operation involving the assignment of numbers to objects to represent the attribute (Torgerson, 1958). Basically the procedure is to assign numbers in such a way as to reflect a one-to-one correspondence between the characteristics of the numbers and the corresponding relations between the quantities of the attribute to be measured.

While all scales have the property of order, their steps may not be equal intervals. On the basis of this property, scales may be classed as ordinal or interval. Either type of scale may or may not have a natural origin or zero point. In an ordinal scale the numbers are so assigned to particular cases of the attribute that the order of the numbers corresponds to the order of magnitude of the particular cases. Examples of ordinal scales are judged loudness of speech and judged elevation in mood. An ordinal scale with a natural origin has the additional restriction that the number zero is assigned to a zero amount of the attribute. For an interval scale, the size of the differences between pairs of numbers corresponds to the distance between corresponding pairs of amounts of the attribute.

In constructing the scales employed in IMPS it was decided to utilize certain findings reported by Cliff (1959). He noted that adverbs like "mildly", "moderately", and "extremely", appear to have multiplicative properties. These words serve to stretch or compress the meanings of other words like adjectives. Consider the effects on adjectives like anxious or sad when combined with "mildly" or "markedly". The adverbs of intensity act as though they multiply the intensity of adjectives they modify.

Cliff, therefore, made the assumption that a number is associated with each adjective, and a separate number associated with each adverb. Thus the intensity of an adverb--adjective combination is the product of these two numbers. Furthermore, the intensity of the adjective used alone is the number associated with it when used in combination. In accordance with these hypotheses, Cliff had three groups of subjects rate the combinations of nine intensity adverbs with fifteen evaluative adjectives on a favorable-unfavorable dimension. By various procedures the degree of correspondence between data and hypotheses were found to be close in all three groups. Cliff concluded that common adverbs of degree act as though they multiply the intensity of adjectives they modify. These principles were utilized in anchoring IMPS scales.

To select a group of nine adverbs about the same "distance" apart, a group of forty adverbs of degree were scaled by the method of successive intervals. Nine adverbs roughly the same "distance" apart were then selected to define a crude interval scale of intensity for forty-five scales. The adverbs chosen were: not at all, very slightly, a little, mildly, moderately, quite a bit, distinctly, markedly, and extremely. By similar procedures a frequency scale was defined by the following: not at all, once or twice, a few times, fairly often, and very often.

THE METHOD OF FACTOR ANALYSIS

Since factor analysis is a principal tool in the experiments to be reported a brief description is necessary.

Earlier in Chapter 2 it was pointed out that a syndrome was basically a statistical concept. It represents a highly correlated set of symptoms or behaviors. When a psychiatrist identifies a syndrome on the basis of his observations on a sample of patients he is engaging in an arm-chair form of factor analysis. He detects certain functional unities and gives them names. Factor analysis is simply a more rigorous way of examining the covariations and the similarities among symptoms evidenced in their intercorrelations. The procedure serves to isolate all relatively independent symptom grouping in a body of data in an objective fashion. Factor analysis is more rigorous and systematic than the clinician because a specific mathematical model is assumed, relatively objective measures are employed, and the data are collected on specific samples.

Speaking more generally, factor analysis is a statistical method for reducing a set of variables to a smaller number of independent categories. Ordinarily this is done through an analysis of the correlations among the variables studied. As a scientific method, factor analysis is of interest because it is a means of discovering one or more unitary traits and abilities. But more importantly the method may be used to test hypotheses concerning functional unities suggested by experience, experiment, or theoretical considerations.

Generally there are two steps involved in a factor analysis. The first step calls for a solution of the minimum number of factors which can account for the empirically obtained correlations. However, there is a basic indeterminacy in the factor problem; any given correlation matrix may be factored in an infinite number of ways. This leads to the second step. The condensed statistical description of the test variables must be transformed mathematically from an arbitrary meaningless set to one that is unique in some sense and psychologically "meaningful" or interpretable. Unique is here used to mean that application of the transformation and the criteria of fit yields the same result no matter who applies it.

At this point a problem arises in choice of a model or form of solution for interpreting a particular set of data. This problem arises in any field of science where observed data are subject to alternative interpretations. A model may be constructed by one investigator and then tested for degree of fit to the data. Yet another model may be devised, also compatible with the data, that provides an equally good fit. A well-known illustration is found in astronomy. The Ptolemaic and Copernican theories describe the motions of the planets with equal accuracy. The final choice of a model, if there is one, depends upon the fruitfulness of the model for further investigations, its simplicity and plausibility, and its consistency with available theory.

The model chosen here is called the multiple factor model and an important basis for it is the concept technically known as "simple structure". The psychological interpretation of the concept is that not all traits are measured by a test variable. Each test in the battery of measures involves at most only one or two of the group factors needed to account for the correlations among the test battery as a whole. Another way of describing the concept is to consider a table or matrix in which the rows represent tests and the columns represent factors. In each row are given the weights or correlations of the test with each of the factors. When simple structure is achieved each row has at least one zero, each column has at least r zeros (r being the number of factors), and for every pair of columns of the factor matrix there is only a small number of tests with sizable values in both columns (Harman, 1960, Chapter 6).

Even if the criteria of simple structure are employed a choice must also be made between an "orthogonal" and an "oblique" reference system. In other words the tests can be described in terms of uncorrelated or correlated common factors. Oblique or correlated factors have greater acceptance among researchers employing such analysis because it is difficult to believe that interacting psychological variables especially in the personality and psychiatric domain are really uncorrelated. Certainly published analyses lead one to conclude that a correlated reference system results in personality constructs and syndromes that psychologically make more sense. Simple structure fit to data is also considerably superior for oblique factors as compared to an orthogonal reference system (Cattell and Dickman, 1962). Another reason for preferring an oblique model lies in the more general factors descriptive of the correlations obtaining among the first-order factors. The first-order factor correlations in turn may be factored to yield "second-order" factors. These higher order factors provide definitions of more inclusive response unities than do the first-order. Finally there is some evidence that oblique factors are more likely to be invariant or experimentally replicable under differing experimental conditions; repeated analyses tend to yield the same pattern of values for the correlations of tests with factors regardless of the combination of tests in which they are presented.

THE INITIAL EXPERIMENT

The first experimental form of IMPS consisted of forty-two nine-point scales and forty-eight dichotomous items. Ratings were collected on four to ten male patients in each of forty-seven federal, state, and private hospitals. A team consisting of an interviewer and a silent observer independently rated each patient. Each of the 296 patients was selected as a representative of one of the following patterns: anxiously depressed, markedly delusional, hostile-belligerent, well integrated but paranoid, apathetic and unmotivated, markedly hallucinated, disorganized in thought processes, retarded and depressed, and manic-excited. The selection of these representatives was usually made by a professional person other than the raters. The intent of this type of stratified sampling procedure was to assure the presence of all known sources of patient variation.

About half of the variables were nine-value scales and the other half were two-value scales. For various technical reasons each of the nine-point scales was dichotomized at the median of the combined rater scores and the individual scores were coded in dichotomous form. Product–moment correlations among the seventy-seven variables selected for the analysis were then computed. A multiple group factoring process was utilized (Guttman, 1952). The first step was to prepare a 77×9 *a priori* simple structure weight matrix consisting of unit and zero weights. The nine columns represented the nine syndromes hypothesized in the first study, while the seventy-seven scales were represented by the rows. Each scale variable was predicted to have its only substantial correlation with one syndrome. This was done by placing a unit weight in the appropriate column and zeros in all other positions in the row. Nine variables were left unassigned to any syndrome. By application of the weight matrix nine syndromes were extracted simultaneously. The residuals showed no evidence for additional factors except for Disorientation. The seven items defining this syndrome had been combined into a single score and thus could not be used to define a separate column. The systematically low correlations of Disorientation with all syndromes, i.e., its low common factor variance, indicated that this group defined an independent syndrome. The final step was to transform the orthogonal factors obtained into a correlated set approximating simple structure.

The criterion chosen for confirmation of the postulated syndromes was that each defining symptom have its only significant correlation (arbitrarily set at 0.30) on the syndrome to which it was allocated. Examination of the transformed syndrome matrix showed that only in one instance did the highest correlation for a variable fall into a column to which it was not allocated. Five of the behaviors defining Conceptual Disorganization, although located as predicted, emerged with correlations less than 0.30. The major reason seemed to be that few relatively inaccessible incoherent patients were represented in the sample; hence the syndrome was defined weakly. A fuller description of the findings is given elsewhere (Lorr, McNair, Klett, and Lasky, 1962). The major findings are also displayed in the tables of Chapters 4 and 5.

THE NORMATIVE STUDY

The initial experimental form was revised on the basis of a study of inter-rater item reliabilities, the initial factor analysis findings, and a number of other considerations. The revised form consisted of forty-six nine-value intensity scales, thirteen five-value frequency scales, and nineteen Yes–No items. The seventy-eight variable form was then employed in obtaining a sample on which score norms, i.e., centile ranks, could be based. The norm sample was comprised of a nucleus of 207 cases selected to secure representation of all likely sources of individual differences in the manner previously described. To this nucleus, ratings of 359 newly admitted schizophrenics were added. The data for the latter were collected in connection with a nation-wide study of the effects of tranquilizers. In all, 566 patients from forty-four private, state, and federal hospitals were included in the sample. In each instance a team consisting of an interviewer and a non-participating observer independently rated each patient. Both psychiatrists and psychologists were represented as raters or observers and many were not only trained clinicians but researchers as well.

Product-moment correlations among the seventy-eight scale variables were next obtained. A 65×10 weight matrix was prepared in which each of sixty-five variables was allocated to one of ten syndromes. One variable, attitude of superiority, was allocated both to Excitement and to Grandiose Expansiveness. The thirteen variables about which there was uncertainty were not used in defining any of the syndromes but their correlations with the syndromes were determined later. Application of the multiple group method of factor extraction yielded ten factors which were easily transformed to a correlated framework.

To what degree were the predictions made for each scale confirmed? The standard used was that the highest correlation should be with the syndrome to which it belonged and no other correlation should be greater than ± 0.25. A count showed that ten of the sixty-five variables had one other correlation above ± 0.25 but only in two instances was the higher correlation with a syndrome other than that predicted. One test of the goodness of fit to simple structure is the number of non-vanishing correlations (>0.25) in a factor column excluding the variables defining the factor. These should be as few as possible. The number exceeding ± 0.25 in the various columns was 2, 1, 1, 2, 1, 3, 1, 1, 0, and 0.

THE ISOLATED SYNDROMES

The ten syndromes isolated will now be described. Only those variables that correlate 0.26 or higher with a syndrome are listed. Whenever a variable j has a correlation r_{jp} above this value with a syndrome p other than the one being described, this syndrome and the correlation of the variable with it will be given. Since the actual scale questions are lengthy, brief descriptive phrases are presented instead. It should be understood that the scales presented in the Appendix were actually used in the study and not these brief descriptions.

The first syndrome represents Excitement (EXC). It is characterized by increased motor activity, elevated mood and self-attitude, and by a lack of restraint in expression of feeling.

No.	Variable	r_{jp}
7	Expresses feeling without restraint	0.40
9	Manifests speech that is hurried	0.58
12	Exhibits an elevation in mood	0.50
15	Exhibits an attitude of superiority	0.34
17	Dramatizes self or symptoms	0.50
20	Manifests loud and boisterous speech	0.49
26	Exhibits overactivity, restlessness	0.38
35	Exhibits an excess of speech	0.58
37	Tries to dominate the interview	0.55

The syndrome labeled Paranoid Projection (PAR) is defined by beliefs or convictions that attribute to others a hostile, persecutory, or controlling intent.

No.	Variable	r_{jp}
44	Preoccupied with delusional beliefs	0.44
59	Believes people talk about him	0.52
60	Believes he is being persecuted	0.41 (HOS 0.47)
61	Believes people conspire against him	0.53 (HOS 0.28)
62	Believes people control his actions	0.54
63	Believes external forces influence him	0.38

An associated syndrome is Hostile Belligerence (HOS). The behavior complex extends from hostile attitude, through multiple complaints, to bitterness and resentment.

No.	Variable	r_{jp}
5	Verbally expresses feelings of hostility	0.76
11	Expresses an attitude of disdain	0.42 (EXC 0.29)
18	Manifests a hostile, sullen attitude	0.74
25	Manifests irritability and grouchiness	0.65
28	Tends to blame others for problems	0.54 (PAR 0.27)
32	Expresses feelings of resentment	0.70
34	Complains and finds fault	0.61
36	Expresses suspicion of people	0.58 (PAR 0.36)

Also related to PAR is the syndrome of Perceptual Distortion (PCP). In early studies such as reported by Moore (1933), the symptom cluster was defined non-specifically by auditory, visual and other hallucinations. In the IMPS Studies, items descriptive of content were introduced. As a consequence the syndrome has broadened and become more meaningful.

No.	Variable	r_{jp}
45	Distressed by hallucinatory voices	0.54
53	Hears voices that accuse or blame	0.65
55	Hears voices that threaten punishment	0.72

No.	Variable	r_{jp}
56	Hears hortatory voices	0.52
57	Sees visions	0.42
58	Reports tactual, gustatory or olfactory hallucinations	0.44
67	Familiar things and people seem changed	0.24

The next syndrome, called Anxious Intropunitiveness (INP), has a resemblance to the psychiatric disorder of Involutional Psychotic Reaction. The major elements that characterize this functional unity are self-directed blame or hostility against the self, lowered mood level, and a variety of anxieties. Interestingly, this is the only syndrome that correlates (negatively) with lack of insight. Intropunitive patients thus are not typically lacking in insight.

No.	Variable	r_{jp}
14	Tends to blame or condemn self	0.74
21	Anxious about specific matters	0.65
24	Apprehensive re vague future events	0.68
27	Exhibits an attitude of self-depreciation	0.80
29	Manifests a depressed mood	0.68 (RTD 0.26)
31	Expresses feelings of guilt and remorse	0.71
39	Does not show a lack of insight	0.44
40	Preoccupied by suicidal thoughts	0.61
41	Preoccupied by unwanted ideas	0.46
42	Preoccupied by specific fears	0.40
66	Believes he is unworthy, sinful	0.62

The syndrome of Retardation and Apathy (RTD) with some association with INP is rather well defined. The elements that characterize it are slowed motor behavior, reduced general reactivity, and apathy. An interesting feature is that the depression variable cuts across both INP and RTD but apathy is confined to the retarded complex.

No.	Variable	r_{jp}
1	Manifests slowed speech	0.61 (INP 0.26)
8	Indifferent to own future	0.41
13	Exhibits a fixed facial expression	0.55
16	Manifests slowed movements	0.60 (INP 0.31)
19	Deficient in recent memory	0.30
22	Manifests blocking in speech	0.45
23	Apathetic to self or problems	0.50
30	Exhibits a slovenly appearance	0.36
33	Manifests low or whispered speech	0.54
38	Fails to answer questions	0.54

The Motor Disturbances (MTR) syndrome is characterized by bizarre and unusual motor behavior such as rigid postures, grimacing, and repetitive movements. A reading of *Mental Disorders* suggests that Schizophrenic Reaction, Catatonic Type, has many similarities. However, certain symptoms listed such as waxy flexibility are now rarely seen and muteness was a basis for excluding a patient. A surprising fact is that the item "talking to self" is correlated not with PCP but with the motor syndrome. This suggests that this behavior which is usually interpreted as an indicator of hallucinatory experiences is probably indicative of other types of disorganization.

No.	Variable	r_{jp}
6	Exhibits peculiar, rigid postures	0.59
10	Manifests overt signs of tension	0.32 (INP 0.30)
46	Grins or giggles inappropriately	0.34
47	Exhibits peculiar grimaces	0.68
48	Exhibits peculiar, repetitive gestures	0.64
51	Talks, mutters or mumbles to self	(0.24)
52	Glances around as if hearing voices	0.30

The behavior grouping labeled Conceptual Disorganization (CNP) has no correlative in diagnostic manuals. Nevertheless, *Mental Disorders* describes the schizophrenic reactions as characterized by disturbances in concept formation and varying intellectual disturbances, The Degan (1952) analysis first identified a factor resembling CNP. This syndrome has appeared regularly since then when appropriate marker variables have been represented. There is evidence in the second-order factors to be described later that CNP is a central element in all of the syndromes except INP.

No.	Variable	r_{jp}
2	Gives answers that are irrelevant	0.54
3	Gives incoherent answers	0.60
4	Tends to drift off the subject	0.38 (EXC 0.32)
49	Uses neologisms	0.42
50	Repeats certain words or phrases	0.42

The Disorientation (DIS) syndrome as represented here is very likely a reversible defect. The test–retest correlation of 0.20 (Table 3.1) supports this hypothesis. Clinicians generally agree that brain-injured persons may be disoriented. The functional psychotic, by definition has no manifest evidence of brain damage. Thus functional disorientation may be a measure of the degree of autism or self-preoccupation so characteristic of schizophrenics. The items defining DIS are all specific queries put to the patient and scored either correct or incorrect.

No.	Variable	r_{jp}
70	Does not know he is in a hospital	0.60
71	Does not know where hospital is located	0.67
72	Does not know name of one other person	0.55
73	Does not know season of year	0.56
74	Does not know calendar year	0.67
75	Does not know own age	0.67

The last syndrome to be described is Grandiose Expansiveness (GRN). Although narrow in scope, it has appeared repeatedly and is associated with EXC and PAR as might be expected.

No.	Variable	r_{jp}
15	Exhibits an attitude of superiority	0.36
54	Hears voices that praise and extol	0.49 (PCP 0.41)
64	Believes he has unusual powers	0.59
65	Believes he is a well-known personality	0.42
69	Believes he has a divine mission	0.69

RELIABILITY OF IMPS

A psychological measurement may be regarded as a sample set of observations from a domain of observations that might be made. Thus an observer's rating in an interview presumably indicates what raters representative of those of a similar class would report about a patient. What is desired is an index or reliability coefficient for use in deciding how confidently the researcher or clinician can generalize from a set of available observations to a class of similar observations (Rajaratnam, Cronbach, and Gleser, 1960). Such a coefficient would be descriptive of generalizability from one or more raters to a universe of similar raters.

A parallel coefficient derives from the scale scores instead of the raters. The set of scales defining a syndrome may be regarded as a random sample of scales from a universe of scales which collectively define the syndrome. Still a third facet of reliability is the set of observations made on different occasions which represents a sample from a universe of similar occasions. The reliability coefficient indicative of the stability of measures over time is usually referred to as the test–retest reliability.

In order to determine the degree of inter-rater agreement for individual scales and for syndromes two independent ratings were obtained on 508 patients in the norm sample. The index of agreement was the intra-class correlation coefficient for average rater reliability with between-rater variance included (Ebel, 1951). To determine consistency between scales comprising a syndrome (the second facet of reliability) the same type of coefficient was

TABLE 3. 1

RELIABILITY COEFFICIENTS OF THE TEN SYNDROME SCORES AVERAGE RATER (r_{av}), INTERNAL CONSISTENCY [KUDER–RICHARDSON F-20] (r_{kk}) AND TEST–RETEST (r_{tr}) COEFFICIENTS

SYNDROME	r_{av}	r_{kk}	r_{tr*}
EXCITEMENT	.88	.90	.48
HOSTILE BELLIGERENCE	.88	.82	.49
PARANOID PROJECTION	.88	.85	.38
GRANDIOSE EXPANSIVENESS	.91	.88	.53
PERCEPTUAL DISTORTION	.90	.82	.35
ANXIOUS INTROPUNITIVENESS	.86	.80	.49
RETARDATION AND APATHY	.86	.92	.50
DISORIENTATION	.90	.89	.20
MOTOR DISTURBANCE	.82	.75	.46
CONCEPTUAL DISORGANIZATION	.87	.82	.48

* Based on 368 newly admitted schizophrenic patients rated before and after eight weeks of drug administration (between drug group differences are not included).

computed. The test–retest correlations were based on 368 newly admitted schizophrenics tested before drug treatment and eight weeks later.

All of these coefficients are presented in Table 3.1. It is quite evident that the inter-rater reliability of the syndromes (for two raters) is quite satisfactory. It compares favorably with objective cognitive tests and questionnaires. The inter-scale reliabilities of the syndromes are also substantial except for MTR which is nevertheless good considering its brevity. It should be noted that the syndromes scores are based on as few as five scales and not more than eleven scales. The test–retest correlations are modest because patients were differentially changed (improved) by the six tranquilizers with which they were treated.

THE FINAL FORM

Three variables were dropped from the second experimental form of IMPS but no further changes were made. The final IMPS consists of seventy-five brief, unlabeled, randomly arranged rating scales and Yes–No items (Lorr, Klett, McNair, and Lasky, 1962). It may be completed following an ordinary thirty to sixty minute psychiatric interview whose focus is on discernible behavior and self-reports of feelings, attitudes, and beliefs. The actual rating process requires about ten minutes and consists in recording each judgment on a separate answer sheet. Norms in the form of centile ranks and standard scores are provided for either one or two raters. Thus each patient may be described in terms of ten dimensions of psychopathology.

SUMMARY

The focus in this chapter was on the construction of an objective standard measuring device and the subsequent isolation of ten syndromes. The historical background of IMPS and the need for an adequate instrument was sketched. Next the criteria guiding scale writing were described and discussed. Two experiments involving the collection and factor analysis of data on IMPS on two independent samples were reported. Finally the ten syndromes isolated were described in detail.

In the chapter that follows a critical review is presented of all published factor analytic studies seeking to isolate psychotic syndromes. Then in the fifth chapter the ten IMPS syndromes are discussed in the context of syndromes thus far discovered and confirmed.

CHAPTER 4

A REVIEW OF FACTOR ANALYTIC STUDIES

THE PRESENT chapter critically reviews all available published factor analyses designed to identify psychotic syndromes which are based on behavior ratings and symptoms. Some analyses are based on behavior manifested in an interview. Another smaller group represents data collected on the ward. Most analyses, however, pool current interview and ward behavior data. A few studies include ratings based on combined social history, interview behavior and ward behavior reports, and observations. The general aim is to sketch the history of such analyses and to offer an evaluative summary of factor analytic approaches to the problem. In the next chapter, the evidence from the various studies with regard to the major confirmed syndromes will be summarized and listed by author and defining variables. But first, some discussion is needed of the principles basic to a valid factor analysis.

CRITERIA FOR AN ADEQUATE FACTOR ANALYSIS

In any definitive factorial experiment, all possible sources of trait variation in a domain should be represented. In the domain of psychotic behavior this principle would require the representation of the symptoms and behaviors characteristic of all types of syndromes known or suspected. The basis of this requirement is readily understood. When major sources of variation are not included, the factors that emerge are likely to be ill-defined, confounded, lacking in stability, and difficult to interpret. A corollary to this principle is that at least three or four measures should be included to represent each factor hypothesized. In more general terms the number of variables included should be sufficient to "overdetermine" the factor. Since a factor is an attribute common to, or involved in, at least two variables, it cannot appear unless it is represented by several experimental variables. In confirmatory studies and in studies extending knowledge of a domain, several "marker" or "reference" variables should be included to represent each established factor. As illustrated later, in the absence of such marker variables, important sources of variation are lost or confounded with other sources.

A parallel requirement to the representation of all sources of trait variation is the necessity to include all known sources of individual variability. If an independent source of individual variation is not represented, or is present only over a limited range, it cannot emerge as a common factor. To illustrate, if none of the patients in a sample exhibit depressive symptoms then no syndrome descriptive of this type of variation can be established even though measures of depression are represented in the analysis. At early stages of exploration a random sample is not required but it is important to include persons who exhibit both a substantial amount and a slight amount of a trait or symptom. For instance if height is a factor in a study it is necessary to include both short and tall individuals to define it. Thus, both adequate representation of fundamental variables in a domain and inclusion of all types of individuals are essential for the definition of common factors.

Hypothesis development is another aspect crucial to a sound investigation. Too often haphazard groupings of measures are factored in the vain hope that the method will magically bring order out of chaos. An investigator must take the time to prepare a set of hypotheses concerning the factors expected. Thurstone (1937) comments that the time spent in thinking about and constructing suitable measures was far greater than that devoted to all of the computing required. Hypothesis-relevant measures constructed or selected in advance are more likely to give clear-cut results than measures whose chief virtue is their availability. Specific hypotheses can thus be confirmed or refuted. The isolation of the Hostile Belligerence syndrome (Chapter 3) may serve as an illustration. Since a hostility syndrome was suspected, seven scales designed to assess various verbal, motor, and ideational aspects of manifest hostility were constructed. Subsequent analyses of data collected confirmed the postulated syndrome. If only one scale had been represented no syndrome could have emerged.

Other more technical requirements need only be mentioned

briefly here. The investigator must provide evidence that the number of factors relative to the number of variables is sufficient. Another condition, described in the previous chapter concerns the existence of a unique solution. Is there evidence of a unique "simple structure" solution? As will be seen shortly "orthogonal" solutions in the area of psychopathology tend not to be satisfactory. The forcing of an orthogonal framework for syndromes that even conceptually are correlated creates hybrids. Two influences that can be isolated clearly in an oblique reference frame become composite factors difficult or impossible to interpret in an orthogonal frame. Cattell and Dickman (1962) have provided a clear demonstration of this effect.

Another requirement for an adequate study is that the measures included be univocal rather than complex composites. Ideally each variable should be a measure of only one factor—the factor hypothesized. A common error is to include total or composite scores which represent the sum of scores on two or more measures. The net effect is to reduce clarity, to increase interpretation difficulties, and to hinder the achievement of simple structure. Measures included in a factor analysis should also be experimentally independent. When two scores, like speed and accuracy, are derived from the same performance they are likely to share some of the uniqueness of that particular performance. The result is an "incidental" factor extraneous to the goals of the factorial study. Another source of incidental factors is found in overlapping scores. Suppose two total scores in a test (e.g., Minnesota Multiphasic Personality Inventory) are derived in part from responses to several of the same questions. Then the correlation between the two scores will be spuriously higher or lower than otherwise and an incidental factor may be obtained. Tests that are near duplicates or equivalent forms, through the presence of shared variance, result in additional common factors of no interest. Guilford (1952) has a clear discussion of various errors made in factoring.

EXPERIMENTAL REQUIREMENTS

Regardless of the type of analyses planned, an elementary requirement for objective behavior observation is specification of the period of observation. Yet obvious as this condition may be, studies in this area are often based on data collected without a specific time reference. In fact some investigators appear to regard neglect of this aspect as a virtue. In some studies social history information is mixed with information concerning current symptoms and behavior. Other studies, by failing to limit the observation period say to three days or a week, confound observations made months ago with current observations. Another common error is to combine interview information with ward observations each obtained by different observers. One consequence is to reduce inter-rater reliability. More importantly the pooling of information of a diverse nature is not justified. The ward represents a broader social stimulus situation than the interview and may reveal syndromes not observable in an interview. When such sources of information are combined it is frequently impossible to judge whether a new syndrome is appearing or whether a pattern is an old one in disguise. In research of this nature it is imperative to separate several sources of evidence and demonstrate that similar appearing patterns emerging from diverse social settings are indeed the same.

THE MOORE–DEGAN STUDY

The first path-breaking factor study on the psychotic syndromes was conducted by T.V. Moore (1933). It occurred to Moore that a table of coefficients of association might throw light on the syndromes. Symptoms that occur together should have a high correlation with one another and a low correlation with the symptoms of other syndromes. A preliminary investigation indicated the need for a more precise definition of symptoms. This led to the development of one of the first published symptom rating scales in the literature.

The thirty-two symptoms included in the rating schedule were descriptive of manic-depressive and schizophrenic disorders. Several frequency and intensity scales defined nearly every variable. Further, each symptom was defined by a separate ward and interview scale. Moore argued that this device served to give an average picture of the patient. The patient should be observed under different conditions; what is manifested on the ward may never appear in the interview and vice versa. The ratings for a given symptom were then weighted and summed. The defect of this procedure, of course, is the pooling of diverse sources of variation observed over different time periods. It is first necessary to demonstrate the validity of combining ward and interview information or, at least, each variable should remain distinct until correlational evidence supports the pooling.

The sample Moore studied consisted of 367 male and female functional psychotics from two hospitals. A group of observers, including the attending psychiatrist, the ward physician, and the ward nurse, rated the symptoms of each patient as to their occurrence. Seven symptoms, such as visual hallucinations, mutism, and stereotyped actions, were termed present if they were clearly evident at any time in the course of the patient's illness. Unhappily, the failure to restrict the ratings to current behavior affects any syndromes isolated in unknown ways. Spurious syndromes may be introduced and symptom correlations are confounded. Some symptoms appear early in a disorder while others appear later. The confounding of ward and interview information and the inclusion of social history data casts doubt on the syndromes isolated and makes interpretation difficult. The legitimacy of relating historical items to current behavior is recognized. It is the mixing of the information from these events in single variables that is objectionable.

Moore used a form of cluster analysis to isolate his syndromes. The syndromes he identified were labeled Catatonic, Deluded and Hallucinated, Paranoid Irritabilitis, Manic, Cognitive Defect, Constitutional Hereditary Depression, and Retarded Depression.

Later Degan (1952) refactored and transformed the Moore data and identified nine elementary syndromes and four higher level syndromes. As will be seen from the tables in the next chapter, six of these syndromes appear to have been confirmed in subsequent studies. These were called Hyperexcitability, Catatonia, Hyperprojection, Depression, Schizophrenic Dissociation, and Traumatic Hysteria. The other three factors, Hyperirritability, Deterioration, and Neurasthenia, are probably ward factors.

SOME EARLY STUDIES

Following Moore's early efforts no factor studies were reported until after World War II. Then several doctoral dissertations appeared. Dahlstrom (1949) abstracted the case records of one hundred neurotic, psychotic, and psychopathic female in-patients seen in a Minnesota hospital . Some eighty-two symptoms and thirteen Minnesota Multiphasic Personality Inventory (MMPI) scores were intercorrelated. A multiple group factoring procedure was applied for forty-one of the symptoms and the thirteen scores. Four of the five factors extracted are labeled Neuroticism, Distortion of Reality, Self Preoccupation, and Control. The syndromes isolated are surprisingly similar to those later identified in rating schedules. The factor termed Neurotic is quite close to syndromes described later as Anxious Intropunitiveness. It is defined by feelings of guilt, anxiety, suicidal thoughts, indecision, obsessions, phobias, depression, and self depreciation. Also defining this factor are the neurotic scales of the MMPI. Dahlstrom's second factor clearly defines a Paranoid Projection syndrome which is marked by delusions of persecution, suspiciousness, and delusions of reference. A third factor includes the schizophrenic and paranoid scales of the MMPI and appears to represent a broad schizophrenic pattern. The fourth factor is defined by disturbances of past memory, apathy, affect-content disharmony, and similar variables.

In 1952 Blair reported a factor analytic study of the social behavior of one hundred schizophrenics. The six factors extracted describe restricted interview behavior and are not concerned with symptoms or ideational data. Some of the factors are General Social Orientation, Socio-Motoric Responsiveness, Curiosity, and Reactive Assertion.

A doctoral dissertation by Guertin (1952) on schizophrenic symptoms was similar in aim and approach to the Dahlstrom analysis. He studied a sample of one hundred newly admitted schizophrenics (sixty-one females and thirty-nine males) with an age range of sixteen to sixty. A check list of seventy-two defined symptoms abstracted from psychiatric texts was used in data collection. However, only fifty-two symptoms were frequent enough to be retained. Each patient was rated for the presence or absence of each symptom following an interview by the investigator. Although attendants were consulted in rating some of the symptoms, efforts were made to study the patient at a fixed point in time. The tetrachoric correlations among variables were factored by means of a multiple group procedure and six correlated syndromes were isolated. The findings should be interpreted with caution as the symptom clusters were not transformed to a unique solution as is usually done following factor extraction. Such a decision is justified if the clusters are hypothesized in advance, but not otherwise. As a consequence the syndromes are not as well defined as they might be.

The six syndromes identified by Guertin were described as Excitement-Hostility, Retardation and Withdrawal, Guilt Conflict, Confused-Withdrawal, Persecutory-Suspicious, and Personality Disorganization. The first, Excitement-Hostility, defined by destructiveness, combativeness, disagreeableness, erratic activity level, disturbed sleep, and uncooperativeness is very likely a syndrome observable only on the ward. It is similar to the Moore–Degan Hyper irritability syndrome. The remaining five factors appear to define syndromes systematically confirmed in other studies. The absence of certain syndromes such as Motor Disturbances and Excitement of a manic quality are simply a function of the restriction of the patient population to schizophrenics and the failure to include suitable marker variables. However, it should be noted that the Guertin study was essentially an exploratory analysis.

THE WITTENBORN STUDIES

In 1950 Wittenborn reported the development of a schedule, the Psychiatric Rating Scales (PRS), for rating mental hospital patients on a representative group of symptoms. The rating schedule consists of fifty-five different unlabeled scales designed to record currently observable behavior and symptoms. Each scale is defined by three or four statements usually arranged in terms of increasing deviance from normality. A novel feature is that the most pathological condition or level observed during the period of observation is to be checked. Most schedules ask for a judgment of what is typical or characteristic. The effect of this unusual requirement seems not to have been investigated. Bias is reduced by the randomized presentation, and by the nature of the scales which are primarily descriptive. The time interval for observation and the source of information, however, is unspecified. This would, of course, tend to leave the rater free to use information from one or more interviews and from ward incidents over unknown time periods in arriving at a judgment.

The first factor analysis reported by Wittenborn (1951) was based on descriptions of 140 male patients at a Veterans Administration Hospital provided by several psychiatrists and two psychiatric nurses on the PRS. The product–moment correlations among the fifty scales were subjected to a centroid factor analysis. The seven factors extracted were then transformed (rotated) to a set of independent (orthogonal) syndromes. The syndromes were described as follows: Hebephrenic or Deteriorated, Mania versus Depression, Conversion Hysteria, Catatonic Excitement, Agitated Depression, Paranoid Schizophrenia, and Paranoid Condition.

In a subsequent investigation Wittenborn and Holzberg (1951) secured ratings on 250 newly admitted patients to a Connecticut State Hospital. The symptom ratings were made by psychiatrists during the patients' second week in the hospital. Alcoholic, senile sclerotic, and paretic patients as well as those over sixty years of age were excluded. The correlations among fifty-one of the scale variables were factored by the centroid method and transformed into an orthogonal framework for interpretation. The seven factors were interpreted as representing the following syndromes: Paranoid Schizophrenia, Excited, Manic versus Depressed, Anxious-Depressed, Conversion Hysteria, Paranoid Condition, and Obsessive-Phobic. The Obsessive-Phobic syndrome defined by phobias, obsessive thinking, anxiety, and compulsive behavior appeared to be a new syndrome appearing in newly admitted patients.

The early Wittenborn studies were exceptionally well planned and meticulously carried out. Nevertheless the findings are limited in several respects. First, the use of an orthogonal reference frame to describe the factors extracted has resulted in a set of syndromes that can only partly be duplicated when an oblique or correlated reference frame is used. It is not unusual in factor analysis of cognitive and perceptual tests to offer both oblique and orthogonal solutions for a given body of data. The degree of fit to the data, the plausibility of inferred constructs, and the extent of consistency with the results of other investigators may then be compared. Typically the cognitive abilities defined by the two solutions are quite similar. When personality and psychopathological variables are involved the oblique and orthogonal solutions are likely to differ considerably. The reason is clear; the syndromes are likely to have substantial negative and positive correlations with each other. Further, from the standpoint of attainment of simple structure, the orthogonal solutions show a distinctly poorer fit to the data than the oblique solutions.

The Wittenborn–Holzberg data were reanalyzed in one study (Lorr, 1957) in an effort to clarify the syndromes. As hypothesized the Excited factor disappeared and a factor of Conceptual Disorganization was identified. Four of the Wittenborn factors, Paranoid Schizophrenia, Anxious Depression, Conversion Hysteria, and Phobic-Compulsive were found to be indistinguishable from those originally isolated. The bipolar Manic-Depressed and the Paranoid Condition syndromes were replaced by a Hostile Belligerence and a unipolar Manic Excitement.

The Wittenborn investigations are also limited by the PRS which is lacking in range of symptoms and behaviors available for rating. There is only one hallucination scale and no scales descriptive of bizarre postures or manneristic movements. As a consequence Motor Disturbances, a catatonic-like factor found by other investigators, can not appear. A Perceptual Distortion syndrome defined by auditory, visual, and other hallucinatory experiences is also missing. Finally ward information is not kept distinct from interview data. Therefore, it is difficult or impossible to judge whether a syndrome is confined to one observational situation or the other.

Wittenborn (1962) has recently reported an analysis of a schedule of ninety-eight new rating scales which were used to describe 150 male veteran patients broadly representative of one hospital population. Two raters, a psychologist and an aide, observed each patient at different times during a two-week period. Some scales were rated on the basis of ward observations alone, some on the basis of interview alone, and some on the basis of either. The final data analyzed were not the work of any one rater or rating. When the raters differed on a given scale, the more extreme rating was included in computing the correlations. Twelve factors were extracted and mechanically transformed to an orthogonal "varimax" solution (Kaiser, 1958). Ten of the factors were interpretable.

Before attempting cross-identification, the several limitations of Wittenborn's procedure require explication. First, scale reliability is acknowledged to be unusually low. Second, the use of the most extreme rating has unknown effects but would appear to be in the direction of inflating correlations. Third, ward and interview observations are inextricably confused in about half of the scales. Fourth, and most seriously, the orthogonal solution yields a poor simple structure as reflected in the large number of scales correlated significantly with two to four syndromes, and the small number with correlations in the ± 0.10 range. As a consequence the factors are mixed hybrids and few can be identified with those isolated in oblique solutions.

Compared with the IMPS syndromes described in the previous chapter, Wittenborn's Schizophrenic Excitement appears to be an amalgam of EXC, MTR, and PCP, and is based on both ward and interview scales. His Depressive-Retardation versus Excited State is seen to be primarily RTD with elements of CNP and DIS. Interview and ward observations are equally prominent. Inspection of the defining scales reveals no manic pole as claimed. The Paranoid Schizophrenic Syndrome corresponds well to PAR and is interview-based. Psychotic Belligerence is mostly based on ward data and corresponds closely to HOS. Wittenborn's Intellectual Impairment syndrome appears to be a combination of CNP and DIS and is derived from interview and ward observations. An Hysteric Conversion syndrome is again isolated. A ward-based Hebephrenic Negativism is defined by a mixture of resistance and anti-social behavior. A Phobic-Compulsive syndrome and a weak Anxiety syndrome are also identified in the interview-plus-ward data. The tenth syndrome, Homosexual Dominance, appears to be new.

THE MSRPP STUDIES

Lorr, Jenkins, and O'Connor (1953) reported a factor analysis of data collected on the Northport Record, a precursor of the Multi-dimensional Scale for Rating Psychiatric Patients (MSRPP). The Northport Record was designed to measure twelve hypothesized factors. The factors postulated were based partly on Thurstone's (1947) analysis of Moore's (1933) data and partly on conventional diagnostic syndromes. The concepts utilized were (a) manic excitement versus depressive retardation; (b) paranoid projection; (c) perceptual distortion (hallucinations); (d) catatonia (postures and movements); (e) anxiety reaction; (f) withdrawal versus sociability; (g) disorientation; (h) obsessive compulsive reaction; (i) hostility; (j) passive resistance; (k) sense of personal adequacy; and (l) loss of reality contact.

Each scale was defined by three to five graded statements. The Interview Section consisted of forty-six scales and the Ward Section consisted of forty-six scales. The first was completed by a psychiatrist or psychologist following an interview. The Ward Section was completed by a professional person on the basis of an interview with the aide or nurse who had observed the patient for a week. The sample consisted of 423 male veteran patients drawn from five hospitals. Representatives of five classes of patients were included: newly admitted, chronic, disturbed, grossly deteriorated, and open ward patients.

The scale variables were dichotomized at the median and the estimated tetrachoric correlations among the eighty-one variables were factored by the multiple group procedure. Eleven syndromes were sufficient to account for the intercorrelations. Seven were based primarily on interview data while four were based for the most part on ward observations. The latter includes Resistiveness, Belligerence, Sociability versus Withdrawal, and Activity Level. The syndromes described as Disoriented, Obsessive-Compulsive reaction, and Sense of Personal Adequacy were not confirmed. Instead the variables defining these postulated patterns were found to correlate with other syndromes to be described.

The Northport Record included a fair number of bipolar scales. These are continua such as lowered mood level versus elevated mood level. Experience has shown that it is sounder to base true bipolar continua on empirical data than to assume their existence on logical grounds. The Manic Excitement versus Depressive Retardation syndrome is exemplary. The presence of opposing behaviors on the same scale does not permit the testing of their possible independence. Subsequent studies to be reported indicate that two distinct syndromes, although negatively correlated, are present and deserve independent representation.

The need for cross-identification of syndromes identified in different rating schedules and the related desire to check the stability of syndromes from one sample to the next prompted an investigation by Lorr, O'Connor, and Stafford (1957). The sample consisted of 116 functional psychotics interviewed and observed in eight psychiatric hospitals. Included were open and closed ward cases, chronic and acutely disturbed, as well as newly admitted and continued treatment cases. Alcoholics and neurologic cases were excluded. Ratings were made on a specially devised rating schedule which included thirty-nine scales from the MSRPP and sixteen scales from Wittenborn's PRS. One aim was to determine the equivalence of the two schedules. Thirteen dimensions previously identified in one or more studies provided the basis for selection. These syndromes were as follows: Retarded Depression versus Manic Excitement, Resistiveness, Paranoid Projection, Activity Level, Melancholic Agitation, Perceptual Distortion, Motor Disturbances, Hostile Belligerence, Withdrawal versus Sociability, Grandiose Expansiveness, Conceptual Disorganization, Obsessive-Phobic reaction, and Hysteric Conversion.

The product–moment correlations among the fifty-two scales retained were factored by the multiple group method and then transformed to an oblique simple structure. Three syndromes failed to emerge and one doubtful syndrome was defined only by compulsive acts. The interpretable syndromes were Excitement, Resistiveness, Paranoid Projection, Anxious Depression, Perceptual Distortion, Motor Disturbances, Activity Level, Grandiosity, and Conceptual Disorganization. Of these nine the first combined the hostile-belligerent elements with excitement to produce what is judged to be a second-order syndrome at the first-order level. Thus only eight syndromes were actually confirmed. The study findings are doubtful principally because of the number and variety of patients included. Because of need for broad representation of patients and the need to reduce sampling errors in the correlation coefficient, from three hundred to five hundred patients are required for a confirmatory study.

ANALYSIS OF A MENTAL STATUS EXAMINATION

A factor analysis of a sixty scale mental status examination has been reported by Bostian, Smith, Lasky, Hover, and Ging (1959). The sample consisted of twenty-two patients in remission assessed by pairs of psychiatric aides, and another twenty-three patients rated by ward psychiatrists and either nurse or psychotherapist. Thus there were fewer patients than test variables! Overlapping portions of the matrix were factored and transformed orthogonally by the "quartimax" method. The syndromes identified in the two matrices were Psychotic Confusion, Hostile Acting Out, Ego Resources, Activity Level, Somatization, Anxious Remorse, Dominance-Submission, and Compulsivity. Of these, Hostile Acting Out and Anxious Remorse alone appear to correspond to syndromes reported in other investigations. Most of the criteria for a sound analysis were violated in this study despite the availability of at least a half-dozen prior analyses. The study was based on a haphazard sample of patients, far too few in number, no marker variables were included, and sources of data were confounded.

THE TROUTON–MAXWELL STUDY

An exploratory study of some interest was reported by Trouton and Maxwell (1956). The experimental variables, taken from an Item Sheet in use at the Bethlehem Royal and Maudsley Hospitals consisted of froty-five major symptoms and social history characteristics. The data analyzed were based on 819 hospitalized males sixteen to fifty-nine years of age manifesting non-organic psychiatric disorders. The centroid factor analysis yielded six factors which were subjected to an orthogonal transformation to "yield factors conforming as far as possible to present psychological knowledge and psychiatric practice . . ." This procedure, *mirabile dictu*, yielded two orthogonal factors identified as Psychoticism and Neuroticism and four additional factors difficult to interpret. Good simple structure was conspicuously absent.

The original data were re-analyzed (Lorr and O'Connor, 1957) with the aim of securing an adequate simple structure interpretation. The transformations were conducted blind, i.e., each variable was coded to minimize bias. The first factor obtained was best defined by the following variables or notations: motor disturbances, schizophrenic type of thought disorder, delusions (other), hallucinations, thought or memory impairment, socially withdrawn, retarded activity, ideas of reference, mood disturbances, gross disturbances of weight and intake, constitutional causes, and denial of symptoms. In addition, a dichotomous notation of psychotic versus nonpsychotic correlated 0.42 with the first factor. The factor is defined by such a wide variety of symptoms that at best it can be regarded as a possible higher level factor appearing at the first-order level (see Chapter 6). The second syndrome correlated —0.52 with the psychotic versus nonpsychotic notation. Other defining notations are: family history of abnormal personality, unsatisfactory early life, frequently unemployed, neurotic traits in childhood, obsessional symptoms (lifelong or episodic), anxiety symptoms (lifelong or episodic), mood variations before present illness, symptoms over twelve months duration, and compulsive acts and/or obsessive thoughts. The common elements appear to be primarily historical in nature with emphasis on long duration, family abnormality, and neurotic characteristics.

The third factor may best be described as an acute situational depression, while the fourth syndrome is suggestive of a possible hostile or paranoid pattern. The fifth factor appears to be an anxious depression, although retardation is present. The final syndrome is characterized narrowly by hypochondriacal attitudes toward illness, and notations of anxiety, other functional disturbances, hysterical symptoms (lifelong or episodic), and family history of neurosis.

As may be seen, the basic data are seriously limited and this the investigators acknowledge: (a) The defining symptoms do not represent all the major diagnostic categories; (b) Some symptoms are combined (e.g., compulsive acts and/or obsessive thoughts); (c) Seven different sources of variance are analyzed; namely, diagnosis, family history of psychiatric disorder, previous adjustment history, previous symptoms, causes and onset of illness, symptoms of present illness, and outcome; (d) Degree of rater agreement is unknown.

If it is assumed that Trouton and Maxwell hoped to establish two general factors of psychoticism and neuroticism, and this appears to be a reasonable guess, what approaches might they have taken? One approach would have been via Burt's (1950) group factor method, which yields a hierarchy of factors. In a hierarchical system, factors are arranged in order of increasing generality, beginning with narrow group factors and ending in a general factor. Another approach would have been through second-order factors (Thurstone, 1937) which are based on correlated first-order factors. If, for the purpose of discussion, it is assumed that the first two Trouton–Maxwell factors represent psychoticism and neuroticism then what are the remaining four factors? Lower order or subordinate factors must be subsumed within a hierarchical arrangement like species to genus or related to more general second-order factors.

ANALYSIS OF SPECIAL GROUPS

Most research workers know that a correlation between two tests will depend very considerably upon the heterogeneity of the sample in which the traits are measured. In general, the more homogeneous the group, the smaller the correlation. In the extreme case, for a group of persons possessing a common test profile, the correlations among the tests may all approach zero. It follows that the results of a factorial analysis of correlations can be affected rather markedly by the degree of "selection" or restriction in the range of subjects on one or more variables. Thomson (1951) has reported a number of studies dealing with univariate and multivariate selection effects. Thurstone (1947), interested more in simple structure, has shown in a broad way that the fundamental meaning of factors may remain unchanged under conditions of partial selection. However, under severe selection not only may there be a loss of one or more dimensions but "incidental" factors of no psychological interest may be introduced. This is the basis for the first criterion described earlier in the chapter. In a factorial investigation an important desideratum is that the experimental subjects vary among themselves as much as possible on a trait being studied.

With this discussion as background, attention can be turned to several analyses of patient symptoms based on samples limited to one or more diagnostic groups. Hamilton (1960) examined the clinical syndromes in depressive states. Grinker and his associates (1961) conducted a most thorough study of over one hundred hospitalized depressives. Both suffer from the limitations described. The syndromes isolated may or may not be confirmable within broader, more heterogeneous populations. Incidental factors may be present. Through failure to include marker variables for the established syndromes, some factors could not appear. In brief these studies, *qua* factorial studies, exhibit the effects of restriction in various sources of population variance and limitations on defining variables.

THE HAMILTON SYNDROMES

Hamilton (1960) constructed a rating scale designed for assessing the condition of patients suffering from depressive disorders. Included were such variables as depressed mood, guilt, several types of insomnia, retardation, several varieties of anxiety, gastro-intestinal symptoms, and loss of weight. Product–moment correlations were computed for the seventeen variables on forty-nine male patients diagnosed as depressives. The correlation matrix was factored by the method of principal components and then transformed to orthogonal simple structure. The first factor is defined by suicidal thoughts or attempts, loss of libido, guilt, retardation, depressed mood, and loss of insight. The second syndrome is characterized by gastro-intestinal complaints, sleep difficulties, loss of interest in work and play, body preoccupation, and loss of weight. Psychic anxiety, agitation, and somatic anxiety mark the third factor. The fourth factor is not very clear.

It is evident that a Retardation syndrome could not have been isolated since only one scale defining such behavior was included. Second, many of the correlations are negative where ordinarily they would be positive in a representative sample of psychotics. For example, depressed mood and guilt are correlated negatively with agitation and psychic anxiety in Hamilton's sample. Thus, despite the care, skill, and acumen exercised by the investigator, the syndromes are of questionable generality.

STUDIES OF DEPRESSION

Grinker and his colleagues Miller, Sabshin, Nunn, and Nunnally in *The Phenomena of Depressions* (1961) have reported a fascinating and imaginative series of investigations directed toward the description of the clinical characteristics of depression. Only limited portions of this multi-faceted investigation will be of concern here. Discussion will be restricted to the factor analyses of the Feelings and Concerns Check List and the Current Behavior Check List developed by the group. The Feelings and Concerns List consisted of forty-seven four-point rating scales completed by psychiatric residents on the basis of interviews. The Current Behavior List consisted of 139 present–absent items which were checked jointly by the head nurse and psychiatric nurse within five days after admission of a patient on the basis of ward observations. A group of ninety-six successively admitted patients diagnosed as "Depression" or "Depressive Reaction" were described on the two check lists.

The correlations among the forty-seven feelings and concerns and the correlations among eighty-four of the more frequently occurring behaviors were factored by the centroid method. For interpretation the factors obtained were transformed by the varimax procedure (Kaiser, 1959) to a unique orthogonal position. Of the five Feelings and Concerns factors, the first is defined by feelings of hopelessness, sadness, helplessness, and a sense of unworthiness. The second factor is defined by concerns and feelings that attribute blame to external events or people for the illness. Concern with guilt and desire to make restitution define the third syndrome. The fourth factor is primarily a tense agitation, and the fifth is defined by feelings of being unloved, inferior, and envious.

Within broader patient populations the characteristics defining the first, third, and fourth factors usually go together as one factor (e.g., Anxious Intropunitiveness on IMPS). However, there is supporting evidence (Schanberger, 1950) in self-report data that the guilt and remorse syndrome may be an independent variable. If additional marker variables for Paranoid Projection had been included, the variables defining the second factor may have been found identical with the projective defense that syndrome implies. However, any judgments concerning the similarity of the Grinker factors with factors found in more varied samples, which include a variety of diagnostic groups, must be made with considerable caution. Factors isolated in studies of restricted samples may be viewed as tentative hypotheses requiring confirmation within fully heterogeneous populations.

The Current Behavior Check List yielded ten interpretable factors. Epitomized briefly they are as follows: (1) Isolated and withdrawn; (2) Slowed and retarded in speech and thought; (3) Disinterested and apathetic; (4) Angrily provocative, demanding, and complaining; (5) Hypochondriacal; (6) Memory impaired and confused; (7) Agitated; (8) Rigid and immobile; (9) Dry depression; (10) Clinging and dependent. In order to compare these syndromes with those isolated in other investigations several facts should be kept in mind. First, the rating factors are derived from the ward situation and not from an interview. Second, although described as a "behavior" check list, many ratings are also based on patient reports such as "complaints". A complaint or an ache is just as subjective as a feeling or a concern. Of the ten syndromes number 5 (Hypochondriacal) and number 7 (Agitated) are primarily subjective, number 4 (Angry and complaining) and number 6 (Confused) are both behavioral and subjective, while the remaining syndromes appear to be behavior-derived.

Syndromes number 1 and number 2, considered as ward factors, resemble the Withdrawal and Activity syndromes obtained by Lorr *et al.* (1962). The Angrily Provocative factor number 4 seems to be the same as the Hostile Belligerence (ward) syndrome. Only with difficulty can the remaining syndromes be compared with those isolated by others. Factor number 7 might be the same as the Lorr, O'Connor, and Stafford (1960) ward factor of Anxious Depression. The fifth factor which is defined by dizzy spells, constipation, "somatic" symptoms, complaints of trouble with eyes, especially sensitive to noise, is suggestive of Hamilton's somatic complaint syndrome.

WARD SCALE ANALYSES

Several factor analyses of ward behavior scales have been reported. Guertin's study (1955) was based on one hundred hospitalized chronically ill veterans who were described on the Hospital Adjustment Scale (McReynolds, Ferguson, and Ballachey, 1952). Tetrachoric correlations were computed among thirty-five of the scale items which were grouped into clusters of positively related variables. Three factors were extracted by the multiple group procedure. However, as no transformations were applied it is virtually impossible for a reader to interpret the findings. Guertin calls his factors lack of General Interest, Social Withdrawal, and

TABLE 4.1

FACTOR ANALYTIC STUDIES OF PSYCHOTIC BEHAVIOR

STUDY	SAMPLE	TYPE AND NUMBER OF MEASURES	DATA SOURCE	RATERS	TYPE OF FACTORS	NUMBER OF INTERPRETABLE FACTORS
DAHLSTROM (1949)	100 NEUROTICS & PSYCHOTICS, BOTH SEXES	41 SYMPTOMS, 13 MMPI SCORES	WARD OBSERVATION & TESTS	PSYCHIATRISTS	OBLIQUE	5
WITTENBORN (1951)	140 MALE PSYCHOTICS	55 DESCRIPTIVE SCALES	INTERVIEW & WARD	PSYCHIATRISTS & NURSES	ORTHOGONAL	7
WITTENBORN & HOLZBERG (1951)	250 NEWLY ADMITTED MALE FUNCTIONAL PSYCHOTICS	51 SCALES	INTERVIEW & WARD	PSYCHIATRISTS	ORTHOGONAL	7
DEGAN (1952)	367 PSYCHOTICS, BOTH SEXES, 2 HOSPITALS	32 GRAPHIC RATINGS	INTERVIEW, WARD OBSERVATION, HISTORY	PSYCHIATRISTS, PHYSICIANS, NURSES	OBLIQUE	9
GUERTIN (1952)	100 NEWLY ADMITTED SCHIZOPHRENICS, BOTH SEXES	52 SYMPTOMS	INTERVIEW, OBSERVATION MAINLY	PSYCHOLOGISTS	OBLIQUE	6
GUERTIN (1955)	100 MALE SCHIZOPHRENICS	35 HAS ITEMS	WARD HISTORY	PSYCHIATRIC CHARGE AIDES	OBLIQUE	3

TABLE 4.1 (CONTINUED)

STUDY	SAMPLE	TYPE AND NUMBER OF MEASURES	DATA SOURCE	RATERS	TYPE OF FACTORS	NUMBER OF INTERPRETABLE FACTORS
LORR, JENKINS, & O'CONNOR (1955)	423 MALE PSYCHOTICS, 4 HOSPITALS	55 DESCRIPTIVE SCALES	INTERVIEW & WARD	PSYCHIATRISTS, PSYCHOLOGISTS	OBLIQUE	11
LORR & O'CONNOR (1957)	500 MALE PSYCHOTICS, 47 HOSPITALS	PRP-- 85 ITEMS	WARD OBSERVATION	NURSES & AIDES	OBLIQUE	8
LORR, O'CONNOR, & STAFFORD (1957)	116 MALE FUNCTIONAL PSYCHOTICS, 8 HOSPITALS	39 SCALES FROM MSRPP, 16 FROM PRS	INTERVIEW & WARD OBSERVATION	PSYCHIATRIC ATTENDANT OR NURSE	OBLIQUE	9
BOSTIAN ET AL. (1959)	23 MALE HOSPITALIZED PSYCHOTICS & 22 POST-HOSPITAL	60 SCALES	INTERVIEW	PSYCHIATRISTS, PSYCHOLOGISTS, PSYCHIATRIC NURSES, SOCIAL WORKERS	ORTHOGONAL (QUARTIMAX)	6
GUERTIN & KRUGMAN (1959)	100 MALE PSYCHOTICS	76 ITEMS	BEHAVIOR RATINGS--WARD, THERAPY, CHURCH	THERAPISTS, CHAPLAINS	OBLIQUE	6
LORR, MCNAIR, KLETT, & LASKY (1962)	296 PSYCHOTICS 47 HOSPITALS	77 IMPS SCALES	INTERVIEW	PSYCHIATRISTS & PSYCHOLOGISTS	OBLIQUE	9
WITTENBORN (1962)	150 MALE PSYCHOTICS	98 SCALES	INTERVIEW & WARD	PSYCHOLOGISTS, AIDES	ORTHOGONAL (VARIMAX)	8

Personal Unconcern. If the titles seem similar it should come as no surprise; the item correlations with each of the three factors are quite similar. In brief, simple structure has not been achieved. A reanalysis showed that one large general factor accounted for most of the variance although two additional narrow factors could be extracted. There are probably two conditions that produce the effects obtained: first, the tetrachoric correlations are systematically biased upward as much as 0.20; second, it is very likely that a substantial "halo" influenced the aides' ratings.

Guertin and Krugman (1959) describe a factor analysis of fifty-five items of a newly devised Activity Rating Scale. Ratings made on one hundred patients provided the data for computing tetrachoric correlations among the fifty-five items. The matrix was clustered and six factors were extracted by the multiple group method. By various techniques the correlations of additional items with the factors were determined. In the final matrix presented, seventy-six items define the six factors which are called Deteriorated Behavior, Interpersonal Tensions, Emotional Controls, Resistive Isolation, Regressive Agitation, and Reality Concern. Mention is made by the investigators that only aides with considerable contact with a patient over a long period could complete these items. Evaluation and comparison of these syndromes is difficult because few analyses have been made with ward data, especially of the type included. However, the Emotional Controls syndrome seems to be the same as the Hostile Belligerence factor found earlier by Guertin (1952) and isolated by Lorr *et al.* in several studies. The other syndromes isolated must await cross-validational studies.

A factor analysis of the Psychotic Reaction Profile (Lorr, O'Connor, and Stafford, 1960) has been reported (Lorr and O'Connor, 1962). The behavior inventory consists of eighty-five statements descriptive of patient ward behavior to be rated true or not true after three days of observation. A test was made for the presence of ten hypothesized patterns likely to be observable on the ward. The dimensions formulated were: Excitement, Withdrawal with Psychomotor Retardation, Paranoid Projection, Perceptual Distortion, Conceptual Disorganization, Resistiveness, Depressive Agitation, Motor Disturbance, Hostile Belligerence, and Dominance. The last was introduced as one potentially useful in differentiating among patient types. The sample consisted of five hundred male psychotics observed and rated in fifty-seven hospitals from all over the United States and parts of Canada.

Product–moment correlations among the eighty-five variables were grouped in agreement with hypotheses and eight factors were extracted. Three clusters, Perceptual Distortion, Conceptual Disorganization, and Motor Disturbance were found to be too highly associated and were accordingly pooled in one syndrome. Of the eight factors obtained, those six regarded as fully confirmed are Paranoid Projection, Hostile Belligerence, Resistiveness, Dominance, Excitement, and Agitated Depression. The remaining two factors, called Withdrawal and Thinking Disorganization are regarded as second-order syndromes appearing at the first-order level.

As an aid in reviewing the findings and as a summarization, thirteen of the studies cited are listed in Table 4.1. Included under each analysis are such characteristics as the nature and size of the sample, the type and number of measures included, as well as sources of data and type of raters used.

SUMMARY

In the present chapter an effort was made to review and summarize the findings of available experiments designed to isolate the major psychotic syndromes by the method of factor analysis. A set of criteria for judging the adequacy of a factor study were sketched. Each reported investigation was then examined and evaluated in terms of these criteria. Major emphasis was thus placed on the methodological strengths and weaknesses of the various experiments. The chapter ended with a summarization of the thirteen investigations that have contributed to the isolation or the confirmation of interview or ward syndromes.

The aim of Chapter 5 is to piece together or integrate available evidence concerning each proposed syndrome. Similar syndromes are assembled, examined, and compared with a view to arriving at some judgment as to which may be regarded as confirmed.

CHAPTER 5

THE CONFIRMED SYNDROMES

IN THE review of the last chapter, the syndromes identified in each of the factorial investigations were briefly mentioned. Emphasis was placed more on a critical evaluation of methods used than upon the syndromes found. The review also served as an historical account of the use of factor methods for the isolation of psychotic syndromes. While such an appraisal is critical, it is perhaps not as interesting intrinsically as a comparison of the findings. In the present chapter an effort is made to assemble the evidence concerning each syndrome and to arrive at some conclusions as to which may be considered "confirmed".

METHOD OF CROSS-IDENTIFICATION

Suppose the same variables are used to describe two distinct groups of individuals. How can the factors resulting from analysis of the two sets of measures be compared and cross-identified? Generally, researchers have used rough methods of inspection and the pooled judgments of colleagues. However, a number of coefficients of factorial similarity comparable to a correlation coefficient are now available (Harman, 1960, p. 256). The basic difficulty is that each investigator uses his own rating schedule, or develops an *ad hoc* list of symptoms. Unless the same measures are represented in the two factors compared, the researcher must rely on judgment for cross-identification.

One method suggested by Young and Householder (1940) and by Bechtoldt (1958) is to solve the problem in the same manner as physical scientists do, i.e., by establishing standards for weight, length, or mass. Thus in the psychological field three reliable tests could be used as a behavioral definition of each established factor. While this procedure has been followed occasionally in studying aptitudes it has not been possible in the area of psychopathology. With such objectively defined factors no problem would arise as to the invariance of factor definitions from study to study. However, in the absence of common measures and common criteria for solution, cross-identification must of necessity be based on judgment. For the same reasons the conclusions reached here should be regarded as tentative. If the conclusions are actually sound and plausible it should be possible to confirm them in future experimental studies.

The first step in cross-identification was to list under each IMPS syndrome all studies that isolated a syndrome judged similar. IMPS was thus given the role of a standard for the interview syndromes. For identification and easy reference, each study is given a code designation derived from the first letter in the principal author's name. Only those syndromes which appeared in at least two factor analyses are regarded as confirmed and only these are listed. A half-dozen studies are not cited. Typically this was because the factors isolated were based on social history or pooled ward and interview data, or because the measures were unstandardized. It seemed neither feasible nor worthwhile to prepare brief descriptions of each variable in each of the thirteen studies. Instead IMPS was used to provide brief descriptions of the variables common to the scales compared. While great care was exercised in matching variables no claim is made for perfect agreement. On the other hand, rating schedules like Wittenborn's PRS and Lorr's Northport Record are very similar, as are Experimental IMPS and the final form of IMPS.

The syndrome titles are the same as those used in Chapter 3. The purpose of a title is to convey the meaning of the behavior-defined unity represented by the complex. No doubt these labels will not please every one but some means of identification other than a number or letter is obviously useful for mnemonic purposes.

For easy reference the code and the authors of the analyses listed are given below:

B : Bostian, Smith, Lasky, Hover, Ging (1959)
D(M) : Degan (1952); Moore's data
G : Guertin (1952)
GK : Guertin and Krugman (1959)
LJO : Lorr, Jenkins, and O'Connor (1955)

LOS : Lorr, O'Connor, and Stafford (1957)
LO : Lorr and O'Connor (1957)
LMKL: Lorr, McNair, Klett, and Lasky (1962)
LKML: Lorr, Klett, McNair, and Lasky (1962)
L (W) : Lorr (1957); WH data
Wa : Wittenborn (1951)
Wb : Wittenborn (1962)
WH : Wittenborn and Holzberg (1951)

THE INTERVIEW SYNDROMES

The first ten tables summarize the evidence with regard to the syndromes identified in interview ratings. Only correlations of 0.30 or higher are listed. Values of 0.30 or higher are arbitrarily judged to be "significant". An alternative procedure would be to list all values unless the variable was not included in an analysis. However, as the primary aim is to give the reader some impression of the extent of replication, the present format is deemed adequate.

The variables defining the Excitement syndrome are shown in Table 5.1. As may be seen seven studies report an Excitement pattern involving increased psychomotor activity, elevated mood and self-esteem, and a reduced emotional restraint. The findings from IMPS are particularly close. The Excitement syndrome thus appears strongly confirmed. Comparison with conventional diagnoses is not made because such categories are judged to correspond to types or classes of patients and not to syndromes which are better regarded as dimensions. The usefulness of the syndromes for identifying psychiatric diagnoses has been explored and is described in the chapter on the validity of the syndromes.

A Hostile Belligerence grouping is well defined in all three studies in Table 5.2. It is expressed verbally in generalized complaining and in reported feelings of resentment. The syndrome is also manifested motorically. The first stages of projective attribution are evident in blaming of others and in suspicion of people and their motives. There is evidence that the next syndrome, Paranoid Projection evolves from and is first exhibited in hostile behaviors and feelings towards others. Table 5.3 lists data from seven independent studies. It is thus evident that Paranoid Projection is one of the most firmly established syndromes. No

TABLE 5.1

CORRELATIONS OF DEFINING VARIABLES WITH THE EXCITEMENT SYNDROME (DECIMAL POINTS OMITTED)

VARIABLE	STUDY						
	D(M)	L(W)	LJO	LOS	B	LMKL	LKML
EXPRESSES FEELINGS WITH LITTLE RESTRAINT		37	63	63		42	40
MANIFESTS HURRIED SPEECH	82*					51	58
EXHIBITS AN ELEVATION OF MOOD	41	63	46	47	55	30	50
DRAMATIZES SELF AND SEEKS ATTENTION		42				46	50
SPEECH IS LOUD, INTENSE OR BOISTEROUS		39	83	72		30	49
EXHIBITS OVERACTIVITY	*	37				46	38
EXHIBITS AN EXCESS OF SPEECH	*		67	53	75	47	58
TRIES TO DOMINATE INTERVIEW						34	55
EXHIBITS ATTITUDE OF SUPERIORITY		34				48	34
EXHIBITS RAPID CHANGE IN IDEAS		53	63				

* Moore's variable combined hurried speech, excessive speech, and overactivity.

scales for delusional beliefs of conspiracy or of influence by external forces (radio waves, electronic devices) were included in the first form of IMPS. This accounts for the absence of significant correlations in the column labeled LMKL.

TABLE 5.2
CORRELATIONS OF DEFINING VARIABLES WITH THE HOSTILE BELLIGERENCE SYNDROME
(DECIMAL POINTS OMITTED)

Variable	Study		
	B	LMKL	LKML
Manifests a hostile attitude	92	53	74
Expresses verbally feelings of hostility		38	76
Manifests an attitude of disdain	86	38	42
Manifests irritability and annoyance	77	47	68
Blames others for his difficulties		28	54
Expresses feelings of resentment	65	45	70
Complains and criticizes others	64	33	61
Expresses suspicion of people		24	58

The six analyses identifying Grandiose Expansiveness are listed in Table 5.4. The syndrome is relatively narrow but well defined and easily recognized. Both Excitement and Paranoid Projection are related to the Grandiose syndrome. One hypothesis is that some persons strong in Paranoid Projection find a solution for their persecutions in ideas of personal superiority and importance. Similarly a sense of mission may follow.

The Perceptual Distortion syndrome has emerged in five studies. Moore first identified the Perceptual Distortion syndrome (Table 5.5) and Degan re-isolated the same pattern. The symptom grouping has appeared whenever sufficient marker variables were included in the analysis. All types of hallucinatory experiences are the principal defining characteristics. Riss (1960) has reported supporting evidence that hallucinations represent distortions of perceptual stimuli, rather than self-initiated reactions in the absence of external stimuli. One hypothesis is that in Paranoid

TABLE 5.3

CORRELATIONS OF DEFINING VARIABLES WITH THE PARANOID PROJECTION SYNDROME
(DECIMAL POINTS OMITTED)

Variable	Study						
	WA	WH	G	LJO	LOS	LMKL	LKML
Believes people talk about him			63	73	65	49	52
Believes he is persecuted	36	64	87	83		54	41
Believes people conspire against him				69	58		53
Believes people influence him	64	65			47	34	54
Believes external forces influence him							38
Exhibits delusional beliefs	62	55	80		32		44

Table 5.4
Correlations of Defining Variables with the Grandiose Expansiveness Syndrome
(Decimal points omitted)

Variable	Study					
	WA	WH	LJO	LOS	LMKL	LKML
Manifests an attitude of superiority			69	30		36
Believes he has unusual abilities, powers	42	32	70	46	(27)	59
Believes he is a well known personality						42
Believes he has a divine mission					55	69
Hears voices that praise or extol					60	49
Seems engrossed in plans	35	40				

Projection, the individual attributes his own fear and hostility to others. Hallucinations from this same viewpoint can be conceived of as a more severe degree of distortion in which inner feelings and attitudes modify incoming sounds and other types of sensory stimuli.

TABLE 5.5
CORRELATIONS OF DEFINING VARIABLES WITH THE PERCEPTUAL DISTORTION SYNDROME
(DECIMAL POINTS OMITTED)

Variable	Study				
	D(M)	LJO	LOS	LMKL	LKML
Hears voices	65	68	62	63	54
Sees visions	68	74	66	39	42
Reports other hallucinatory expressions (tactual, gustatory, olfactory)	73			40	44
Hears voices that accuse				67	65
Hears voices that threaten				52	72
Hears hortatory voices				53	52
Reports bizarre delusions	55	37			
Believes familiar things have changed					67
Disoriented for self		64	46		

The syndrome called Anxious Intropunitiveness has been isolated in the eight studies listed in Table 5.6 as well as in several others mentioned in the previous chapter. The Degan confirmation is the most doubtful of those listed as many of the variables defining the syndrome were based on previous history. The syndrome is characterized by anxiety, both "free-floating" and specific, by self-directed blame and hostile feeling, by feelings of guilt and by a sense of sinfulness. Of all the syndromes only Intropunitiveness is not characterized by a lack of insight as usually defined. Further research may evolve additional syndromes related to those found by Grinker *et al.*

Studies isolating the Retardation and Apathy syndrome are shown in Table 5.7. The syndrome is most clearly defined in the two IMPS analyses. The characteristic elements are slowed or delayed motor activity including slowed speech, and manifestations

TABLE 5.6

CORRELATIONS OF DEFINING VARIABLES WITH THE ANXIOUS INTROPUNITIVENESS SYNDROME (DECIMAL POINTS OMITTED)

Variable	Study							
	D(M)	WA	WH	LJO	LOS	B	LMKL	LKML
Anxious about specific problems	53	78	44	58	71	68	58	65
Vague apprehension		69	65		35	48	63	68
Blames self for difficulties							59	74
Self depreciatory in attitude							56	80
Depressed in mood	63			46		27	57	68
Expresses feelings of guilt								71
Preoccupied with suicidal thoughts		59	56				43	61
Distressed by specific fears		51			48		46	40
Believes he is unworthy and sinful		73	72		43		41	62
Distressed by unwanted thoughts		48	34		50	36	46	46
Manifests insight into problems		50	36	37				44
Difficulty in sleeping		41	34					

of apathy and indifference. The Wittenborn findings are not listed because a comparable syndrome is defined by what appear to be ward scales. It is possible that in future research the elements of apathy can be shown to be independent of psychomotor slowing. In studies thus far reported these two elements cannot be differentiated; when one is present the other is also present.

TABLE 5.7
CORRELATIONS OF DEFINING VARIABLES WITH THE RETARDATION AND APATHY SYNDROME
(DECIMAL POINTS OMITTED)

Variable	Study				
	G	LJO	LOS	LMKL	LKML
Speech slow and deliberate				53	61
Body movements slowed or deliberate	92			48	60
Voice low or whispered		83	65	48	54
Apathetic and unresponsive in feeling	66	56	74	52	50
Manifests blocking in speech				37	45
Fails to respond to questions		67	53	36	54
Exhibits deficit in recent memory				(20)	30
Indifferent to treatment or release					41
Facial expression fixed, immobile				52	55
Exhibits a slovenly appearance				(29)	36

The Disorientation syndrome was first identified by Degan (1952) although not in a convincing fashion. Only two highly correlated symptoms, disorientation for time and disorientation for space, defined the syndrome. Blewett (1958) identified a group of questions, very similar to those found in IMPS, in a study of schizophrenia. Although the study did not involve a factor analysis the item intercorrelations implied the presence of a single common factor. The experimental form of IMPS included the disorientation items but these were represented in the table of correlations as a single variable. It is for this reason that it did not emerge as an independent syndrome. The two IMPS study findings strongly support the existence of an independent syndrome of disorientation.

Table 5.9 presents the evidence for the Motor Disturbance syndrome. It is defined by unnatural manneristic postures, body movements and grimaces, giggling, and signs of overt body tension. The early Wittenborn studies failed to emerge with this syndrome because no scales descriptive of manneristic movements and postures are included in the PRS. In IMPS the Motor Disturbance syndrome relates to Psychomotor Retardation on the one hand and to Disorientation on the other. It has been hypothesized that symptoms defining this syndrome represent symbolic ways certain patients have of communicating with others.

TABLE 5.8
CORRELATIONS OF DEFINING VARIABLES WITH THE DISORIENTATION SYNDROME
(DECIMAL POINTS OMITTED)

Variable	Study		
	D(M)	LMKL	LKML
Does not know where he is		*	60
Does not know hospital location	82	*	67
Knows no one's name in hospital			55
Does not know season of year		*	56
Does not know calendar year	71	*	67
Does not know own age		*	67

*See Text.

The tenth interview syndrome is labeled Conceptual Disorganization (Table 5.10). The pattern was first isolated in the Degan analysis, and appeared again in Guertin's analysis as Personality Disorganization. The IMPS analyses leave no doubt concerning its existence. The incoherent and rambling speech, peculiar verbalization, and stereotyped speech suggest thinking disorder. Thought-feeling disharmony, i.e., a dissonance between the content of what the individual is saying and his affect, is probably characteristic but not easily elicited. For this reason it has been omitted from IMPS. The pattern as a whole corresponds to Bleuler's concept of what is central to a schizophrenic disorder.

The syndrome is also related to Excitement and to Motor Disturbances. It has been shown to correlate with defective concepts (F-) on the Rorschach.

THE WARD SYNDROMES

In this section those syndromes defined by ward-observed behaviors are listed. While there should be fairly good agreement between the behaviors exhibited on the ward and those in an interview, the stimulus situation is obviously more complex. A greater range of interpersonal behaviors can be manifested by an

TABLE 5.9
CORRELATIONS OF DEFINING VARIABLES WITH THE MOTOR DISTURBANCE SYNDROME
(DECIMAL POINTS OMITTED)

Variable	Study				
	D(M)	LJO	LOS	LMKL	LKML
Assumes peculiar postures	58	45	49	50	59
Exhibits peculiar repetitive movements	36	56	53	60	64
Grimaces peculiarly		41		58	68
Manifests signs of overt tension				27	32
Grins or giggles inappropriately	40			(21)	34

TABLE 5.10
CORRELATIONS OF DEFINING VARIABLES WITH THE CONCEPTUAL DISORGANIZATION SYNDROME
(DECIMAL POINTS OMITTED)

Variable	Study					
	D(M)	G	LJO	LOS	LMKL	LKML
Irrelevant answers to questions			72	69	26	54
Grammatically incoherent answers			59	62	51	60
Rambles or drifts off the subject					42	38
Uses Neologisms					(20)	42
Repeats words or fixed phrases	65	81	60			42
Talks to voices	53				32	(23)
Thought-emotion disharmony		51	61			
Self-preoccupied	32	70	38			

individual in the process of interacting with other patients, aides, nurses, and doctors. Wittenborn and Plante (1961) report a most interesting comparison of physician and nurse symptom ratings that throws much light on the relative contributions of ratings obtained from these two data sources. Physicians appear to see and rate more severe levels of psychopathology than nurses. The subjective aspects of a patient's illness such as delusions of guilt, hopelessness, suicidal thoughts, and indecisiveness are more likely to be rated as present by physicans than by nurses. Relative to physicians, nurses tend to generalize their impressions and are less discriminating in reacting to symptomatic distinctions. There is, in other words, more "halo effect" evident in nurse's ratings. The findings suggest that the nurses' observations are guided by the need to maintain ward routine and are especially sensitive to characteristics that complicate her work. In contrast the physician emphasizes how the patient feels and what he thinks.

TABLE 5.11
CORRELATIONS OF DEFINING VARIABLES WITH THE HOSTILE BELLIGERENCE SYNDROME (WARD)
(DECIMAL POINTS OMITTED)

Variable	Study					
	D(M)	LJO	GK	LO	L(W)	WB
Exhibits irritability	51	65			53	
Loses temper or throws tantrums	47			48		55
Swears or uses obscene language		65		53		65
Spontaneously assaultive			85	35		56
Bullies others		59	54			
Combative and assaultive		64		50	71	75
Shouts and yells				48	52	36
Impudent or impolite			63		56	

The Hostile Belligerence (W) pattern is well defined and will be recognized by most clinicians (Table 5.11). The irritable hostility, the assaults, and temper tantrums suggest an impulsive acting out. As will be shown in Chapter 7 the syndrome is correlated with the interview pattern of the same name and may be synonymous with it. The expression of the pattern is, of course, somewhat different on the ward since peers and ward aides rather than doctors are involved. Certainly its appearance in so many studies provides ample confirmation.

The Resistiveness (W) pattern (Table 5.12) has appeared in four analyses all based on ward data. Although narrow in scope it relates to Retardation, to Hostile Belligerence (W), and to Paranoid Projection. A study is needed to explore the full meaning of Resistiveness which at present is quite narrow in content. Another possible extension is to the interview. There may be an interview analogue of Resistiveness.

TABLE 5.12
CORRELATIONS OF DEFINING VARIABLES WITH THE RESISTIVENESS SYNDROME (WARD)
(DECIMAL POINTS OMITTED)

Variable	Study			
	LJO	LOS	GK	LO
Reluctant to cooperate	84	40	75	
Resists doing expected activities	60	36		41
Requires urging to do what is expected		46	54	
Does the opposite of what he is asked				38

TABLE 5.13
CORRELATIONS OF DEFINING VARIABLES WITH AN OVERACTIVITY SYNDROME (WARD)
(DECIMAL POINTS OMITTED)

Variable	Study			
	LJO	LOS	LO	L(W)
Livelier than most		63		
Moves faster than average		59		
Restless		55		37
Hard to stop if spoken to	53	39		
Usually found with others	49	37		
Is always doing something	57		84	
Busy with plans and projects			66	60

Table 5.13 presents a somewhat doubtful syndrome. It is unclear whether the factor defines an excitement, a temperament characteristic, or an overactivity in response to inner problems. It is tentatively called overactivity.

SUMMARY

The chapter was devoted to the cross-identification of syndromes isolated in thirteen factor analyses. The evidence reviewed was in the form of tables of correlations of defining variables with syndromes. It was concluded that ten interview syndromes could be considered confirmed. These syndromes are Excitement, Hostile Belligerence, Paranoid Projection, Grandiose Expansiveness, Perceptual Distortion, Anxious Intropunitiveness, Retardation and Apathy, Motor Disturbances, Disorientation, and Conceptual Disorganization. In addition three ward syndromes have the necessary supporting evidence.

How valid are the psychotic syndromes? How do they relate to conventional psychiatric diagnostic classes? Are the syndromes sensitive to the influence of the tranquilizing drugs? Are they useful in treatment? These and other questions will be discussed in the chapters that follow.

CHAPTER 6

HIGHER LEVEL SYNDROMES

IN THE previous three chapters evidence was presented concerning ten syndromes of deviant behavior and how they may be measured in a carefully conducted interview. In this chapter data are offered concerning a hierarchical organization of deviant behavior, thinking, and perception. The conceptual scheme consists of a hierarchy of graded categories beginning with specific symptoms which join in first-order syndromes. The first-order syndromes define a smaller number of second-order syndromes which in turn define a higher order syndrome.

HIGHER ORDER SYNDROMES

While factor analysis is a useful tool in hypothesis formation, it cannot provide a theory of the organization of the syndromes. Unifying conceptual schemes or models must be provided by the investigator. Tucker (1940) and Thurstone (1947) have developed the concept of higher order factors which can be isolated from the correlations among the first-order factors. The factoring procedure is no different from that involved in analyzing the correlations of individual measures to identify first-order factors. The higher order factors provide, in the domain of psychosis, tentative definitions of more inclusive categories than the first-order syndromes. It should be noted, however, that higher level syndromes represent linear combinations of the first-order syndromes and not independent dimensions. The relations among the first-order, the second-order and the third-order syndromes may be represented diagrammatically as in Figure 6.1. Several individual scales define each first-order syndrome. Two or more first-order syndromes participate in and serve to define each second-order syndrome. The third-order syndrome is, in this case, based on contributions from all of the second-order syndromes. The arrangement as a whole offers a hierarchical organization of a set of categories. Evidence towards the tenability of such a structure is offered in subsequent sections of the chapter.

TABLE 6.1
SECOND-ORDER FACTORS
DEGAN ANALYSIS
(DECIMAL POINTS OMITTED)

	Second-Order				
First-Order	W	X	Y	Z	
Hyperirritability	61		-37	33	HOS
Manic Hyperexcitability	56				EXC
Schizophrenic Dissociation		68			CNP
Traumatic Hysteria		45	-20	35	DIS
Hyperprojection		40	-52		PCP
Neurasthenia	-26		63		RTD (?)
Depression			51	-42	INP
Catatonia				71	MTR
Deterioration	22			32	?

CRITERIA FOR AN ADEQUATE ANALYSIS

Earlier, in Chapter 4, some of the experimental and statistical requirements essential to an adequate factor analysis were sketched. These same basic requirements must be satisfied in a second-order analysis. All known sources of trait and individual variation should be represented. Excited and depressed, confused and deluded, agitated and retarded, anxious and apathetic—all such varied types of patients and symptoms should be included. The necessity of achieving a clear simple structure becomes crucial as the direction and size of the correlations among the first-order syndromes determine the nature of the higher order solution. For these reasons, it is especially difficult to satisfy the invariance requirement. It will be recalled this principle demands that the factor analyses yield the same test-factor correlations, apart from errors, regardless of the test battery in which they are included. In brief, the test-factor correlations should not depend upon what other measures are included. As the data are presented, it will be seen that some second-order factors are nevertheless confirmed.

In the sections that follow, an effort is made to review those findings currently available. Studies mentioned, naturally, correspond closely to those already discussed in the context of first-order syndromes. Following this review, tentative hypotheses are presented concerning the nature of these broader syndromes.

DEGAN'S HIGHER LEVEL PATTERNS

The correlations among the first-order syndromes obtained from Moore's data were also factored by Degan (1952). The four second-order factors as defined by the first-order variables are given in Tables 6.1 and 6.2. The labels on the left side of Table 6.1 are Degan's, while those on the right represent a translation into IMPS syndromes. In the review of Chapter 4 it was pointed out that only six of Degan's Syndromes appear to have been confirmed in subsequent studies, namely: Hyperprojection, Depression, Manic Hyperexcitability, Catatonia, Schizophrenic Dissociation, and Traumatic Hysteria.

The four higher order patterns obtained are interpreted by Degan as Mania (W), Hebephrenic Schizophrenia (X), Paranoid-Depressive Psychosis (Y), and Catatonic Schizophrenia (Z). Factor W is very probably a ward factor as the defining syndromes are based on ward observations of excitement, destructiveness, euphoria, irritability, tantrums, and talking to voices (Table 6.2). It is very similar to what Lorr *et al.*, (1954) have called Hostile Belligerence. The Hebephrenic Schizophrenia (X) is most similar to the Schizophrenic Disorganization pattern found in IMPS.

Factor Y is interpreted by Degan as Paranoid-Depressive. This interpretation of Y is very doubtful. Moore included no specific paranoid scale variable. The scale most indicative of paranoid ideation concerns rational delusions (Scale 3, Table 6.2). Further, the Hyperprojection factor is defined principally by hallucinations and bizarre delusions. It would appear best to regard Y as a depression with retardation in which projection in the form of hallucinations and delusions is absent. Factor Z is defined primarily by motor disorganization and some disorientation, and the absence of thinking disturbances.

TABLE 6.2
CORRELATIONS OF SCALE VARIABLES WITH DEGAN'S SECOND-ORDER FACTORS (LORR ANALYSIS)
(DECIMAL POINTS OMITTED)

	Second-Order			
	W	X	Y	Z
1. Disorientation in Time	02	48	-12	29
2. Disorientation in Space	-05	36	-06	25
3. Rational Delusions	06	33	-09	-04
4. Bizarre Delusions	-03	29	-44	35
5. Hypochondriacal Delusions	-05	19	-10	01
6. Auditory Hallucinations	00	38	-25	18
7. Visual Hallucinations	17	41	-36	00
8. Tactual Hallucination	00	36	-40	03
9. Other Hallucinations	14	31	-38	07
10. Absence of Insight	01	22	-28	26
11. Shut-in	-14	32	19	43
12. Loss of Finer Sensibilities	19	25	16	30
13. Mutism	-08	-05	11	63
14. Negativism	00	01	09	63
15. Refusal of Food	07	-05	38	46
16. Stereotypism of Attitude	-16	25	07	45
17. Stereotypism of Actions	-01	38	00	32
18. Sterotypism of Words	07	60	-12	12

TABLE 6.2 (CONTINUED)

	W	X	Y	Z
19. GIGGLING	02	26	-16	36
20. DESTRUCTIVENESS	44	06	04	33
21. TALKING TO VOICES	43	46	-22	13
22. IRRITABILITY	54	06	-33	33
23. TANTRUMS	47	-04	-12	21
24. HOMICIDAL TENDENCY	20	03	-14	22
25. EXCITEMENT	55	12	-06	-01
26. EUPHORIA	34	-16	-43	01
27. DEPRESSION	-07	-21	50	-41
28. ANXIETY	26	-02	24	-40
29. TEARFULNESS	12	-23	21	-16
30. RETARDATION	-20	-06	43	-13
31. NEURASTHENIA	-11	11	41	04
32. SUICIDAL TENDENCY	-05	-29	22	04

WITTENBORN SCALE FACTORS

Reanalysis of the Wittenborn–Holzberg data (Lorr, 1957) yielded seven first-order and three second-order factors. The second-order factors are presented in Table 6.3. The first factor (X), defined by Anxious Intropunitiveness and Phobic-Compulsive, represents a more general turning against the self. The second factor (Y) represents a Paranoid Belligerence that has been found elsewhere (Lorr, Jenkins, and Holsopple, 1954). It is defined by paranoid ideation, belligerence, combativeness, and motor restlessness. The third factor (Z) represents thinking disorganization joined with slowed psychomotor activity.

Total score correlations may also be analyzed to determine higher-level factors. One published table of correlations among

Wittenborn's PRS (Fruedenberg and Robertson, 1956) was analyzed and three factors were obtained. However, interpretation must be guarded as some of the scores are not experimentally independent, i.e., certain rating scales contribute to several of the scores and thus spuriously increase correlations. Factor X in

TABLE 6.3
SECOND-ORDER SYNDROMES
LORR ANALYSIS OF WITTENBORN–HOLZBERG DATA
(DECIMAL POINTS OMITTED)

First-Order	Second-Order		
	X	Y	Z
A. Paranoid Projection	-02	44	-11
B. Conceptual Disorganization	00	-02	52
C. Hostile Belligerence	02	49	09
D. Anxious Intropunitiveness	58	-07	-27
E. Hysteric Conversion	-15	26	13
F. Excitement	-06	34	-39
G. Phobic-Compulsive	64	07	04

Table 6.4 is seen to be very similar to Factor X in the Wittenborn–Holzberg data. Factor Y appears to represent an excitement with some schizophrenic coloring. Factor Z appears to represent a schizophrenic disorganization similar to that found by Degan and by Lorr in IMPS.

MSRPP HIGHER ORDER SYNDROMES

In a study of 153 chronic schizophrenics Lorr, Jenkins, and Holsopple (1954) obtained the correlations among eleven factor scores based on the Multidimensional Scale for Rating Psychiatric Patients (Lorr, 1953). A factor analysis yielded three second-order factors labeled Alpha, Beta, and Gamma (Table 6.5). Alpha, a bipolar continuum, represents excitement versus a retarded, resistive withdrawal with motor disturbances. Most scales defining the first-order syndrome Excitement versus Depression were

TABLE 6.4
SECOND-ORDER SYNDROMES BASED ON
PRS FACTOR SCORES (LORR ANALYSIS)
(DECIMAL POINTS OMITTED)

First-Order	Second-Order		
	X	Y	Z
Anxiety	79	07	02
Phobic	78	-08	-01
Depressed State	39	68	-21
Schizophrenic Excitement	00	77	56
Paranoid Condition	16	61	27
Paranoid Schizophrenia	11	87	08
Hebephrenic Schizophrenia	-06	74	47
Hysteric	10	-27	44
Manic State	00	05	63

TABLE 6.5
MSRPP SECOND-ORDER FACTORS
LORR, JENKINS, HOLSOPPLE ANALYSIS
(DECIMAL POINTS OMITTED)

	Alpha	Beta	Gamma
Excitement vs. Retardation	55		
Resistance	49	36	66
Paranoid Distortion		47	
Overactivity		20	
Melancholy Agitation	-60	-27	
Perceptual Distortion		85	
Motor Disturbances	-60		31
Belligerence			86
Withdrawal	-85		77
Grandiosity		37	48
Conceptual Disorganization	64	65	22

bipolar. Hence a negative sign preceding its correlation with the higher order factor may be interpreted as retardation. Beta is defined principally by PCP, CNP, PAR, and GRN. In the original report, Beta was interpreted as a Thinking Disorganization. A more valid interpretation perhaps is that Beta is Paranoid Process. This interpretation will be elaborated shortly. The third factor, Gamma, is clearly a ward syndrome of Hostile Belligerence similar to Degan's W (Mania).

TABLE 6.6
SECOND-ORDER SYNDROMES
IMPS EXPERIMENTAL DATA
(DECIMAL POINTS OMITTED)

First-Order	Second-Order		
	X	Y	Z
Excitement	74	-05	04
Hostile Belligerence	55	44	-02
Paranoid Projection	-06	68	02
Grandiose Expansiveness	-07	27	63
Perceptual Distortion	10	20	62
Anxious Intropunitiveness	12	17	10
Retardation and Apathy	-54	-21	23
Motor Disturbances	28	-16	19
Conceptual Disorganization	41	36	40

HIGHER LEVEL SYNDROMES IN IMPS

Two analyses of the correlations among IMPS syndromes are available (Tables 6.6 and 6.7). The first analysis is based on data collected on an experimental form of IMPS, while the second derives from the normative sample for IMPS. In order to indicate fully the relations of the second-order syndromes, the correlations of the individual scales with the second-order patterns were also derived and are presented in Table 6.8.

TABLE 6.7
SECOND-ORDER SYNDROMES
IMPS NORMATIVE DATA
(DECIMAL POINTS OMITTED)

FIRST-ORDER	SECOND-ORDER		
	X	Y	Z
EXCITEMENT	79	-08	06
HOSTILE BELLIGERENCE	59	10	-26
PARANOID PROJECTION	15	66	-01
GRANDIOSE EXPANSIVENESS	-05	43	-04
PERCEPTUAL DISTORTION	00	67	01
ANXIOUS INTROPUNITIVENESS	-29	20	-11
RETARDATION AND APATHY	-42	-10	59
DISORIENTATION	-06	-02	63
MOTOR DISTURBANCE	14	-01	58
CONCEPTUAL DISORGANIZATION	15	22	56

Factor X in both analyses represents a bipolar variable. At one pole, X is defined by Excitement and Hostility and at the opposite pole by retardation and apathy. Of course, when one set of behaviors is present the other is absent. The variable may well correspond to the classical Manic-Depressive classification. The bipolar nature of X suggests that some antagonistic but reversible biochemical substances may underlie the pattern. It is also noteworthy that while Intropunitiveness is linked to the retarded aspects of X, its contribution to the pattern is not a major one. One possible explanatory hypothesis is that X represents a defensive over- or underactivity in response to threat or anxiety.

The second factor Y in both analyses is defined most prominently by Paranoid Projection. Associated are Perceptual Distortion, Grandiose Expansiveness, Hostility, and to a lesser extent, Conceptual Disorganization. In previous reports this pattern has been labeled Thinking Disorganization. A more fitting hypothesis is that the pattern implies an externalization or attribution of distrustful and hostile feelings to others. To the paranoid individual, people are unfriendly towards him, persecute him, or even try to control him. In time, disembodied voices accuse or threaten him. This may lead him to an insight that he is persecuted because he is important and superior. The diagnosis of Schizophrenic reaction, paranoid type, corresponds fairly closely to Factor Y.

TABLE 6.8

CORRELATIONS OF SCALES WITH SECOND-ORDER FACTORS. IMPS NORMATIVE DATA (DECIMAL POINTS OMITTED)

	Second-Order		
	X	Y	Z
7. Unrestrained Feeling	57	-03	09
9. Hurried Speech	70	01	03
12. Elevated Mood	37	-05	04
15. Attitude of Superiority	56	07	-02
17. Self-Dramatization	57	-03	-05
20. Loud and Boisterous	67	-03	07
26. Overactive	48	00	23
35. Excess Speech	68	-03	07
37. Dominates Interview	68	-03	04
36. Suspicious of People	38	37	-16
59. Ideas of Reference	13	48	12
60. Ideas of Persecution	38	36	-15
61. Ideas of Conspiracy	29	46	-09
62. People Controlling	20	49	-04
63. Forces Controlling	14	45	04
14. Blames Self	-17	15	-16
21. Anxiety (Specific)	-01	17	-23
24. Vaguely Apprehensive	-13	25	-14
27. Self-Depreciating	-23	13	-07

TABLE 6.8 (CONTINUED)

	X	Y	Z
8. LACK OF GOALS	-18	-02	40
13. FIXED FACIES	-49	02	31
16. SLOWED MOVEMENTS	-46	08	35
22. SPEECH BLOCKING	-25	04	45
23. APATHY	-41	00	41
33. WHISPERED SPEECH	-51	00	43
38. FAILURE TO ANSWER	-33	-13	51
54. VOICES EXTOLL	08	44	-01
65. GREAT PERSON	03	33	01
64. UNUSUAL POWERS	27	32	-06
69. DIVINE MISSION	02	40	00
2. IRRELEVANT ANSWERS	25	21	50
3. INCOHERENT ANSWERS	21	19	44
4. RAMBLING ANSWERS	43	19	32
49. NEOLOGISMS	22	16	21
50. STEREOTYPED SPEECH	-02	04	36
70. DISORIENTED AS TO HOSPITAL	-06	01	30
71. DISORIENTED AS TO STATE	-06	-08	48
72. KNOWS NO ONE	-08	-04	38
73. DISORIENTED AS TO SEASON	-06	-10	46
74. DISORIENTED AS TO YEAR	-05	-04	47
75. DISORIENTED AS TO AGE	-09	-09	46
30. SLOVENLY APPEARANCE	09	-07	44
39. SHOWS INSIGHT	21	04	28

TABLE 6.8 (CONTINUED)

	X	Y	Z
29. Depressed in Mood	-31	06	03
31. Guilt and Remorse	-21	21	-11
40. Suicidal Thoughts	-12	17	-12
41. Recurring Thoughts	-02	34	-19
42. Morbid Fears	01	23	-05
66. Ideas of Sinfulness	-19	21	01
45. Hallucinatory Voices	-01	49	11
55. Voices Threaten	00	53	-05
53. Voices Accuse	02	50	00
56. Voices Order	-03	45	08
57. Visions	02	43	03
58. Other Hallucinations	03	33	00
6. Rigid Postures	04	-04	57
46. Giggling	14	05	27
47. Grimacing	12	-01	50
48. Repetitive Movements	10	-02	46
5. Verbally Hostile	45	14	-20
11. Attitude of Contempt	56	-02	-03
18. Hostile Attitude	39	-08	00
25. Irritability	47	-08	-03
28. Blames Others	46	28	-26
32. Bitter and Resentful	46	26	-25
34. Complains and Gripes	52	10	-16
1. Slowed Speech	-33	-08	44

TABLE 6.8 (CONTINUED)

	X	Y	Z
43. COMPULSIVE ACTS	-01	18	06
44. DELUSIONAL BELIEFS	24	53	02
10. OVERT TENSION	24	08	21
51. TALKS TO SELF	10	15	32
52. STARTLED GLANCES	08	18	32
67. IDEAS OF CHANGE	-09	41	02
68. IDEAS OF BODY DESTRUCTION	09	21	-01
19. MEMORY DEFICIT	-16	01	38

There appears to be little agreement on Factor Z in the two IMPS analyses. Because of greater confidence in the final form of IMPS, only its factor Z will be discussed. Factor Z is defined by Motor Disturbances, Disorientation, Retardation, and Conceptual Disorganization. Degan's Factor Z is most similar to IMPS Factor Z. Only Retardation is absent from the Degan pattern. A Schizophrenic Disorganization evidenced both in bizarre motor behavior and thinking disturbances (CNP) is implied. A reading of the description of Schizophrenic reaction, hebephrenic type, reveals little correspondence. Comparison with Schizophrenic reaction, catatonic type, is difficult as the diagnosis really includes two states: generalized inhibition, and excessive motor activity and excitement. IMPS Z appears to cut across both diagnoses.

Figure 6.1 presents schematically the obtained relations between the first- and higher order syndromes of IMPS. It shows, for example, how the first-order syndromes of EXC and HOS contribute positively to the excited pole of Excitement versus Retardation. RTD and INP contribute to the retarded and depressed pole (as shown by dotted lines). All three second-order syndromes participate in a third-order syndrome.

The third-order factor was extracted by means of Spearman's single-factor formula (Thurstone, 1947, p. 274). Through use of a suitable transformation, the correlations of the scales with the third-order factor were derived. Table 6.9 presents those variables

TABLE 6.9

CORRELATIONS OF SCALES WITH THIRD-ORDER FACTORS. IMPS NORMATIVE DATA (DECIMAL POINTS OMITTED)

		CORRELATION
2.	IRRELEVANT ANSWERS	44
3.	INCOHERENT ANSWERS	39
4.	RAMBLING ANSWERS	34
50.	STEREOTYPED SPEECH	25
49.	NEOLOGISMS	22
6.	RIGID POSTURES	38
47.	GRIMACING	35
48.	REPETITIVE MOVEMENTS	32
46.	GIGGLING	22
74.	DISORIENTATION: YEAR	30
71.	DISORIENTATION: STATE	29
73.	DISORIENTATION: SEASON	27
75.	DISORIENTATION: AGE	27
72.	KNOWS NO ONE	23
70.	DISORIENTATION: HOSPITAL	20
51.	TALKS TO SELF	28
52.	STARTLED GLANCES	28
59.	IDEAS OF REFERENCE	25
39.	NO INSIGHT	23
19.	MEMORY DEFICIT	23

TABLE 6.9 (CONTINUED)

	CORRELATION
45. HALLUCINATORY VOICES	22
44. DELUSIONAL BELIEFS	21
30. SLOVENLY APPEARANCE	29
22. SPEECH BLOCKING	28
38. FAILURE TO ANSWER	25
8. LACK OF GOALS	23
26. OVERACTIVE	23
1. SLOWED SPEECH	22
23. APATHY	21
33. WHISPERED SPEECH	21
10. OVERT TENSION	20

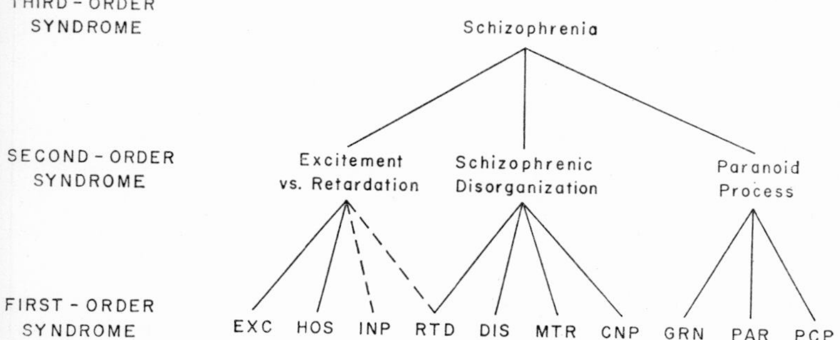

FIG. 6.1. Diagram of the relations among syndromes identified in IMPS (Dotted line indicates negative relationships)

correlating 0.20 or higher with the third-order factor. The correlations among the second-order factors and their correlations with the third-order factor are given in the Appendix. The impression one gets is that of symptoms and behaviors typical of schizophrenia. Alternatively anxiousness, depression, manic excitement and hostility are absent. In brief, affective elements that define EXC, HOS, and INP play no role. A tentative hypothesis is that the third-order factor represents the elements common to the schizophrenic process.

CROSS-STUDY COMPARISONS

The extent of agreement on the second-order syndromes across studies can now be examined. As an aid to interpretation, the syndromes identified have been labeled with IMPS titles. Comparison of columns of Table 6.10 indicates that there is fair agreement on an Excitement versus Retardation factor. The retarded pole of the factor possibly should be labeled depression as it is accompanied by a dysphoric mood. Inspection of the first column of Table 6.8 provides a more concrete notion of the nature of this syndrome than the correlations of 6.10.

Three studies agree fairly well in the definition of a Paranoid Process (Y). This factor (Table 6.11) is hypothesized to represent a tendency to distort and to reorganize thinking and perception. The defense mechanism implied is clearly projection. Mechanisms of defense facilitate the inhibition of needs and the selection of indirect substitute outlets for needs. The reason is that direct expression of such needs would create social difficulties, elicit guilt feelings, and create anxiety. The mechanism of projection requires the disowning of a need and its displacement to a substitute. The individual's mistrust of, and hostility towards, himself and others are attributed to others. The process results in delusions of persecution, hallucinations and eventually ideas of grandeur. The hostility and the conceptual disorganization appear to be peripheral correlates of the process of externalizing blame.

From the viewpoint just described it would appear that the projective mechanism is a form of cognitive reorganization. Both Cameron (1947) and Jenkins (1952) have conceptualized paranoid thinking as a form of cognitive reorganization. Supportive data

TABLE 6.10
THE SECOND-ORDER SYNDROME
EXCITEMENT VS. RETARDATION AND APATHY
(DECIMAL POINTS OMITTED)

	Analysis		
	Experimental	Normative	
	IMPS	IMPS	MSRPP
First-Order	X	X	Alpha
Excitement	74	79	55
Hostile Belligerence	55	59	04
Retardation and Apathy	-54	-42	-85
Conceptual Disorganization	41	15	64
Motor Disturbance	28	14	-60
Anxious Intropunitiveness	12	-29	-60

for this viewpoint has been recently reported by McReynolds (1963). He tested the hypothesis that highly delusional schizophrenics, when presented with an ambiguous stimulus (Mooney's Closure Test), would attempt the identification of more pictures

TABLE 6.11
THE SECOND-ORDER SYNDROME
PARANOID PROCESS
(DECIMAL POINTS OMITTED)

	Analysis		
	Experimental	Normative	
	IMPS	IMPS	MSRPP
First-Order	Y	Y	Beta
Paranoid Projection	68	66	47
Perceptual Distortion	20	67	85
Grandiose Expansiveness	27	43	37
Hostile Belligerence	44	10	14
Conceptual Disorganization	36	22	65

than minimally delusional patients. His data supported this notion as far as delusions are concerned. Riss (1959) tested the hypothesis that an auditory hallucination is a perception involving distortion of a stimulus rather than a perception in the absence of an external stimulus. He found that auditory hallucinations do indeed occur significantly more frequently in the presence of sound stimuli. The findings of Riss and of McReynolds are thus consistent with the proposed hypothesis that paranoid delusions and auditory hallucinations represent a Paranoid Process.

Confirmation of the IMPS second-order factor Schizophrenic Disorganization in data reported earlier is uncertain. Degan's Factor Z is a possible match for IMPS factor Z. The central element to the syndrome appears to be a profound disturbance in thinking, motor behavior, and orientation. Meehl's (1962) signs of schizophrenia, such as cognitive slippage (associative dyscontrol), psychomotor dyscontrol, vestibular malfunction, body image anomalies, and spatial aberrations, are suggestive of the above syndrome. All of the syndromes defining factor Z are significantly correlated with duration of hospitalization (see Chapter 7). Research may also reveal that the syndrome correlates highly with a social biography characteristic of a "process" schizophrenia.

The fourth second-order syndrome is called Intropunitiveness, as it appears to represent a turning against the self. Philips and Rabinovitz (1958) have reported a similar broad category. The defensive mechanism implied corresponds to Rosenzweig's (1938) concept of intropunitiveness, from which the label derives. The syndrome fails to appear in IMPS at a second-order level for the simple reason that at least two variables sharing variance must be present before a factor can be defined. The pattern appears only when the Wittenborn PRS scales are analyzed, mainly because a Phobic syndrome is included which overlaps with the Anxiety syndrome. The factor resembles the diagnoses of Involutional psychotic reaction and Phobic reaction combined.

A second-order ward syndrome of Hostile Belligerence, identifiable in ward observations, has also been noted in Moore's data (Factor W), in the Wittenborn–Holzberg data (Factor Y), and in MSRPP data (Factor Gamma). A closely similar symptom has been found by Lorr and O'Connor (1962) in the Psychotic Reaction Profile.

SUMMARY

Available reports of second-order factors in the domain of psychotic behavior and ideation observable in an interview were reviewed. Four second-order or higher level interview syndromes appear to be confirmed in at least two studies. These syndromes are Excitement versus Retardation, Paranoid Process, Schizophrenic Disorganization, and Intropunitiveness. Together, the scales, the first-order syndromes, the second-order syndromes, and a third-order syndrome provide a hierarchical conceptualization of psychotic psychopathology.

CHAPTER 7

VALIDITY OF THE SYNDROMES

TRADITIONALLY, the validity of a psychological test or rating scale has been defined as the extent to which the instrument measures what it purports to measure. However, it has been found useful to distinguish several kinds of validity labeled construct, content, predictive and concurrent validity (Amer. Psychol. Assoc., 1954). The point of view taken here is that construct validity is central (Loevinger, 1957) and that the remaining concepts may be regarded as components of construct validity. By a construct is meant some postulated attribute or trait of persons, assumed to be reflected in behavior or test performance. The validity of a construct (trait, attribute, syndrome) is established by convergence of several sources of evidence. One source is substantive or content validity, which should be consistent with the proposed interpretation. Content validity is evaluated by demonstrating how well the content of the test samples the domain of behavior about which inferences are to be drawn. Further, the proposed interpretation of the test should be consistent with its substance or content. For example, a measure of psychomotor retardation should sample broadly the universe of behaviors believed to define retardation.

A second component of construct validity may be called structural. It is assessed by comparing the psychometric relationships among the test variables with the relations among non-test manifestations of the same trait. The relations among symptoms of psychoticism are illustrative. They vary in intensity and frequency and nearly every symptom may be manifested by a patient. These relations suggest a quantitative model of measurement. It would follow that symptoms of psychotic behavior should not be treated as though they were qualities invariantly present (or almost so). In brief, a class model as described in an earlier chapter is not consistent with the facts, while a quantitative model fits well.

A third component of construct validity may be described as

external validity (Loevinger, 1957). If relevant external criteria are collected at the same time as the test, and correlated with it, concurrent validity is at issue. Correlations with criteria secured at a later time represent evidence of predictive validity. Predictive validity is assessed by showing how well predictions made from the test are confirmed by evidence gathered at a later date. Concurrent validity is evaluated by determining how well the test scores on the instrument to be validated correspond to scores on other measures of the same trait. Concurrent validity is also shown if the test discriminates between several groups who differ on some relevant variable. A test may have concurrent validity but not have predictive validity. Concurrent validity would be demonstrated if IMPS scores were shown to be highly related to independent estimates of clinical status made by the ward psychiatrist. If IMPS scores accurately predicted length of stay in the hospital, it would possess predictive validity for that purpose. In general, to the extent that correlates can be specified, either present or future, from a knowledge of the proposed construct or from the theoretical system within which it is embedded, the construct gains support.

In the present context it is important to distinguish between the validity of the concepts, i.e., the syndromes themselves, and the validity of the IMPS which purports to measure them. The syndrome set that has been described is one way of organizing and conceptualizing psychopathological behavior. Evidence of these syndromes has been found repeatedly in independent factor analyses of a variety of item material. In two independent factor analyses of essentially the same form of the IMPS on separate and sizeable patient samples, the ten hypothesized syndromes emerged as predicted and prior to conventional transformations. The syndromes can be accepted as stable recurring clusters of behavior, hypothesized and confirmed.

In the IMPS the behavioral items that define the syndromes demonstrate considerable homogeneity of content and they possess "face" validity, i.e., they appear to be related on the basis of content to what they are supposed to measure. But how do the syndrome scores relate to external criteria? On the simplest level is the expectation that they differentiate between known groups in predicted directions. For example, open ward patients are typically less disturbed than closed ward patients; most of the syndromes should then discriminate between open and closed ward patients. Table 7.1 shows that the means of all syndromes are in the predicted direction and all mean differences are significant except INP, RTD, and DIS. Possibly DIS failed to discriminate between ward groups because disorientation is relatively rare in the sample studied. Syndromes such as EXC and HOS may be more often considered as determinants of closed ward assignment than INP or RTD, although depression and fear of suicide are often the basis for closed ward assignment and might be reflected by high scores on these two syndromes.

PATIENT TYPE

In the nucleus normative sample, selection of patients for rating was stratified with respect to nine areas of prominent symptomatology so that a wide range of psychopathology would be represented. Patients were sought who were actively hallucinatory, exhibiting bizarre postures, manic excited, hostile and belligerent, highly paranoid, anxious and depressed, retarded and depressed, apathetic and unmotivated, or showing disturbed thinking. The categories were not intended to be independent or mutually exclusive; a highly paranoid patient, for example, might have also been markedly hostile and belligerent. When the IMPS syndrome scores were analyzed by patient type, there were a number of predictable relationships confirmed. Patients selected as manic excited, for example, were expected to have high scores on EXC and low scores on RTD. Patients selected as retarded and depressed were expected to show just the opposite. Actively hallucinatory patients were expected to have high scores on PCP and highly paranoid patients were expected to have high scores on PAR. These and many other relationships were evident by inspection of the means. Table 7.2 contains point biserial correlations computed between each patient type versus all other patients and syndrome score for each of the ten syndromes. These correlations are not high but present a very consistent and convincing picture of the extent to which each syndrome is related to the patient type. The way the table is arranged, most of the predicted positive relationships are clustered around the main diagonal.

The correlations are substantially higher if contrasts are made between patient types expected on theoretical grounds to manifest the syndrome and those not expected to do so. For example, when manic excited patients were compared only with retarded depressed patients, the point biserial with EXC rose to 0.74. When manic excited, hostile belligerent and highly paranoid patients all of whom were expected to manifest EXC and HOS were contrasted with all other patients the correlations were 0.50 and 0.57

TABLE 7.1

SYNDROME SCORES OF OPEN AND CLOSED WARD PATIENTS

Syndrome	Open Ward (N=61)		Closed Ward (N=146)		t
	Mean	S.D.	Mean	S.D.	
Excitement	20.1	30.26	33.5	33.15	2.76**
Hostile Belligerence	16.7	22.54	36.7	34.15	4.27**
Paranoid Projection	15.9	24.33	34.2	31.30	4.14**
Grandiose Expansiveness	4.5	10.97	11.8	17.01	3.14**
Perceptual Distortion	6.9	11.60	10.9	16.58	1.72*
Anxious Intropunitiveness	14.7	29.28	22.2	34.70	1.51
Retardation and Apathy	35.9	28.73	36.8	32.35	.07
Disorientation	1.3	2.54	1.8	3.23	.05
Motor Disturbance	15.4	17.16	25.2	21.44	3.23**
Conceptual Disorganization	8.7	14.13	16.4	16.83	3.18**

* $p < .05$; one tailed test.
** $p < .005$; one tailed test.

respectively. Both anxious depressed and retarded depressed patients were expected to manifest INP and there was no particular reason to expect the other groups to do so; the point biserial was 0.53. All of these correlations provide supportive evidence for the concurrent validity of the syndromes.

The bottom row of Table 7.2 also gives the correlation ratio (eta). This is an index of curvilinear correlation between the syndrome score and the nine patient types considered simultaneously. The

TABLE 7.2

POINT BISERIAL CORRELATIONS BETWEEN SYNDROME SCORES AND PATIENT TYPES (DECIMAL POINTS OMITTED)

PATIENT TYPE	N	EXC	HOS	PAR	GRN	PCP	INP	RTD	DIS	MTR	CNP
MANIC EXCITED	17	51*	10	01	03	-07	08	-22*	-07	-01	13
HOSTILE BELLIGERENT	14	14*	31*	10	-03	-01	-12	-06	05	15*	04
HIGHLY PARANOID	33	15*	42*	48*	30*	01	-07	-25*	-20*	-06	01
ACTIVELY HALLUCINATORY	21	-08	-06	02	01	31*	-04	00	14*	-01	04
ANXIOUS, DEPRESSED	17	-02	-04	-05	-09	13	38*	-09	-12	07	-13
RETARDED DEPRESSED	29	-25*	-24*	-24*	-17*	-06	33*	22*	-11	-14*	-23*
APATHETIC, UNMOTIVATED	23	-23*	-25*	-21*	-12	-09	-12	21*	16*	-10	-07
BIZZARE POSTURES	16	-04	-12	-15*	-06	-09	-18*	05	02	18*	02
DISTURBED THINKING	23	-10	-11	-03	09	11	-14*	11	17*	00	22*
ETA	193	62	62	56	36	37	55	45	36	29	36

* $p < .05$; two tailed test.

index is high if the differences between the patient types in mean syndrome scores are marked compared to the overall dispersion of scores. The index is low if the differences between the types are small and also members within a type vary considerably in score. As may be seen, eta is substantial for about half of the syndromes.

DIAGNOSIS

Conventional psychiatric diagnoses were also available for most of these patients. These diagnoses were made by many psychiatrists at many hospitals and are subject to all of the sources of unreliability previously discussed. Some diagnostic groups were combined because so few cases were represented. Schizophrenia includes cases of simple, undifferentiated, and affective schizophrenia. Depression includes cases diagnosed psychotic, involutional, agitated and manic-depressive depression. Table 7.3 presents the point biserial correlations computed as previously described between syndrome scores and diagnostic group membership. According to these data, the paranoid patients as compared with all other patients are characterized by HOS, PAR, GRN, and CNP but are lacking INP. Depressed patients compared with all others are high on INP and low on EXC, HOS, PAR, GRN, and CNP. The manic patients are high on EXC but low on PCP and RTD when compared with other types of patients. The other relationships are similarly interpreted.

Multiple correlations between diagnostic class and the ten syndrome scores were also computed. The diagnostic groups most accurately classified by the multiple regression analyses were manic-excited, depression (mixed type) and paranoid schizophrenia. Paranoid schizophrenia was differentiated from the other groups fairly well (R=0.56) by means of five syndromes: high scores on PAR and HOS; low scores on INP, EXC, and PCP. Manic-excited patients were differentiated (R=0.57) by four syndromes: high scores on EXC and low scores on HOS, MTR, and CNP. Depressed patients were differentiated (R=0.60) by high scores on INP and low scores on PAR. Diagnoses of hebephrenic, catatonic, and mixed schizophrenics were not accurately differentiated. As with the data on patient types, the multiple correlations and the comparisons in Table 7.3 were made between

TABLE 7.3

POINT BISERIAL CORRELATIONS BETWEEN SYNDROME SCORES AND DIAGNOSES
(DECIMAL POINTS OMITTED)

DIAGNOSIS	N	EXC	HOS	PAR	GRN	PCP	INP	RTD	DIS	MTR	CNP
SCHIZOPHRENIA	53	-14*	-19*	-08	01	13	-06	00	-02	-01	-04
PARANOID	71	13	42*	40*	16*	-01	-19*	-11	09	06	17*
HEBEPHRENIC	19	-02	-10	-02	03	11	-11	18*	-13	09	08
CATATONIC	10	-09	-18*	-17*	-11	-02	-03	14*	-02	02	-08
DEPRESSION	27	-18*	-20*	-24*	-20*	-13	52*	09	05	-12	-22*
MANIC-EXCITED	10	42*	06	-11	05	-14*	-09	-19*	10	-04	02
ETA	190	49	48	44	26	24	54	32	20	17	28

* $p < .05$; two tailed test.

one diagnostic class and all others. This tends to obscure the differentiating features between any two classes. If a greater number of cases had been available, particularly for the smaller groups, it would have been informative to compare each pair of diagnostic groups.

CORRELATES OF THE SYNDROMES

Table 7.4 presents the correlations (eta) of age, education, and duration of hospitalization with the syndrome scores for this sample of patients. EXC and INP scores are slightly associated with age. There is also modest, though significant, association between EXC, PCP, and MTR, and education. The correlations of duration of hospitalization with RTD, DIS, MTR, and CNP are more meaningful. These four variables together define the morbidity score described as Schizophrenic Disorganization and high scores simply represent the end process of long term hospitalization. On the other hand this morbidity score may be of value in predicting duration of hospitalization. As expected, Anxious Intropunitiveness is negatively related to duration. Patients with high INP scores do not stay in the hospital long *or* by the time a patient has been in the hospital a long time, he no longer manifests high INP. Both are reasonable hypotheses although the latter seems a better interpretation of these data. The direction of the remaining non-significant correlations is consistent with expectation.

AN APPLICATION OF THE IMPS

The IMPS has now been used in three large scale cooperative drug studies (Casey *et al.*, 1961; Overall *et al.*, 1962; Lasky *et al.*, 1962). The results of each of these is pertinent to the validity of the syndromes but only the last will be discussed in any detail as the other two used an earlier experimental version of the IMPS. This was a comparative study of the relative clinical effectiveness of six tranquilizing drugs with newly admitted schizophrenic patients: chlorpromazine, chlorprothixene, fluphenazine, reserpine, thioridazine, and triflupromazine. All of these drugs were assumed to be effective agents on the basis of at least some reliable evidence from earlier studies. Reserpine was expected to be relatively less effective than some or all of the other drugs but not enough was known to make any other predictions with confidence. Comparisons of chlorpromazine and thioridazine (Azima *et al.*, 1959; Somerville *et al.*, 1960; Woldrop *et al.*, 1961) had failed to demonstrate differences in clinical effectiveness.

TABLE 7.4
CORRELATIONS (ETA) OF AGE, EDUCATION, AND DURATION OF HOSPITALIZATION WITH SYNDROMES
(DECIMAL POINTS OMITTED)

SYNDROME	AGE	EDUCATION	DURATION OF HOSPITALIZATION
EXC	24*	26*	-14
HOS	15	20	-15
PAR	20	15	12
GRN	07	20	11
PCP	18	22*	16
INP	21*	13	-37*
RTD	13	16	34*
DIS	06	15	38*
MTR	18	23*	26*
CNP	12	17	28*

* $p < 0.05$; two tailed test.
Negative sign attached as an aid in interpretation.

In evaluating any form of treatment, it is necessary to have measuring instruments that are sensitive to change when it does occur. After eight weeks of treatment with these six agents significant improvement was observed on all syndromes for two of the drug groups, on most of the syndromes for the other drug groups. Improvement in PAR, INP, RTD, and CNP was significant at the 0.01 level or better for all drug groups. Improvement in HOS, PCP, and MTR was significant at the 0.05 level or better for all groups. Patients receiving reserpine and triflupromazine did not change significantly on EXC although the other four drug groups did. GRN and DIS also failed to reach significance for some drugs. Of the sixty "*t*" tests computed, forty-nine were significant at the 0.01 level or better, five were significant at the 0.05 level and only six failed to reach significance. This implies that all of the syndromes are sensitive to change with treatment at least as perceived by the interviewers making the ratings, and are valid for this purpose.

In a comparative drug study it is desirable to have a rating instrument sensitive enough to detect differences in action among drugs. This is a much finer discrimination than testing differences between pre- and post-treatment ratings or comparing an active agent with a placebo. Most comparative drug studies that have been reported have been unable to distinguish between two active compounds. Failure to reject the hypothesis of no difference is the no man's land of statistical inference. It may be that the drugs are truly equivalent in clinical effectiveness; it may also be that they are quite different but because the measurement of differences is so crude or other uncontrolled aspects of the experiment have introduced so much "noise", these differences are obscured. No conclusion is justified other than the lack of reliable evidence of difference. If a significant difference is found, however, and the experimenter is not willing to consider it a chance occurrence, it implies not only that there is a difference in drug action but that the measuring device is sensitive to it. This reasoning is particularly relevant to the reliability of a test or scale but has implications for its validity as well.

After eight weeks of treatment, significant differences were found among drugs on the following syndromes: EXC, HOS, RTD, and MTR. The first three of these syndromes considered jointly define a higher order bi-polar factor which has been named *Excitement versus Retardation*. A multiple discriminant analysis of the changes in the ten syndrome scores (and four scores from another rating scale) showed that all differences among drugs in amount of change, considered simultaneously, could be accounted for by one significant dimension. The syndromes contributing most to this dimension of change were those already enumerated. This finding made sense both clinically and in terms of previous research. The drugs seem to have their most profound effect on those syndromes associated with activity level; there is reduction of excitement and hostility and paradoxically also a reduction in withdrawal, retardation and apathy.

A MULTIMETHOD TEST OF VALIDITY

Campbell and Fiske (1959) have proposed an approach to validation through inspection of the "multitrait–multimethod matrix". Although our data do not fit their model well, some of their principles can be used in discussing relationships between the syndrome scores and scores obtained from another behavior rating scale. First, measures of the same trait should correlate higher with each other than they do with measures of different traits involving separate methods. Second, these validity values should also be higher than the correlations among different traits measured by the same method.

In the drug study just discussed, patients were assessed by two methods. They were interviewed by a psychologist and a psychiatrist who recorded their impressions on the IMPS. They were also rated by a nurse and a nursing assistant, on the basis of a three-day ward observation period, using the Psychotic Reaction Profile (PRP) (Lorr *et al.*, 1960). The PRP is scored on four areas of psychopathological behavior: Thinking Disorganization, Withdrawal, Agitated Depression, and Paranoid Belligerence. The first three of these correspond respectively to Conceptual Disorganization, Retardation, and Intropunitiveness. Paranoid Belligerence was expected to be correlated with both PAR and HOS. Table 7.5 contains the intercorrelations of the pooled ratings on the IMPS and the PRP for 439 schizophrenic males prior to treatment.

In this particular multitrait–multimethod comparison, method differences are numerous. The two scales are psychometrically quite different. The IMPS contains nine-point severity items, five-point frequency items and dichotomous present–absent items while the PRP is a checklist on which all items are dichotomous, i.e., rated true or not true. The scoring keys of the IMPS were derived from a factor analysis of the items while the scoring keys of the PRP were developed by a method of homogeneous keying (Loevinger *et al.*, 1953) which probably yields variables comparable to higher order factors. The behavior sample to be rated is different; in the one case being of one hour duration and in the other case being three days. Ward behavior is also not expected to be completely comparable to interview behavior. The raters

(DECIMAL POINTS OMITTED)

	IMPS									PRP			
	HOS	PAR	GRN	PCP	INP	RTD	DIS	MTR	CNP	THN	WIT	BEL	AGT
Excitement	51	27	44	11	-01	-24	00	30	47	23	-19	37	-25
Hostile Belligerence		50	25	15	11	-10	-09	13	21	-01	-11	30	-13
Paranoid Projection			37	50	21	-03	-06	16	27	09	07	08	00
Grandiose Expansiveness				30	02	-08	00	08	29	17	04	20	-06
Perceptual Distortion					37	23	08	30	30	13	21	-05	15
Anxious Intropunitiveness						20	-06	07	-02	-16	-03	-10	19
Retardation and Apathy							38	48	25	24	51	-11	39
Disorientation								43	29	28	32	04	20
Motor Disturbance									56	47	39	10	16
Conceptual Disorganization										45	22	12	01
Thinking Disorganization											54	28	23
Withdrawal												03	60
Paranoid Belligerence													00
Agitated Depression													

are different in terms of professional training and in terms of their motivation, their attitudes and opinions about patients. Even the attributes themselves are different, both conceptually and at the level of the item domain being sampled. All of these method differences would tend to decrease cross-method correlations. Another aspect of these data that detracts from the usefulness of the multitrait–multimethod comparison is that the IMPS syndromes were conceived as an intercorrelated set; it is not expected that all intercorrelations will be low.

In spite of these considerations, there is support for the concurrent validity of corresponding scores. CNP correlates higher with Thinking Disorganization (0.45) than it does with any of the other PRP variables and higher than its correlation with most of the other IMPS syndromes. MTR, however, correlates with Thinking Disorganization at a slightly higher level than CNP. If Thinking Disorganization is a higher order factor comparable to those found on the IMPS this association is to be expected. RTD correlates higher with Withdrawal (0.51) than with any of the other IMPS or PRP variables but Withdrawal shows a higher intramethod correlation with Thinking Disorganization (0.54) and Agitated Depression (0.60). INP correlates only 0.19 with Agitated Depression but all of the correlations involving INP tended to be low. The cross-method correlation of HOS and Paranoid Belligerence is satisfactory (0.30) when compared with the correlations of HOS and other PRP variables. However, HOS correlated a good deal higher with PAR (0.50). Paranoid Belligerence and PAR are apparently unrelated at least in this sample. Paranoid Belligerence showed a higher correlation with EXC (0.37) than it did with HOS and a comparable intramethod correlation with Thinking Disorganization (0.28). As the highest values in the matrix are heterotrait–monomethod correlations (i.e., between different scores within a single method), the principles of Campbell and Fiske are not completely satsified.

The Psychotic Reaction Profile has also been factor analyzed (Lorr and O'Connor, 1962) and the eight factors obtained might be expected to be psychometrically more comparable to the IMPS syndromes than were the four cluster scores. Table 7.6 presents these correlations. The correlations among the IMPS syndromes were omitted as they were already presented in Table 7.5. The intercorrelations of the eight PRP factors are shown but are of little value for the multitrait–multimethod comparisons as there is item overlap among factor scores. As a consequence some of the correlations are spuriously high. The cross-method correlations are of the greatest interest and although they tend to be lower than might be desired, they do support again the validity of the IMPS

TABLE 7.6
INTERCORRELATIONS OF IMPS SYNDROMES AND PRP FACTORS
(DECIMAL POINTS OMITTED)

	PRP							
	THN	PAR	ACT	RES	WIT	DOM	AGT	HOS
Excitement	20	08	18	09	-17	33	-25	33
Hostile Belligerence	-02	13	07	09	-11	19	-12	26
Paranoid Projection	09	17	-02	12	05	00	-01	08
Grandiose Expansiveness	14	15	04	14	-01	17	-06	18
Perceptual Distortion	13	07	-11	11	17	-08	14	-03
Anxious Intropunitiveness	-13	-04	-04	-07	-02	-05	20	-07
Retardation and Apathy	26	-05	-39	21	51	-19	40	-11
Disorientation	29	00	-23	22	33	-08	19	01
Motor Disturbance	49	02	-25	27	39	-06	17	08
Conceptual Disorganization	42	03	-10	22	22	02	00	11
Thinking Disorganization		-01	-42	42	58	12	30	22
Paranoid Projection			45	59	-02	-12	-19	24
Overactivity				-13	-75	-05	-68	-03
Resistiveness					46	09	19	41
Withdrawal						-17	61	00
Dominance							-04	61
Agitated Depression								00
Hostile Belligerence								

syndromes. As has been stated previously there is little reason to expect that ward factors and interview factors will be equivalent.

RTD correlates highest with Withdrawal (0.51) and Agitated Depression (0.40), and negatively with Overactivity (—0.39). CNP correlates highest with Thinking Disorganization (0.42). In the factor analysis of the PRP it was possible to isolate both a Paranoid Projection factor and a Hostile Belligerent factor where previously there had been a Paranoid Belligerence cluster. The cross-method correlations of PAR are uniformly low as are those of Paranoid Projection from the PRP. Apparently this syndrome as observed in the interview is not manifested in the ward situation and vice versa. HOS shows a somewhat stronger relationship with its PRP counterpart although EXC is also significantly related to both measures of hostility.

SOME ADDITIONAL DATA

Although somewhat tangential to the question of validity, Table 7.7 contains data which further define the syndromes in

TABLE 7.7
MULTIPLE CORRELATIONS OF EACH IMPS SYNDROME WITH ALL OTHERS
(DECIMAL POINTS OMITTED)

	MULTIPLE CORRELATION	COEFFICIENT OF NONDETERMINATION
EXC	82	33
HOS	79	38
PAR	80	36
GRN	64	58
PCP	59	65
INP	44	81
RTD	65	58
DIS	53	72
MTR	62	62
CNP	76	42

terms of their inter-relationships. To the extent that a syndrome score can be predicted from the other syndrome scores, it is measuring the same thing or combination of things measured by the other syndromes. To turn this around, the extent to which it fails to be predicted may be an indication of its uniqueness. The coefficient of nondetermination can be interpreted as the per cent of variance of the syndrome not held in common or not predictable from the other syndromes. By this criterion, INP is the most unique, while EXC, HOS, and PAR are the least unique. These relationships were based on data from the nucleus normative sample previously discussed.

SUMMARY

The establishment of validity can be considered a task which is never really complete. As new correlates are determined and new predictions confirmed, the definition of a construct becomes firmer and its role in reference to other constructs becomes clearer and clearer. In this chapter a variety of evidence for the concurrent validity of the syndromes has been presented. The syndromes have been shown to be related to open or closed ward assignment, to prominent features of psychopathology and to conventional diagnostic class membership. The syndromes have also been found to be sensitive to change with drug treatment and related to independent estimates of psychopathology derived from another behavior rating scale. In most instances the strength of these relationships is quite satisfactory, particularly when it is recalled that the basic data were collected by many raters, often untrained, at many hospitals under a variety of conditions. In this sense the data presented represent a severe test of the validity of the syndromes.

There is still much work to be done. As yet there is no clear evidence of the predictive validity of the syndromes although it seems reasonable that the level and configuration of syndrome scores might be predictive of treatment outcome, length of stay in the hospital and other criteria. The discussion of the syndrome circle that follows in the next chapter can be considered one type of construct validity.

CHAPTER 8

THE SYNDROME CIRCLE

IN THE sixth chapter, evidence was presented for a hierarchy of syndromes. In the chapter just preceding, some data were offered in support of the functional unity of these more general patterns. In the present chapter, the concept of a circular ordering of the syndromes is developed. Data from several independent sources are cited in support of this conceptual scheme. Finally, some explanatory hypotheses are developed to account for the patterns common to segments of the circular orders obtained.

THE CIRCULAR ORDER CONCEPT

Earlier it was stated that some conceptual framework was needed to relate the various syndromes into a unified network. A hierarchical model of higher order syndromes was suggested as one possible solution. However, such a model is better suited to an all positively correlated set of variables as in the domain of intellect. It seems less appropriate to the often found bipolar variables of personality and psychopathology. Guttman (1954) has proposed a circular ordering of such qualitatively different traits in a domain. This approach also appears capable of accounting for the relationships among the psychotic syndromes. The ordering, which he calls a "circumplex", takes into account both unipolar and bipolar elements and is productive of needed insights into symptom-generating antecedents. Guttman and later Jones (1960) have proposed certain algebraic factor structures to explain a matrix exhibiting "circumplicial" form. Neither of the proposed theories has been tested here. Only the concept of a closed sequence of ordered variables is utilized in what follows.

In a correlation matrix exhibiting a circular order, the correlations are highest next to the principal diagonal which runs from the upper left corner to the lower right corner as in Table 8.1.

Along any row (or column) the correlations decrease in size as one moves further away from the main diagonal, and then they increase again. Thus there are two areas of high correlation: along the principal diagonal and in the lower left-hand corner of the table. Since a correlation table is symmetric, there is a corresponding area of high correlation in the upper right-hand corner. Guttman shows that a table of correlations that can be so arranged represents a circular rank ordering of variables. The arrangement is circular because it represents a sequence without beginning or end. Figure 8.1 depicts how the variables in Table 8.1 may be arranged on a plane surface. The symptom-groupings are equally spaced but this is for esthetic reasons as only a rank ordering has been established. Nor are syndromes opposite each other on the circle necessarily opposing. If the table and figure are studied in relation to each other, it will be seen that contiguous variables are always positively correlated. As one moves around the circle, the correlations of any particular variable, say Excitement, with other variables decrease with distance from it and then increase again as one approaches it on the other side.

TABLE 8.1

CORRELATIONS AMONG EIGHT SYNDROMES BASED ON IMPS NORMATIVE SAMPLE (DECIMAL POINTS OMITTED)

	EXC	GRN	PAR	INP	RTD	DIS	MTR	CNP
EXCITEMENT		44	27	-12	-37	-04	28	46
GRANDIOSE EXPANSIVENESS	44		38	-05	-13	-02	10	31
PARANOID PROJECTION	27	38		16	-12	-06	18	29
ANXIOUS INTROPUNITIVENESS	-12	-05	16		14	-11	-03	-14
RETARDATION AND APATHY	-37	-13	-12	14		36	34	15
DISORIENTATION	-04	-02	-06	-11	36		34	30
MOTOR DISTURBANCE	28	10	18	-03	34	34		51
CONCEPTUAL DISORGANIZATION	46	31	29	-14	15	30	51	

Stated somewhat more rigorously, it can be said that the correlations of any specified variable with its neighbors decrease monotonically (continuously) in size as a function of their sequential separation. Half-way through the sequence, the correlations increase in size monotonically until the main diagonal is reached on the other side. Should personality variables be represented in the matrix, then some of the correlations of X_j with its more

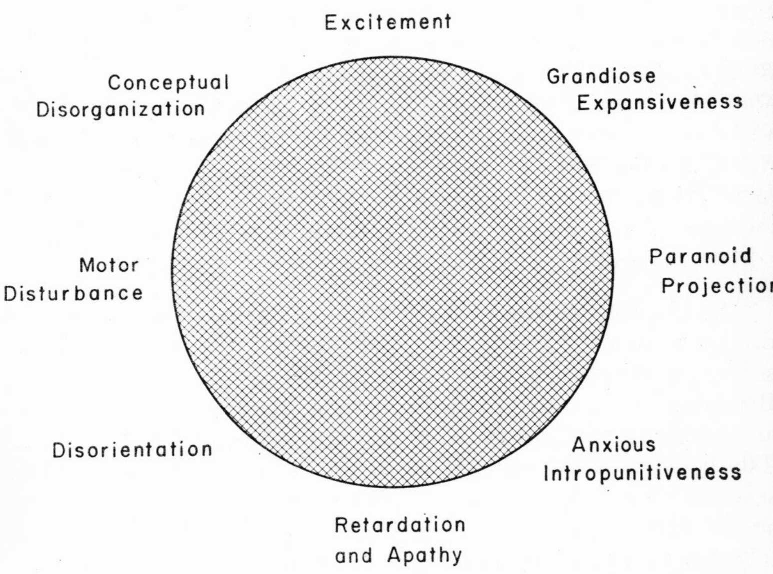

FIG. 8.1. The psychotic syndrome circle.

remote neighbors are likely to be negative rather than zero or positive. Implied here is the presence of common bipolar elements that enter positively into some variables and negatively into others.

The central notion of this conceptualization is order, a sequence of qualitatively different trait variables "which has a circular law of order" (Guttman, 1954, p. 325). In this concept, the idea of dimensionality is extraneous. Of course, the participating variables *could* be regarded as linked together by a number of higher level factors. However, the concept for Guttman is essentially ordinal; the notion of dimensionality has no fundamental role as it has in conventional factor theory.

To test the hypothesis of a circular rank order or law of neighboring, as Guttman refers to it, the variables in a domain are initially arranged in a sequence suggested by knowledge of variable similarity. Next a table of correlations is assembled with a view to satisfying the conditions described, i.e., with the highest correlations along the main diagonal followed by decreasing correlations which then increase again. The question is whether the correlations of each of the variables decrease and increase monotonically in size as a function of the sequential separation between any two. By graphing the variables, a visual check is possible. The size of the correlations can be represented on the ordinate axis and the ordered variables on the abscissa. When the correlations of a variable with all other variables are so plotted, a smooth curve resembling a sine function should appear.

A PSYCHOTIC SYNDROME CIRCLE

The clearest evidence for a circular ordering of psychotic syndromes is shown in Table 8.2. The correlations are based on the scores of the final form of IMPS. Two syndromes, Hostile Belligerence and Perceptual Distortion, do not fit into this sequence and are omitted. Table 8.2 represents an extension of Table 8.1. The correlations of each of the syndromes with the remaining seven is shown in a separate column of Table 8.2. Inspection shows that by and large the expected pattern of decrease and increase in the magnitude of the coefficients in each column is fairly regular. For example, the Excitement syndrome values are $0.44 > 0.27 > -0.12 > -0.37 < -0.04 < 0.28 < 0.46$. The rise and fall of values in the columns is not always continuous, nor are the differences of the same magnitude. The presence of chance errors and the effects of sampling preclude a perfect fit. However, judged subjectively, the fit is fairly good.

Table 8.3 presents the correlations among a set of syndromes based on the experimental form of IMPS (Lorr *et al.*, 1962). The defining variables are very similar to but not identical with those involved in the final form. The correlations among scores were computed by means of the usual formula for correlation among scores of variables (Gulliksen, 1950). Again, while the pattern is not as smooth as in Table 8.1, the same circular order is evident.

TABLE 8.2

CORRELATIONS AMONG EIGHT SYNDROMES BASED ON IMPS NORMATIVE SAMPLE (DECIMAL POINTS OMITTED)

	EXC	GRN	PAR	INP	RTD	DIS	MTR	CNP
Excitement								
Grandiose Expansiveness	44							
Paranoid Expansiveness	27	38						
Anxious Intropunitiveness	-12	-05	16					
Retardation and Apathy	-37	-13	-12	14				
Disorientation	-04	-02	-06	-11	36			
Motor Disturbance	28	10	18	-03	34	34		
Conceptual Disorganization	46	31	29	-14	15	30	51	
Excitement		44	27	-12	-37	-04	28	46
Grandiose Expansiveness			38	-05	-13	-02	10	31
Paranoid Expansiveness				16	-12	-06	18	29
Anxious Intropunitiveness					14	-11	-03	-14
Retardation and Apathy						36	34	15
Disorientation							34	30
Motor Disturbance								51

To rule out the possibility that the circular order obtained was unique to the rating schedule used, supporting data was sought in other investigations. The most likely sources appeared to be the correlations presented by Moore (1933) for his scales, the data presented in the two Wittenborn studies based on PRS, and the Lorr *et al.* (1958) data based mainly on the MSRPP. Since the methods of factoring and the nature of the solutions varied considerably from one analysis to the next, there was a problem in deciding what variables should be combined to form a syndrome. The solution chosen was to define syndromes on the *a priori* basis of knowledge of the IMPS. Correlations among the variables comprising each of the defined clusters were assembled, and correlations among the clusters were then computed.

TABLE 8.3
CORRELATIONS AMONG EIGHT SYNDROMES
BASED ON AN EXPERIMENTAL FORM OF IMPS
(DECIMAL POINTS OMITTED)

	EXC	GRN	PAR	INP	RTD	DIS	MTR	CNP
EXCITEMENT		25	31	03	-48	-07	-17	33
GRANDIOSITY	25		49	-13	00	12	18	54
PARANOID PROJECTION	31	49		06	05	03	12	46
INTROPUNITIVE	03	-13	06		13	-03	12	-12
RETARDED	-48	00	05	13		18	31	36
DISORIENTED	-07	12	03	-03	18		11	17
MOTOR DISTURBANCE	-17	18	12	12	31	11		44
CONCEPTUAL DISORGANIZATION	33	54	46	-12	36	17	44	

The Moore rating schedule does not include variables descriptive of Grandiose Expansiveness nor of Paranoid Projection. As a consequence only six syndromes can be assembled and correlated: Excitement, Anxious Intropunitiveness, Retardation, Disorientation, Motor Disturbances, and Conceptual Disorganization. By a similar process seven syndromes can be assembled from data reported by Wittenborn (1951) and by Wittenborn and Holzberg (1951). The absence of a sufficient number of variables precluded defining a Motor Disturbance syndrome. On the other hand, an Obsessive-Phobic syndrome isolated by Wittenborn could be included. It was hypothesized to fit between PAR and INP. The remaining symptom groupings were Excitement, Paranoid Projection, Grandiose Expansiveness, Intropunitiveness, Retardation, and Conceptual Disorganization.

The seven Moore syndromes were arbitrarily defined in terms of the following variables: (a) *Excitement*: destructiveness, excitement, euphoria; (b) *Intropunitiveness*: depression, anxiety, tearfulness, suicidal tendency, insight; (c) *Retardation*: retardation, neurasthenia, absence of euphoria; (d) *Disorientation*: disorientation for time and for space; (e) *Motor Disturbances*: mutism, negativism, stereotyped postures and actions, giggling, shut-in; (f) *Conceptual Disorganization*: stereotyped words, talking to voices.

The variables used to define each Wittenborn cluster were as follows: (a) *Excitement*: insomnia, ideas change, in constant movement, shouts and sings, variation in speech, mood changes, exaggerated affect, exaggerated well-being, attention demanding; (b) *Paranoid Projection*: feels persecuted, believes others influence him, clearly delusional, opinions contrary to physical laws; (c) *Grandiosity*: grandiose notions, engrossed in plans, speech stilted; (d) *Intropunitiveness*: believes he is evil, feeling of impending doom, has attempted suicide, distressed by anxiety, feels hopeless, shows blocking, fears abhorred act; (e) *Retardation*: avoids people, activity at minimum, affective failures; (f) *Conceptual Disorganization*: unaware of others, slovenly, memory faults, irrelevant speech, cannot make decisions, unable to carry out plans; (g) *Obsessive-Phobic*: phobias, obsessive thinking, compulsions.

The circular pattern appears in two of the three sets of data (Tables 8.4 and 8.5). The correlations are positive and highest next to the main diagonal and they decrease with distance from the diagonal. In the Wittenborn data the Obsessive-Phobic syndrome is located as expected between PAR and INP. The evidence thus supports the hypothesis of a definite circular arrangement of symptom groupings. The successive correlations in these tables decrease as expected but not as consistently as they do in Table 8.1. If due weight is given the armchair derivation of the syndromes, the sequences are in fair agreement with expectations.

A final table of correlations based on a rating schedule consisting of a combination of PRS and MSRPP scales (Lorr *et al.*, 1957) was clustered (Table 8.6). The syndrome correlations, when arranged in the order expected, exhibit a pattern relatively consistent with the requirements of a circular order involving both unipolar and bipolar variables.

Thus the evidence from six independent samples based on four different scales (Moore, PRS, MSRPP, and IMPS) and on different raters, while not strong, tends to support the hypothesis that many of the syndromes may be arranged in a consistent circular rank order. Except for the IMPS symptom groupings, which are

TABLE 8.4
CORRELATIONS AMONG SEVEN SYNDROMES BASED ON WITTENBORN DATA
(DECIMAL POINTS OMITTED)

(STUDY #1 BELOW AND STUDY #2 ABOVE DIAGONAL)

	EXC	GRN	PAR	OBS	INP	RTD	CNP
EXCITEMENT		71	31	24	05	-18	34
GRANDIOSITY	38		62	10	-03	-15	07
PARANOID PROJECTION	46	59		07	16	19	13
OBSESSIVE-PHOBIC	21	-12	02		49	17	08
INTROPUNITIVE	-12	-29	-19	54		24	-04
RETARDED	-40	-35	-03	19	26		67
CONCEPTUAL DISORGANIZATION	19	-18	01	26	10	70	

TABLE 8.5
CORRELATIONS AMONG SEVEN SYNDROMES BASED ON MOORE'S DATA
(DECIMAL POINTS OMITTED)

	EXC	INP	RTD	DIS	MTR
EXCITEMENT					
INTROPUNITIVE	-13				
RETARDATION	-59	39			
DISORIENTATION	17	-31	06		
MOTOR DISTURBANCE	15	-51	17	50	
CONCEPTUAL DISORGANIZATION	21	-44	-02	46	65

based in both instances on the factor analysis, the symptom groupings in other cases were assembled (a) by examining the content of the scales and (b) by categorizing them consistent with the IMPS factor analysis. The correlations themselves were not permitted to enter into these determinations, although if this had been done some of the relationships might have been in closer agreement with expected values.

TABLE 8.6
CORRELATIONS AMONG SIX SYNDROMES
BASED ON LORR, O'CONNOR, STAFFORD DATA
(DECIMAL POINTS OMITTED)

	EXC	GRN	PAR	INP	RTD	CNP
EXCITEMENT		65	21	-09	-69	29
GRANDIOSITY	65		31	-20	-06	28
PARANOID PROJECTION	21	31		23	-04	41
INTROPUNITIVENESS	-09	-20	23		20	-04
RETARDATION	-69	-06	-04	20		48
CONCEPTUAL DISORGANIZATION	29	28	41	-04	48	

MERITS OF THE PSYCHOTIC SYNDROME CIRCLE

The principal virtue of the circular ordering of the eight syndromes is its capacity to link conceptually together a number of independent syndromes. Each syndrome becomes more meaningful when it is seen as imbedded in a network of relationships. Each symptom-grouping is most similar to the two on either side. This relationship suggests that contiguous syndromes possess some characteristic in common. Possibly common biochemical or psychological processes are associated with related segments of the circle. Another possibility is that closely associated syndromes have common origins in distinctive defense mechanisms. In patients who utilize projection as a major defense GRN and PAR may be prominent. INP and RTD may be exhibited by those whose tendency is to direct hostility and blame towards the self. MTR and DIS may represent the extreme results of withdrawal.

The circular sequence also has predictive utility. If two contiguous variables correlate less than might be expected, then a syndrome may be missing. Examination of symptom content of the participating syndromes may suggest the nature of the missing symptom-group. For instance, it is possible that an Apathy syndrome belongs between Psychomotor Retardation and Disorientation. Additional behavioral scales can be constructed, data collected, and the proposed syndrome tested for independence. Also, when the cross-correlations in the circle matrix are too high or too low, the model requirements are not satisfied. The content of the symptoms can be inspected and the correlations examined. Some symptoms can be dropped and others introduced to modify one or both syndromes involved. The degree of fit of the modified syndromes can then be checked on fresh data.

The conceptual scheme may provide a basis for understanding certain clinically observed shifts in patient psychopathology. Patients scoring high on Disorientation and Motor Disturbances go through periods when they are described as excited (EXC) and disorganized in their speech (CNP). In conventional psychiatric language, the catatonic has phases of stupor and excitement. Another illustration may be found in the Anxious Intropunitive patient. Following electro-shock treatment such patients may exhibit Paranoid Projection. And contrarywise patients high on Paranoid Projection may grow increasingly grandiose, or become anxious, depressed (INP), and attempt suicide. The observations suggest that contiguous syndromes are related as far as their natural course in the individual is concerned. Further study may show that changes in syndromes are not only in the direction of increase or decrease in intensity or severity, but also in pattern. It is hypothesized that ordinarily these changes in pattern will be in the direction of the syndrome to the right or to the left on the circle. An exception to this suggested generalization occurs when a syndrome exhibits high negative correlations with another as, for example, EXC and RTD. A shift to the syndrome opposite in the circle would appear to be a possibility. An excited patient may become retarded and depressed; while a depressed patient may subsequently exhibit excitement.

The circular sequence is consistent with known difficulties in symptom differentiation. Even skilled clinicians may confuse apathy with dysphoric mood. It is difficult to differentiate a "flight of ideas" from thinking disorganization. In general, symptoms and behaviors defining adjoining or touching syndromes in the circle are more difficult to differentiate and are more easily confused than more distant symptoms.

THE MISSING SYNDROMES

Some comments seem needed concerning the syndromes missing from the proposed circular sequence. There is also the question of additional sequences. It is not clear why HOS does not fit into the sequence. One possibility is that Hostile Belligerence is secondary or subsidiary both to Excitement and to Paranoid Projection. The circular Manic-Paranoid order in Table 8.7 is supportive of this hypothesis and consistent with clinical observation. It is well known that manic patients, depending upon circumstances, may alternately be hostile or euphorically grandiose. The paranoid patient similarly may exhibit alternately a belligerency or a grandiosity. Thus the circular arrangement implied in Table 8.8 is a plausible one.

TABLE 8.7

CORRELATIONS AMONG FOUR IMPS SYNDROMES (DECIMAL POINTS OMITTED)

	EXC	HOS	PAR	GRN
EXCITEMENT		50	27	44
HOSTILE BELLIGERENCE	50		56	29
PARANOID PROJECTION	27	56		38
GRANDIOSE EXPANSIVENESS	44	29	38	

The other syndrome missing from the larger circle is Perceptual Distortion. Examination of the correlations between PCP and other ordered variables (0.26, 0.11, 0.06, −0.22, −0.24, 0.05, 0.33, 0.49) indicates a monotonic decrease and increase except with MTR and CNP. Examination of scale content and intercorrelations suggests that with some modification of MTR and CNP, PCP would also fit into the major circular sequence.

TABLE 8.8
CORRELATIONS AMONG SEVEN SYNDROMES
BASED ON IMPS NORMATIVE SAMPLE
(DECIMAL POINTS OMITTED)

	PAR	PCP	RTD	DIS	MTR	CNP	GRN
Paranoid Projection							
Perceptual Distortion	49						
Retardation and Apathy	-12	11					
Disorientation	-06	06	36				
Motor Disturbance	18	22	34	34			
Conceptual Disorganization	29	24	15	30	51		
Grandiose Expansiveness	38	33	-13	-02	10	31	
Paranoid Projection		49	-12	-06	18	29	38
Perceptual Distortion			11	06	22	24	33
Retardation and Apathy				36	34	15	-13
Disorientation					34	30	-02
Motor Disturbance						51	10
Conceptual Disorganization							31

THE SCHIZOPHRENIC CIRCLE

Another circular rank order, applicable to a subdomain of psychopathology and defined by seven syndromes differing in content, is presented in Table 8.8. Inspection of Table 8.8 reveals a consistent, continuous drop and increase in the magnitude of the coefficients in every column. The contents of the symptom-complexes making up the circular order are strongly suggestive of schizophrenic symptomatology. For this reason the order is tentatively labeled a Schizophrenic Circle. Table 8.9 provides partial corroborative data from the experimental form of IMPS. It is interesting to note that not all of the correlations are positive. This implies some of the behaviors such as disorientation and retardation are antithetic to paranoid and grandiose behaviors. On the other hand, they are all linked together in the circular order by common psychological properties.

TABLE 8.9
CORRELATIONS AMONG SIX SYNDROMES OF EXPERIMENTAL FORM IMPS
(DECIMAL POINTS OMITTED)

	PAR	PCP	RTD	MTR	CNP	GRN
PARANOID PROJECTION		50	05	12	46	49
PERCEPTUAL DISTORTION	50		10	23	44	54
RETARDATION AND APATHY	05	10		31	36	00
MOTOR DISTURBANCE	12	23	31		44	18
CONCEPTUAL DISORGANIZATION	46	44	36	44		54
GRANDIOSE EXPANSIVENESS	49	54	00	18	54	

Upon inspection, the circular order appears plausible and meaningful. As in the major circle of psychopathology, the order is consistent with observed changes in patients over a period of time. Changes in pattern of symptoms are probably not a chance matter; they relate closely to the position of the patient's predominant syndrome on the circle. Unfortunately, no longitudinal or directional data are yet available to confirm or disconfirm these possibilities.

SUMMARY

Several circular rank orders were proposed as conceptual schemes for linking together the established psychotic syndromes. One circular sequence embraces all syndromes except Hostile Belligerence and Perceptual Distortion. Another circular sequence ties together seven syndromes descriptive of schizophrenic behavior. These syndrome circles are suggestive of a fairly wide range of hypotheses for experimental testing.

CHAPTER 9

CLASSIFICATION AND TYPING

THUS FAR attention has been focused on the psychotic syndromes. The various experiments out of which a set of confirmed syndromes evolved were evaluated and compared. One chapter was devoted to the evidence supportive of their validity. Then two schemes for conceptualizing and linking together the syndromes or dimensions of psychoses were described. The remainder of the book will now be devoted to the problem of naturally occurring patient types or classes. The present chapter will focus on theoretical issues of classification and typing. This will be followed by a brief history of clinically derived classes of psychiatric disorders. Then the results of an experiment designed to offer a beginning to a syndrome-based set of types will be presented at length.

One of the basic procedures in scientific investigation is classification, or the recognition of groups of entities or attributes as having certain characteristics in common. In this chapter some of the concepts underlying the groupings of persons are presented and various proposed indices of similarity and their limitations are discussed. Then some methods for identifying types or classes when the defining criteria are unknown are briefly sketched to provide the reader with a broad view of what is involved in identifying classes.

THE CONCEPT OF TYPE

The most general notion is the idea of a class. A class may be said to consist of entities that belong to it and are called members of the class. There are one or more criteria for deciding whether or not an entity belongs to a class. If an entity satisfies the criteria it is a member; otherwise it is not. A "type" is here defined as a class of persons. As with class, when the term type is used the conditions for membership must be specified. A person who satisfies all conditions is a member; otherwise he is not a member. The characteristics common for one type must, of course, be different in one or more respects from those defining another type.

Type defining variables may be quantitative continuous or qualitative categorical. In the case of continuous variables upper and lower bounds on the continuum must be specified. Suppose, for example, the variable was systolic blood pressure, then the range for inclusion within a class might be 110–170. Categorical variables may be unordered or ordered. Examples of unordered categories are Catholics, Protestants, and Jews; doctors, lawyers, and engineers. Examples of ordered variables are social class and army grade (private, corporal, sergeant). Distinctions between qualitative and quantitative may become blurred when quantitative differences are found to inhere in the trait that led to the categorization. Marital status for instance can be ordered as follows: single (never married), single (divorced), separated, married (divorced and remarried), and married (first and only).

Should the defining criterion be a single continuous variable, the class will be a "scission" type (Stephenson, 1953) defined by a region below or above a cut on the continuum. If several continuous variables are involved each divisible by scissions then the resulting types are "supraordinate". Examples of scission types based on single dimensions or trait extremes are the dull and the bright, introverts and extroverts, hermits and sociophiles. Types based on several dimensions considered simultaneously are exemplified by hysterics, schizophrenics, and psychopaths.

Cattell (1961) reports no less than forty-five possible meanings of the term type. In Cattell's terminology, the word pattern is reserved as a generic term for configuration and profile. A profile is a set of elements on which the order of elements has no relevance. A configuration is a set of elements in which the order or sequence of the elements is relevant. Examples of profiles are a set of syndrome scores for a patient and a set of primary ability scores for a pupil. The rank order of elements is arbitrary. Since time is not involved and the elements are independent any other order would be as meaningful. A learning curve and a developmental curve are examples of configurations. Cattell restricts the term type to a profile with a high frequency of occurrence. The emphasis on frequency of recurrence would appear to be an important but not a necessary requirement. For instance, cyclic manic-depressives are rare but worthy of recognition.

VALUE OF TYPING

What are the practical and scientific implications of grouping persons into types? Unique combinations of attributes make members of a type more easily recognized, remembered, understood, and differentiated from non-members in a given area. A dachshund is easily distinguished from a Boston bulldog, and a chimpanzee from a baboon. To label a person a psychopath or to say he is schizoid immediately suggests a broad pattern of traits and to-be-expected behaviors. A depressive will be slowed down, pessimistic, dejected, hopeless, and withdrawn. A well integrated paranoid is likely to be hostile, evasive, suspicious, and defensive. In brief, knowledge of class membership is immediately useful in predicting behavior.

Some classes of persons like physicists and psychiatrists, bakers and bankers, are defined by occupation. But there are broad domains where groups are not ready made through occupation, educational, or situational circumstance. It is in such domains that there is a special need to discover types. The military psychologist is interested in identifying job families for assigning recruits for training and for more efficient development of selection test batteries. The dress designer can use body types to simplify the task of designing suits and dresses. The personality theorist looks for stable temperament and interpersonal trait constellations in order to better comprehend his data. Kraepelin and Bleuler have suggested well known psychiatric groups for similar reasons. Their hope was that patient classes would lead to etiology, more effective treatment and a better understanding of the duration and course of these disorders.

The integrity of the individual is preserved in types as compared to its fractionation in single trait measures. This is what is meant when a clinician says a patient's scores must be considered simultaneously to be meaningful. However, this line of argument must not be carried too far as any global index has its own defects. Classification makes possible the enhancement of predictive accuracy through the operation of higher order dependencies and the utilization of interactions, if they exist in the data. This statement can be clarified by first looking at linear predictive equations. Each predicted score Y is the simple weighted additive sum of a set of scores. The weights are constants (applied the same way to every person's score) which maximize the correlation between the tests and the criterion Y. Interactive effects like the simultaneous presence of two high scores or two low scores are ignored. The effect can be illustrated by an example from Meehl (1950). Two items (Yes or No) can each be unrelated to a criterion, such as whether a person is schizophrenic or normal, when scored singly. Yet if scored for the simultaneous presence of Yes in both items, prediction of the criterion may be theoretically perfect.

Toops (1948) has stated a number of relevant generalizations in connection with the concept of unique patterns that apply to types. Any sample of persons of identical or homogeneous trait-profile will tend to be more homogeneous as to behavior than the parent population. Such a sample of persons is also by definition more homogeneous in respect to any dependent behavior variable or criterion, if that dependent variable bears a greater than zero correlation with the trait-profile. Suppose, for example, an anxious-depressed patient group is treated by a tranquilizer. Their response-behavior can be expected to be more alike than that of psychotics in general. It also follows that the more valid and relatively independent the traits involved in the trait-profile, the more homogeneous will be the behavior of the persons comprising the group. These principles support the desirability of the typing process.

A taxonomy of natural occurring types is an important scientific objective in its own right. Types are the correlatives of trait-dimensions. Both are of scientific interest and provide an increased understanding of a group of phenomena. Types are a potential basis for developmental studies that might throw light on antecedents as well as causal agents. Such antecedents and influences in the case of psychotic types can be parental patterns, biochemical substances, or physiologic variables.

SINGLE AND MULTIPLE PURPOSE TYPES

There are two major approaches or philosophies of typing. Proponents of one approach argue that any particular classification will be meaningful only to the extent that it is based on variables related to a broader class of behavior which one desires to predict or control (Gleser, 1961). This single purpose approach tends to be that of the practical clinician and administrator. Should the patient be placed in a closed or in an open ward? Will this patient's stay in the hospital be long or short-term? Will the patient attempt suicide or not? Emphasis is on the uses to which a type may be put for prediction or decision making.

Proponents of the opposing philosophy of typing contend that a type need have no apparent utility but it should be of scientific interest. Types are multipurpose and represent a way of advancing psychological theory. In many areas, due to special situational and developmental conditions, traits combine in unique ways and are exemplified in types. For example, some individuals are dominant, aggressive, and socially active. Others are passive, dependent, inhibited, and self-abasive in relation to others. Character and personality types may represent an organization of behaviors that have resulted from child rearing patterns and from the operation of defensive mechanisms.

The proponents of the "Typing for what?" approach would say there is no single meaningful way to classify people. Persons similar on one set of variables are not necessarily more similar than persons in general on another set of variables. Since there is no one "true" or "real" way to classify people, a type is simply a useful means for making predictions.

Methods of type identification are distinctively different in the two approaches. Procedures for determining profile similarity or of matching profile elements are applied in the multipurpose approach. In the single purpose approach some mathematical function of the profile elements is found or constructed in order best to predict the external criterion. Emphasis is thus on the criterion rather than on the profile which is merely a means of differentiating several groups or intervals of the criterion. Suppose, for instance, one wants to predict a measure of response to a tranquilizer from test patterns. The profile elements of improvers and non-improvers are examined statistically (Lubin & Osburn, 1957) with a view to identifying patterns predictive of improvement. A polynomial function is then written relating various profile element combinations to the criterion. Thus, interest in the profiles is secondary.

There are indeed an endless number of ways of classifying people. But the basic difficulty of classification schemes tied to external criteria and to special purposes is that they lack scientific generality. Each new treatment modality, each new decision calls for another classification, another task of establishing patterns that differentiate between the criterion groups on the external behavior variable. This has been called "cook-book" or "recipe" research. While useful for a period, criterion-based types are soon outdated as new treatment modalities appear. Further, such criterion-specific types usually tell little about the nature of the type or the criterion. Classifications are of general interest in so far as they convey knowledge about common processes and common structures in particular domains. This is the role classification plays in biology. It is unlikely that classification will ever be of comparable importance in psychology but the process can yield generalizations of interest.

SOME METHODOLOGICAL PROBLEMS

Given a sample of individuals each with a score on K identical profile elements there are three steps to the definition of types. The first step is to assess the degree of similarity between each person and every other in the sample. The next task is to find any existing clusters or groups of individuals on the basis of the similarity indices. The final step is to set bounds and define the criteria of inclusion.

There are a number of methodological problems in assessing similarity between two or more individuals over a set of measures. First it is necessary to recognize that similarity is not a general quality. Similarity in profiles or in the persons whom they describe can be defined only in terms of specified dimensions of comparison. This dictum is recognized as related to the definition of membership in a class given earlier. Persons similar on one set of definitional variables are not necessarily more alike on another set of criteria than people in general. There would, however, be a tendency to be more alike. For instance, persons classed as Republicans differ widely if classed on the basis of their physiques, their intellectual talents, their preference for foods, or their interpersonal behavior. This implies that diverse measures may evolve very different classes. It should thus surprise no one if symptom syndromes, MMPI scores, and Rorschach scores yield very different patient groups. Nevertheless, some clinicians as well as researchers often express an expectation in this direction.

Another restriction that should be recognized concerns the loss of information about the unique individual in the process of classification. Typing involves selection, abstraction, and condensation of information. Some information must be discarded in the process. Any global index of similarity like a correlation coefficient loses certain kinds of facts. From another point of view the problem is more one of reducing the number of descriptive variables. There are more than 18,000 trait names listed by Allport and Odbert (1936) and they are surely not all independent. Suppose only ten symptoms are noted as present or absent in a sample of patients. Then there are 2^{10} or 1024 different symptom combinations possible. It follows that some condensation or reduction in variables is needed.

A related problem concerns the assumptions made in combining scores on distinctive dimensions in the single index. For instance, if one score measures excitement and another degree of paranoid tendency, any index based on both assumes that one unit of excitement is the same as one unit of paranoid tendency. This difficulty is typically by-passed by converting all measures into the same standard scale units with a common origin. However, this in itself involves assumptions not easily defended. For example, one trait could truly be twice as variable as another, or one trait could be twice as important as another and should be given special weight. Yet one degree of difference in, say, anxiety is treated as equal to one unit of difference in thinking disorganization. In using indices of similarity one must be willing to assume equality of intrinsic value for the k defining profile elements. Otherwise, the elements should be weighted in accordance with judged social or clinical importance.

MEASURES OF PROFILE SIMILARITY

An extensive literature on methods of measuring profile similarity has developed. Examples of some of these indices are Du Mas' r_{ps} (1947), Kendall's Tau (1948), Cattell's r_p (1949), Spearman's

Rho (McNemar, 1955), Meehl's index (1950), Sagebeer's index (1938), and the intraclass correlation (Haggard, 1958). Cronbach and Gleser (1953) have proposed a generalized concept of pattern similarity. They show that most indices may be subsumed under the general Pythagorean formula for the linear distance between two points in k-dimensional space, where k is the number of profile elements. A related literature on "agreement analysis" has developed independently. Recently Stilson (1955) has formulated this procedure in terms of the algebra of sets and relations. The geometrical formulation of profile similarity will be considered first.

Let j be any of the measures 1, 2, 3, . . . which are k in number and let x_{ja} be the score of any person a on test j. Then if just two persons are considered, there will be a set of scores $x_{ja}(x_{1a},x_{2a}, \ldots x_{ka})$ for person a, and a set $x_{jb}(x_{1b},x_{2b}, \ldots x_{kb})$ for person b. Each score x_{ja} may be regarded as a coordinate of a point p_a in k-dimensional space. Let x_{jb} define a point p_b. The closer the scores of the two individuals, the closer the points p_a and p_b will be in space. A measure of distance or dissimilarity can then be defined as

$$D^2{}_{ab} = \sum_{j}^{k} (x_{ja} - x_{jb})^2$$

providing each measure is assumed to be linearly independent.

Conventionally a profile is represented as a two dimensional curve uniting the points representing an individual's scores and relative positions on each of several dimensions with all scores rendered comparable by statistical treatment. It can be shown that a profile for an individual is separable into three components. The elevation or "level" component of the profile is the mean of all scores for a person. The "scatter" component is the dispersion of the individual's scores about his own mean. The "shape" represents such information as remains, the particular form of the curve. All three characteristics should be considered when comparing profiles to ascertain their similarity.

The D^2 measure considers all k dimensions in the data. Most other indices proposed tend to have the effect of measuring similarity in $k-1$ space, or $k-2$ space, that is, with the consequent loss of information about the elevation of the scores and their scatter. An important question is whether similarity between score sets should take the elevation component into account. In psychopathology data this would correspond to the over-all severity of illness. If the elevation component is of no interest, the investigator may get rid of it by converting to deviation scores around the individual mean or level. In general it appears unwise to eliminate elevation. A similar question concerns the value of scatter. If the individual's deviation scores are divided by the measure of his scatter, the scatter of profiles is equalized. The effect is to increase the jaggedness of flat profiles and to decrease the variability of jagged profiles.

While D^2 or D loses no information concerning level or scatter it fails to take the "direction" of differences into account. It does not recognize that two profiles are mirror-images of each other in shape (e.g., introvert and extrovert). A covariance and a correlation coefficient Q between two profile scores do recognize such directional differences. A high positive correlation implies a parallel profile while a high negative coefficient signifies opposing scores on similar profile elements. The covariance index, which is the average of the cross-products of the deviation scores of the two individuals compared, loses information only about level. The person–person correlation is an index of similarity in profile shape only. Despite the loss of level and scatter, Q may in certain areas of similarity convey much of the resemblance between two persons.

AGREEMENT AS SIMILARITY

An agreement score may be defined as the number of variates on which a pair of persons receives an identical score. The variates are typically unordered qualitative categorical variates. Moreover, no assumptions are made concerning metric in computing an agreement index. Suppose, for example, several patients were described on five categories ratable as true or not true. The highest possible number of agreements is then five. The agreement score for a pair of patients is simply the number of instances that both were categorized the same way on the same variates.

Agreement scores can be conceptualized geometrically, if

desired, just like distance measures. Suppose there are given k two-alternative variates, then there are 2^k possible different profiles. The k items form a k-dimensional space containing 2^k possible points. Each person may be assigned to one point in space according to his profile on the k variates. A classification procedure will subdivide this space into regions.

CONDITIONS FOR AN ADEQUATE TYPING ANALYSIS

Typing has as its goal the identification of homogeneous classes or groups. It proceeds without resort to any *a priori* concepts as to the nature of the classes, the correct assignment of individuals to such classes, or the number of classes. What are some of the conditions for an objective and meaningful analysis? The reader will recognize that some of the criteria are similar to those proposed for a factor analysis.

(1) It is essential that all major sources of trait variation in the defined area of behavior be represented. This would mean that measures of all the psychotic disorders should be represented in an analysis aimed at identifying psychotic types. Suppose several major sources of behavior variation are differentially absent in studies by two investigators. Then the classes involved in the two studies are likely not to be reciprocally confirmed. Addition of new dimensions can alter the profiles defined in unknown ways. Totally different groups can appear in such studies. If all known sources of trait variation are present, then a relatively complete profile will be delineated.

(2) A related requirement is that the defining variables be descriptive of independent dimensions or concepts. The distance function (D^2) and many related indices of similarity assume that the profile elements are independent. This condition, therefore, must in a measure be satisfied for valid use of a similarity index. It can be shown that, when the defining variables are uncorrelated, they contribute to D^2 in proportion to their variances (Cronbach and Gleser, 1953). When these variates are correlated, D^2 is additionally influenced by these correlations. The presence of a general factor can strongly influence the agreement

in profiles. Further, the contributions of any factor to the D^2 measure depends upon the number of variates in which it appears. The investigator may wish to give greater weight to some factors than to others. In any case, he should be aware that what is included will determine the profiles. Stephenson (1953) suggests constructing items which sample a domain of traits. If such sampling were possible, representative and uniform coverage of a domain would be assured. However, construction of factorially pure items is not presently possible and item sampling is presently a fiction. The investigator is usually pleased to use the items he constructs; he does not sample.

Cronbach and Gleser (1953) suggest the pooling of items into clusters to obtain subtest scores for each individual. Such scoring can be based on statistical analyses (e.g., factoring) or on *a priori* grouping of items. Cluster scoring serves to reduce the weight of factors specific to one item and gives greater weight to the common element running through the group of items. It also reduces the weight given to differences between persons arising from errors of measurement. Hence, cluster scores on profile elements and the similarity indices based on them are more reliable than scores based on items.

(3) The classes evolved should be invariant or replicable under any arbitrary changes in the scales of measurement (Saunders and Schucman, 1962). Any classification arrived at should not be a function of particular scales or items scored in a particular way. For example, it should be possible to arrive at a set of types starting either with IMPS or with Wittenborn's PRS, providing both assess all important dimensions. This condition will rarely be satsified in exploratory studies.

(4) The classes evolved should be invariant or replicable under changes in the sample of persons examined. This means that each type should be replicable within other representative samples. Another view of this requirement is that the type to which a person is assigned should be the same regardless of the persons who are included in the sample analyzed.

(5) Evidence should be provided that the classes evolved are not achieved by chance. In other words, it should be possible to show that the classes have been "over-determined" by the data. This problem has no easy solution.

APPROACHES TO TYPING

There is general recognition that there are no formal rules for finding clusters because a cluster is not a well-defined term. The term cluster is used here as the progenitor of a type which does have defined limits. A type is evolved from a cluster. Resort may be made to the geometrical model in order to visualize the problem of isolating groups of people on the basis of a limited number of relatively independent variables. Each of N persons can be represented as a point in k-dimensional space where k is the number of variables considered as dimensions. Consider that k is 10 so that each person is represented in 10-dimensional space. Imagine that there is a swarm of red dots for Excited patients, a swarm of blue dots for Retarded and Apathetic patients and another swarm of yellow dots for Disorganized Schizophrenics and so on. Suppose further that these swarms overlap each other and you are color-blind. One problem is how to set boundaries and how to separate the regions. Another problem is to determine the number of distinct groups. As Thorndike (1953) points out there is no simple answer as to the question of how many families there should be. One solution at early stages of research is the practical one of excluding any clusters below a given size. In brief, the problem of classification is one of discovering and defining swarms or nodes in the score space.

TYPING BY AGREEMENT ANALYSIS

The method called agreement analysis was independently described by Zubin (1938) and by Jenkins and Ackerson (1933). McQuitty (1954) has contributed a great many specific procedures for fractionating a sample of people into subsamples. The process begins with an agreement score, the number of variables on which a pair of persons receive an identical score, are categorized in an identical way, or respond in the same way. Agreement scores are calculated for all pairs of individuals in the sample to be classified and may be entered in a two-way table or agreement matrix.

The first class is defined as the largest set of persons such that the agreement score between every pair in the set is at least c. The first class is then removed and a second set or class is defined in the same way. The process is continued until all persons have been classified. In this way, at each stage, the next class is the set of persons containing the maximum number of persons subject to the restriction that each pair in the class is similar on at least c of the variables. Thus c is an integer lying between zero and k, the number of variables, and is called the classification criterion. Varying the value of c will alter the number of classes defined. If c is set high enough, no classes would exist. Or c can be set so low that all persons are assigned to one sample. The value of c is usually chosen on statistical grounds.

In this form of agreement analysis, each pair of persons in a given profile group agree on some subset of at least c of the variates. However, two separate pairs in a class need not agree on the same subset of variates. In a variation of the first procedure, the criteria are more stringent. At each stage, the next class is defined as the largest set of persons who receive identical scores on each variate in a subset containing at least c variates. For every variate in this subset, every person in the class must receive the same score.

For either of the two methods the classes defined may overlap. In other words, a person may be assigned to two or more of the classes. This occurs also when person–person correlations are factored and each person may correlate significantly with several type-factors. Since only counting operations are used in defining the classes, and no metric is assumed, the question of independence of profile dimensions is not directly faced.

Stilson (1956) has shown that, under certain conditions, the results of factor analysis and the results of agreement analysis are quite similar. It is clear that this classificatory scheme leads to unique classes in the sense that any two investigators following the same procedure would arrive at the same classes for the same data, providing only that the same c-value is applied. A detailed analysis and critique of the method can be found in Stilson's study.

One problem that seems not to have been explored is the influence of the variates used on agreement analysis. Should continuous variates be converted into a smaller number of categories? Do the same generalizations concerning cluster scores versus items apply in agreement analysis?

TYPING BY FACTOR ANALYSIS

Factor analysis has often been proposed as the method of choice for locating groups within a heterogeneous population. In such an analysis the data factored usually consist of correlations among individuals across a set of traits. The procedure is fundamentally inappropriate as factor analysis isolates dimensions rather than clusters or groups. For similar reasons the simple structure concept appears inapplicable to the isolation of groups. The method may miss groups altogether or dismember them in the process of transformation to simple structure. If a cluster falls between two type-factors, each type-factor is defined by persons marginal to the major cluster.

Groups with opposite score profiles like Manic-Excited and Depressed Retarded, or like endomorphs and ectomorphs emerge in an analysis as bipolar type-factors (Lorr and Fields, 1954). In a more general way, because correlations between person profiles tend to be negative (Ekman, 1951; Humphries, 1957), bipolar factors are common. Intercorrelations among ipsative scales (centered on person's own mean) will tend to be negative. The size of the negative correlation will be a function of the number of ipsative scales. As a consequence the investigator must decide whether or not two groups are being defined by each such factor. Hence the number of factors does not indicate the number of groups present. Another drawback is that the method yields many small type-factors hazily defined by two or three persons. However, other procedures also have this limitation.

Type-factors tend to yield a multiple classification of persons. The usual goal is a set of mutually exclusive classes. The multiple classification may be seen in any factor table. Each row in a table of type-factors represents the correlation of each person with a type-factor. Typically a person has substantial correlations with several type-factors. Only a few persons correlate highly with one and only one type-factor and thus constitute "pure" representatives of a type. In addition the method provides no boundaries as to the members of a type-factor. At some point it is necessary to decide arbitrarily which persons are sufficiently correlated with the type and sufficiently "pure". Then a composite profile can be constructed from the score profiles of the persons selected.

One old argument, mathematical in nature, against factoring person correlations is that type-factors yield the same results as trait-factors (Burt, 1940). Assume here that both trait sources and person scores are standardized. Suppose all sources of individual variation (and thus all types) and all sources of trait variation are represented in a data table. Then, the argument goes, the number and kinds of trait-factors will be the same as the number and kinds of type-factors. By either procedure it is possible to identify the same dimensions. In the case of type-factors this is done by comparing persons correlated positively, negatively, or not at all with the type-factor and infering the dimension on which individuals differ. Hence factor analysis of inter-person correlations yields dimensions and not person classes.

TYPING BY CLUSTER ANALYSIS

The third procedure, for lack of a better name, is called cluster analysis. One of the earliest compilations of cluster search methods was reported by Cattell (1944). He labeled these Ramifying Linkage, Matrix Diagonal, Correlation Profile, and Approximate Delimitation. Thorndike (1953) has outlined a procedure which results in clusters which are maximally compact, i.e., the mean distance of persons from their clusters is minimized. Recently, Sawry, Keller, and Conger (1960) outlined an objective method of grouping profiles based on distance measures. The methods discussed by Cattell and by Sawry *et al.* are relatively independent of the indices employed. Appropriately modified, they represent useful procedures for obtaining clusters of profiles once a matrix of similarity indices has been assembled.

Briefly, the procedure selects clusters from a matrix of correlations (D^2s, covariances, or other indices). Based initially on a small number of nuclei, highly homogeneous clusters which are simultaneously dissimilar to each other are formed. To these homogeneous clusters, the remaining profiles in the sample are added or excluded.

Step 1. Form an $N \times N$ matrix of indices where N is the number of persons.

Step 2. Select a potential nucleus of a cluster. Decide on a minimum correlation for the definition of "similarity". Construct a table of the N persons, listing with each person the code numbers of all of the others in the matrix who are above the limit set for similarity. Select as a potential nucleus any two similar persons, proceeding from the person who has the largest number of other profiles similar to it. Any selected profile is crossed out from the table. This procedure is repeated until no similar profiles remain.

Step 3. Select a second nucleus cluster which is dissimilar to the first cluster. Decide on a maximum correlation for the definition of "dissimilarity". Add members to the nucleus cluster who are simultaneously similar to other nucleus members but dissimilar to the initial cluster. Continue this procedure until no similar profiles remain.

Step 4. Select additional nuclei which are dissimilar to each other and to those already selected. Add other profiles to each nucleus until no others satisfy both bounds for similarity and dissimilarity for any cluster.

Step 5. Compute the centroid (mean) of each cluster and determine the mean of the cross relationships. Plot the profiles of members of each cluster and decide on upper and lower bounds for each profile element for each cluster. Determine the means of the profile elements within each cluster. Once the upper and lower bounds are set the type is defined.

The steps just sketched represent only a rough outline of the method. Greater detail is provided in the references. Perhaps it will suffice to say that the nature of the similarity index will affect the specific details of the procedure.

Several other procedures have been proposed that fit into the category of cluster search methods. Holzinger (1941) has developed a method of grouping by *B*-coefficient. This method is based on the assumption that the variables of a group identifying a factor should have higher intercorrelations than with other variables in the set. The coefficient of belonging, *B* is defined as one hundred times the ratio of the average of the intercorrelations of a subset or cluster of variables to their average correlation with all other remaining variables. The *B*-coefficient has long been used and represents a fairly efficient and economical computation scheme for an initial grouping of variables into homogeneous sets.

The clustering process is begun by selecting two variables which have the highest correlation. To these is added the variable for whom the sum of the correlations with the preceding is highest. The process is continued always adding a variable which correlates highest with those already in the nucleus, until a sharp drop occurs in the value of *B*. One arbitrary standard for "belonging" proposed, is that a cluster have a minimum *B*-coefficient of 130.

Another method for evolving homogeneous clusters has been developed by Loevinger, Gleser, and DuBois (1953). One restriction of importance is that the procedure assumes that the variables are given as dichotomous or can be reduced to dichotomous form. This means that the profile elements must first be reduced if they are continuous variates. The method also assumes a very sizable number of profile elements say on the order of five hundred to one thousand for the task of typing.

The process begins with a nucleus of three or four persons with high covariances *inter se*. A saturation coefficient, defined as the ratio of inter-person covariance to total covariance, is applied to maximize the homogeneity of each cluster. All persons are excluded from a cluster who lower the saturation of the three-person nucleus. The one person is added who maximizes the saturation of the resultant four person cluster. The process terminates when all persons are either included in a cluster or excluded. The method could prove useful if the profile elements are numerous as in a questionnaire, and if the items have been explored to determine the dimensions measured.

SUMMARY

The concept of a type as a class of persons having certain characteristics in common was elaborated. The practical and scientific implications of classification were discussed. The importance of developing an objective taxonomy was stressed. Two philosophies of approach, single purpose and multipurpose, were contrasted and judged in favor of multipurpose typing. Various methodological problems such as metric, loss of information, and the meaning of similarity were discussed. Following this, some geometric and non-geometric indices of similarity were examined. Some tentative conditions for an adequate typing analysis were proposed. Finally, a brief description and critique was given of typing by factor analysis, by agreement analysis, and by cluster analysis.

In the next chapter, a history of the clinical evolution of present-day psychiatric classes is sketched. The aim is to link such clinical efforts and findings to statistical findings later presented.

CHAPTER 10

A BRIEF HISTORY OF PSYCHIATRIC CLASSIFICATION

IN THE previous chapter an effort was made to sketch the concepts central to the sorting of patients into groups. Some statistical procedures for evaluating classes of patients were next reviewed. In this chapter a capsule review of the historical events leading to the present standard nomenclature is offered. This brief history will highlight the gradual introduction of the disease concept into psychiatry. This concept is shown to be based on ancient views which were revived during the Middle Ages in the struggle to escape the web of theology. Psychiatric classification is also seen to be derived from Linnaeus' eighteenth century scheme for classifying plants. These two historical elements led on the one hand to the adoption of the physical disease model and the idea of syndromes or symptom-complexes. On the other hand the Linnaean concept led to the notion of classes of patients with which the next few chapters are concerned.

THE CLASSICAL TRIAD

Relatively little is known about pre-Greek medicine aside from details of its intimate connection with religions and superstitions. Greek and Hindu scientists were the first to consider illness a natural phenomenon to be studied scientifically, but only the Greeks considered psychiatric conditions as sickness. In addition to epilepsy and hysteria, Hippocrates (*c.* 460–377 B.C.) and other Greek physicians recognized the overt symptomatology of a major triad of disorders: mania, melancholia, and phrenitis (febrile delirium). All were diagnosed on the basis of overt symptomatology. "Paranoia" seems to have been a general term which covered most conditions later subsumed under "insanity". It disappeared from the literature about A.D. 200 until the eighteenth century (Cameron, 1959). Although the Greek labels were facsimiles of recent and current diagnoses, mania and melancholia were extremely heterogeneous classes. Mania simply meant an agitated form and melancholia a quiet form of insanity.

Hippocrates' triad remained essentially intact until the sixteenth century. Throughout the Graeco-Roman classical period, further clinical observations were added and various etiological theories were introduced but the triad remained the core descriptive concept. Aristotle (384–322 B.C.) questioned the accuracy of a qualitative distinction between the normal and pathological. He saw no sharp dividing line and suggested a quantitative difference. Asclepiades in Rome (*c.* A.D. 90) distinguished illusional, delusional, and hallucinatory behavior—differences Esquirol rediscovered in the nineteenth century (Schneck, 1960). The acute–chronic dichotomy of diseases, including psychiatric conditions, is traceable to Asclepiades. It is still with us both as a principal diagnostic sign (e.g., acute situational maladjustment) and as an implicit cue (e.g., personality disorder).

Aretaeus of Cappadocia (*c.* A.D. 100) introduced the concept of age-related psychiatric disorder. For him, age of onset became the basis for differentiating involutional and senile disorders. Lewis (1942) and Arieti (1959) think he anticipated Falret, Baillarger, and Kraepelin by 1800 years in seeing a manic-melancholic cycle. While he observed the alternation of quiet and excited states in the same person, the generality of the manic and melancholic categories makes it doubtful that he was talking about the same thing as later authors. Aretaeus was also one of the first to consider prognosis as a basis for reaching a diagnosis.

Soranus and Caelius Aurelianus (second century A.D.) placed less emphasis on the classical triad and more on the acute–chronic dichotomy in their diagnostic formulations. Examples of symptoms and symptom complexes they classed as acute disorders were: phrenitis, lethargy, stupor, hydrophobia, and satyriasis. Headaches, melancholia, and nocturnal emission were grouped as chronic brain conditions. They thought most disorders were due to humors affecting the brain or to malfunctioning of the diaphragm, uterus, or hypochondrium.

SIXTEENTH TO EIGHTEENTH CENTURY PSYCHIATRY

Religion, theology, witchcraft, and the Inquisition gradually arrogated the fields of psychiatry, psychology, and philosophy and dominated them until the sixteenth century. For 1300 years there was no substantial scientific progress. Then, during the sixteenth century, two trends of enormous importance began to develop almost imperceptibly. The concept of "mind" began to be divorced from the concept of "soul" and it became possible for scientists to look into the body for causes of characteristics and functions of the mind. Sir Francis Bacon's concept of a measurable, quantitative, physiological psychology exemplifies this trend. A fuller development of the approach was eventually to lead to a descriptive, empirical, and experimental psychology of human behavior. Another major trend was the rise of individualism accompanied by a shifting of attention and emphasis to the roles that human drives and emotions play in man's behavior.

Paracelsus (1492–1541) constructed a classification scheme he considered more precise than the classical triad. Besides epilepsy, he described four other psychiatric conditions: mania, vesania (true insanity), chorea lasciva (St. Vitus' Dance), and suffocatio intellectus (hysteria). Mania was a disorder of reason, not of the senses as in true insanity. There were five subgroups of true insanity, including melancholias and obsessions. Paracelsus thought all disorders were due to disturbances of the vital spirits by food, drink, vapors, the moon or stars, or combinations of these agents. He introduced the constitutional view in discussing the etiology of another subclass of the vesaniae, insani. The insani were born mad (or defective) as a result of diseased semen or the influence of the moon on the uterus (Ackerknecht, 1959).

Johann Weyer (1515–1588) was the first physician to devote the major share of his interest and time to the study of psychiatric problems. His detached but humane objectivity was almost miraculous in a world obsessed with demonology. His views brought him into repeated conflict with the inquisitors whom he persistently attacked obliquely. Weyer argued that most witches and sorcerers were either sick or criminal and that the sick should be segregated and treated humanely and intelligently, with an emphasis on understanding the individual's problems. Because of Weyer's attention to the individual case, Zilboorg (1941) considered him a predecessor of modern dynamic psychiatry. Because of his objective, detailed case reports and histories, Weyer is also seen as a father of descriptive psychiatry. Unfortunately, it was more than a century after his death before his work began to attract followers instead of detractors.

Felix Plater (1536–1614), a Swiss physician, was one of the early well-known nosologists and he made a distinction between hereditary, congenital, and acquired disorders. He believed strongly enough in observation and description to live for awhile in the dungeons with the insane. He believed strongly enough in medieval theology and Galen to emerge with unoriginal views about etiology. Plater advanced four diagnoses for the classification of the insane: imbecility, consternation, alienation, and defatigatio. Imbecility included mental defectives, bizarre psychotic states, and other conditions. Consternation apparently included the stupors of both febrile delirium and catatonia. Alienation was Plater's diagnosis for an extremely heterogeneous group of abnormalities ranging from phrenitis, St. Vitus' Dance, melancholy and dementia to hypochondriasis, alcoholism, jealousy, and possession by the devil. Defatigatio was due to God or the devil, and insomnia was its principal symptom (Ackerknecht, 1959).

Many other nosologies were born during the seventeenth and eighteenth centuries. Most were based on brief, cursory, and uncontrolled examinations of patients in varied settings. The fact that criminals, defectives, brain injured, and functional psychotics were all tossed into the same hopper did not ease the sorting effort. Antecedents of modern psychiatric nomenclatures tended to be of two types. They were either sets of a few labels for broad, mixed classes of disorders based on obvious group differences, or they were long arrays of names of symptoms. Orderly classification awaited the nineteenth century when the psychiatric hospital movement stimulated prolonged observation of patients and compilation of detailed clinical records and histories.

Organic psychiatry, a discipline divorced from psychology and philosophy as well as theology, emerged as a distinct orientation in the sixteen hundreds with the resurgence of Hippocrates' theory that the brain is the locus of behavioral abnormality. Organicism did much for neurology, little for psychiatry. Working in their laboratories, dissecting rooms, and morgues, the organicists monotonously ascribed psychological disorders to brain and body fluid malfunctions. There was some justification for the organic approach since a large proportion of patients were retarded, brain injured, paretic, or apoplectic. But the functional psychoses, the neuroses, and the personality disorders received relatively little attention.

George Ernst Stahl (1660–1734) reacted strongly against organicism and dualism and had a marked but delayed effect on French psychiatry during the eighteenth century enlightenment and on German psychiatry in the nineteenth century. Stahl thought the prevailing dualism had a deleterious effect on understanding abnormal behavior. He observed the powerful physiological responses that accompanied emotional states and saw how such states could interfere with recovery from common diseases. Without appealing to physiological, mechanical, or metaphysical causative forces, Stahl was able to establish the fact that psychological events could produce abnormal reactions. He made the distinction between functional and organic disorders that later became a fundamental criterion in psychiatric diagnostic schemas.

The habit of looking at behavior disorders in the Hippocratic tradition spread from general medicine to psychiatry in the eighteenth century, largely through Thomas Sydenham's influence. Classification of symptoms was pursued rigorously as the initial phase of discovering disease entities with a characteristic onset, course, and outcome. No historically important diagnostic criterion was added to the literature. Hippocrates' classification of diseases into febrile and afebrile types was widely accepted, as was his division of abnormal behavior into manic and melancholic sub-classes.

Francois Boissier de Sauvages (1706–1767), a follower of Stahl, was a leading French nosographer. He wrote a three-volume *Nosologie Methodique*, which was published posthumously. His system was based directly on Linnaeus' botanical model. De Sauvages distinguished ten classes, forty orders, and seventy-eight genera in which to pigeonhole 2400 diseases (Veith, 1957). The eighth class was Folies and subsumed four orders: errors of reason, bizarreries, deliria, and anomalies. Each order was divided into genera, such as the fourteen melancholias and other disturbances classified as errors of reason. "Vaporous affections" were in another class entirely and illustrate the confusion of description and etiology that has always plagued psychiatric diagnosis. The vaporous affections were classified on the basis of assumed etiology, while other labels such as bizarreries referred to manifest behavior.

PINEL TO KRAEPELIN

At the turn of the nineteenth century, Chiarugi in Italy, Pinel in France, and Tuke in England led the wave of enlightenment which eventually brought about humanitarian reforms in the care of psychiatric patients. Their work and results sparked the spread of reform in hospitals and the concomitant opportunities for careful and prolonged observation of patients. To a considerable but unappreciated extent, the fact that observations were made in a hospital setting must have molded the resulting nosologies of the psychoses, just as the later study of the "minor" disorders manifested by outpatients, analysands, and armed forces personnel determined the categories of neuroses. As Szasz (1957, 1961) has suggested, a schema useful in one setting may have little or no utility in another. It is probably equally true that the actual observations made were to a marked extent a function of situational determinants. The bewitched, the sorcerers, the eccentrics, the impulsives, and the scapegoats as well as the paretics, the epileptics, the retarded, the senile, the alcoholics, and the demented became "sick" by definition long before there was any clear delineation of specific illness, damage, or incomplete development of the organism. As medical problems, they were rescued from theology and placed in hospitals before an adequate disease nomenclature could be developed.

NINETEENTH CENTURY FRENCH PSYCHIATRY

Generally speaking, the French and English were not as addicted to classification as the German psychiatrists. The French originated no complex nosologies, although occasionally they focused on a set of symptoms considered to be a clinical entity.

Pinel, for instance, thought nosological edifices were premature and adopted a modified Hippocratic schema of four categories. Like Hippocrates, he classified on the basis of observable symptomatology. Mania included agitated and excited cases. Melancholics were quiet, tended to be preoccupied with one train of thought, and could be either sad or grandiose. Incoherent thinking and speaking separated dementia from mania. Patients with severe intellectual deficits were diagnosed as idiots. Pinel not only thought melancholia could change into mania but also observed the almost imperceptible transitions between disorders. He thought two disorders could co-exist in the same person and that some individuals could alternate between one diagnostic group and another (Vieth, 1957). Pinel's emphasis on the development of systematic procedures for recording clinical notes and case histories was a boon to later classification attempts.

Esquirol (1772–1840), Pinel's student, was influenced by the trend toward somaticism and cerebral localization but he also considered the roles of social crises and the aloneness of man in the development of abnormality. Esquirol was one of the first to introduce statistical (tallying) methods into psychiatry. He used them to demonstrate that nearly one-third of the males in the Bicetre and one-fourth of the women in Saltpiêtre were there due to some psychological pressure, such as financial worry. He rediscovered the difference between illusions and hallucinations, introduced the latter term into psychiatry, and gave it its modern meaning. He separated psychotics who were preoccupied with a single thought or set of thoughts (monomania) from Pinel's melancholic group. His observations on monomania were important to later studies of paranoia.

In 1820 an issue emerged which yet provokes theoretical controversy. E. J. Georget (1795–1828) attempted to present a unitary concept of abnormal behaviors in his *Dissertation sur les Causes de la Folie* (Zilboorg, 1941; Schneck, 1960). Georget argued that there is only one psychosis, and it is due to a single brain disease. The many symptoms are but various forms of the same disease. Proponents of this theory had an antidotal effect on the prevailing preoccupation with symptoms as disease entities, but it is notable that the issue arose even before general paresis was clearly delineated as a clinical entity. Modern variants of the issue are seen in debates about the number of schizophrenias and in the division among experimenters as to whether there is a single psychoticism factor or several such factors.

Falret (1794–1870) and Baillarger (1809–1890) identified manic-depressive psychosis almost simultaneously. Falret called the syndrome "*folie circulaire*", and Baillarger named it "*folie á double forme*". Kraepelin in 1899 adopted into his classification system essentially the same picture Falret and Baillarger described. The alternation of elated and depressed states had been recognized through the centuries. The obviousness of such states and their impact on the observer may account for it being the first psychosis generally accepted as a separate entity.

Stahl's distinction between functional and organic psychoses had never been widely accepted. Adolph Wachsmuth revived it in 1859, stating that brain damage does not necessarily produce abnormal behavior, nor does abnormal behavior necessarily reflect brain damage. The more dramatic results of research on general paresis, however, impeded acceptance of this distinction, reinforced the already powerful position the somaticists, and retarded the growth of interest in psychological and sociological aspects of abnormal behavior.

The somatogenic orientation found an influential proponent in Benedict Augustin Morel (1809–1873) who advanced his infamous degeneration theory in 1860. The theory was to have a marked effect on French psychiatry up to the modern period. A minor variant is seen in Janet's theory of the neuroses. Morel considered abnormalities as degenerations. They were transmissible by heredity and deteriorated progressively towards extinction. They could result from intoxicating agents, moral sickness, toxins, acquired damage, or hereditary weakness. By the "law of progressivity of degeneration", a disorder in one generation could be traced to a vastly different disorder in one's ancestors. Valentin Magnan (1835–1916) followed Morel as a leader of French psychiatry, although by now the world leadership had passed to Germany. Magnan adopted the essentials of Morel's degeneration theory but emphasized the hereditary rather than the moral aspects. Degeneration was Darwinian regression, and all the diverse symptoms of the functional psychoses were merely psychological stigmata of hereditary insanity.

NINETEENTH CENTURY ENGLISH PSYCHIATRY

English psychiatric views were closely linked with the French. In the early part of the nineteenth century, there was more interest in reform, in development of treatment methods, and in forensic psychiatry than in classification. Probably this was a function of the prevailing attitude that symptoms were unimportant except as indicants of brain disease or injury. Only a few phrenologists attempted to relate specific symptoms to brain lesions. The English were greatly interested in problems related to anti-social behavior and in the separation of non-punishable from punishable legal offenders. James Cowles Prichard (1766–1848) originated the concept of "moral insanity" which was ill-defined but widely accepted.

In the latter part of the nineteenth century, the need for classification was more strongly felt. A mass of observational data had accumulated and some systematization was imperative. One of the two general views prevalent was that classification should start with factual knowledge about patients' symptoms, not with fictitious and fantastic etiological assumptions about neurochemical events. The other view placed emphasis on etiological conditions.

David Skae (1814–1873) led and spoke for the first group. Skae developed categories for idiots, chronic masturbators, epileptics, sthenics, asthenics, and idiopaths (Zilboorg, 1941). "Sthenic" and "asthenic" were borrowed from John Brown to describe states of increased and decreased excitement. As was usual in the early schemas, "idiot" subsumed dilapidated psychotics as well as the intellectually retarded. Maudsley (1835–1918) classified patients on the basis of his speculations about causation. All mental conditions were due to brain disease and causes of the latter were toxicity, anemia, poisons, circulatory defects, infections, and overwork. Daniel H. Tuke (1827–1895) complained that Skae's use of Greek etymology solved no psychiatric problems, but his own system straddled the symptomatic and etiological approaches. Tuke saw twenty-two groups of disorders falling into three major classes. These groups were mostly names of symptoms, but each represented a putative specific disease with a definite but unproven etiology.

NINETEENTH CENTURY GERMAN PSYCHIATRY

For the first half of the century, German psychiatry was split between psychic and somatic theorists. The former were influenced by romanticism and viewed mental conditions as products of a disembodied soul. In 1818 Heinroth (1773–1843) published a text in which he treated abnormality as due to a diseased and unfree soul. He substituted for Plater's categories a forty-eight-disease system which mixed symptomatology and etiology as classification criteria. Most of the disorders were varieties of mania and depression to which he attached Greek and Latin names. They fell into three broad classes of hypersthenias, asthenias, and hyposthenias. About the same period, Stark divided psychiatric conditions into dysthenias, dysbulias, and dysnoesias. Each had a hyper-form, an a-form, and a para-form (Zilboorg, 1941).

William Griesinger (1817–1868) established not only the somatogenic orientation but also the one psychosis (brain disease) school in Germany. Griesinger saw no difference between functional and organic disorders since he believed that physiological damage was always the causative agent. Like a high temperature, abnormal behavior was merely symptomatic. He tried to trace behavioral symptomatology to localized brain lesions but resorted to the grossest speculations in correlating the patient's symptom history with post-mortem findings. Griesinger thought a psychosis developed in two stages: a beginning phase characterized by emotional and behavioral disturbances; a later phase, marked by disturbances of thinking and other intellectual functions and irreversible organic changes. The distinction between the two phases amounted to diagnosing curable and incurable psychoses, and it led to a pessimistic treatment philosophy.

Gradually, after Griesinger, the emphasis on somatology diminished. More attention was then devoted to the study of clinical pictures. Snell, basing his ideas on Esquirol's and Lasegue's studies of monomania, tried to demonstrate a third psychosis apart from mania and melancholia. He called the disorder "primary insanity" and noted a preoccupation with a restricted delusional system without gross thinking and judgmental impairment. Sander and Cramer described the picture with greater clarity. Sander named it "paranoia" in 1868. Since Kraepelin the disorder has been considered a distinct clinical entity in most nosologies.

Karl Ludwig Kahlbaum (1828–1899) spoke more about forms of abnormal behavior than about diseases. He was particularly concerned with describing what he called "symptom complexes". In 1869 he published a monograph on a disorder he called "catatonia" (*spannungsirrsein*), describing in detail the peculiar but characteristic posturing, motor tension, attitudinizing and stuporous states. Kahlbaum first named the symptom of "verbigeration" and introduced "cyclothymia" as a synonym for circular insanity. In 1871 a student of Kahlbaum, Ewald Hecker (1843–1909), presented a description of hebephrenia ("paraphrenia hebetica") that was to become part of Kraepelin's system. Hecker related the onset of the disorder to puberty and noted the rapid deterioration. Hebephrenia was classified under paraphrenia (age-related disorder) which also included the neophrenias and presbyophrenias (Braceland, 1957).

There was little further delineation of functional psychotic syndromes until Emil Kraepelin's (1856–1928) first *Lehrbuch* appeared in 1883. The *Lehrbuch* reached its classical form in 1899 and was periodically revised until the late 1920's. Kraepelin was a consolidator, not an innovator, and his principal contribution was to bring order to a confused scene by synthesizing the work of the preceding forty years into a single somewhat coherent nosological schema. Kraepelin was quite aware that his system utilized multiple diagnostic criteria. In fact he argued that a classification scheme could not be confined to physiological, etiological or symptomatic criteria but must be based on all clinical findings. In actual practice Kraepelin weighted symptoms, course, and outcome more heavily than etiology which could rarely be established. He stressed prolonged and unremitting recording of observations of the entire course of a disorder in order to discern common patterns among patients.

Kraepelin dichotomized psychiatric conditions into endogenous and exogenous types. He borrowed his terms from Moebius to reflect the prevailing psychiatric dichotomy of acquired and congenital diturbances (Zilboorg, 1941). Exogenous factors produced certain states that precipitated cortical damage which was then reflected in abnormal behavior. Among such states were ex haustion, intoxication, metabolic disease, and emotional distur bance. Endogenous factors included age, sex, and heredity Manic-depressive psychosis and paranoia were due to endogenou factors and dementia praecox to exogenous causes. Other endo genous psychoses included senile conditions, severe retardation and some neuroses. Other exogenous psychoses were paresis an syndromes associated with alcoholism.

During the thirty years following the 1883 *Lehrbuch*, Kraepeli filled in the details of the manic-depressive disorders. He con ceived of the group as representing varied manifestations of th same basic syndrome. Four principal manic-depressive sub categories or states occurred—manic, depressed, mixed, an fundamental. The fundamental states were marked moo deviations which preceded or replaced manic or depressiv episodes. Manic and depressive states could occasionally coexis A common prognosis was the major reason for grouping thes states into a single class. Other reasons were their commo features, difficulty of differentiation, and alternation of manic an depressive states in some patients.

Prognosis was even more heavily overemphasized as a criterio for diagnosing dementia praecox. Kraepelin considered dementi praecox as one disease with many forms and gloomily prognosti cated eventual deterioration. If the patient had a remission o recovery, the diagnosis was usually revised. Kahlbaum's catatoni Hecker's hebephrenia, and a number of other patterns wer grouped under a common rubric. Following work by Bleule Kraepelin added the simple type of dementia praecox to hi system. Paranoid, depressive or stuporous, circular, and child hood forms were also diagnosed.

By Kraepelin's time, paranoia had again become a loosely usec over-inclusive label. He restricted the diagnosis to cases mani festing systematic delusions accompanied by otherwise clear an orderly thinking. His description of the condition was essentiall the same as those drawn by Snell and Lasegue.

Whatever the defects of Kraepelin's system, it certainly brough some sense of order into the field of psychiatry. It served as nodal point from which more intensive explorations could pro cede. Bleuler, Meyer, and countless others could now push th study of abnormal behavior beyond the bounds of the clinical history into the patient's life history. Shortly before Kraepelin, Charcot's studies of hysteria had helped make outpatient psychiatry respectable and observations of outpatients led to many modifications of Kraepelin's system.

BLEULER, MEYER, AND THE ANALYSTS

Next to Kraepelin, Eugen Bleuler (1857–1939) and Adolph Meyer (1866–1950) probably have had the greatest influence on the current American nomenclature. Though Bleuler generally opposed diagnostic labels, his work with schizophrenia led to pronounced changes both in the labeling and the concept of the disorder. Bleuler demolished Kraepelin's ideas that deterioration is inevitable and affect is flat and indifferent in schizophrenia. While believing schizophrenia to be an organic disease, he saw the many forms of schizophrenia as a group of reactions whose common feature was a primary loosening of associations. He thought many symptoms, such as hallucinations and delusions, were secondary reactions originating in the patient's attempt to adjust to the primary pathology. Bleuler was first to recognize simple schizophrenia and to focus attention on the schizoid personalities, preparing the way for the recent concepts of sub- and pre-schizophrenias.

Meyer objected to the overemphasis on the study of symptomatology that preceded and accompanied the Kraepelinian wave. He opposed the view that symptoms were indicants of specific brain lesions and the resulting search for minute differences among similar symptoms. Meyer rejected the disease concept and substituted a concept of abnormal "reaction types". Reaction types, he thought, represent faulty life adaptations by biological organisms. A matrix of psychological, social, physiological and constitutional demands impinge upon the organism. Psychological and physiological reactions are equally important aspects of the adjustment of the total organism. He considered reaction types as results of "experiments of nature". Meyer's diagnostic scheme included five reaction types or "ergasias": merergasia (neurosis), thymergasia (affective disorder), parergasia (schizophrenia and paranoia), dysergasia (deliria), and anergasia (brain injury). His classes were much less influential than his reaction-type concept (Muncie, 1948).

The Freudians have had more influence on the substance of the Standard Nomenclature than on its formal categories. Many of the mechanisms first elaborated by Freud have been adopted as signs for differential diagnosis but, in general, the analysts have paid little attention to problems of description and differentiation of psychotic syndromes. They have been more concerned with the psychogenic basis, developmental history, and adaptive function of the disorder. Freud paid little attention to diagnostic labels and used them rather loosely to suit his own purposes.

In highly condensed form, the Freudian view is that there are two psychoses—depression and schizophrenia. They have in common a collapse of the reality-testing functions of the ego and a regression to narcissistic, pre-Oedipal stages of psychosexual development. The principal difference between them is the depth and specificity of regression. The depressed patient regresses to a specific level of development, the oral-sadistic stage. The schizophrenic regresses to a deeper but less specific state which accounts for the greater variety of schizophrenic symptoms. Paranoia is not considered a separate psychosis. It differs from schizophrenia only in that the paranoid break with reality is confined to a relatively narrow area. Much like Bleulerians, Freudians distinguish two types of schizophrenic symptoms. Symptoms, such as depersonalization, delusions of grandeur, and bizarre physical sensations reflect the central regressive disorder. Symptoms such as hallucinations and paranoid delusions reflect an effort at restitution (Fenichel, 1945).

In the orthodox analytic view, depression includes both involutional and affective psychoses. A neurotic depression is essentially the same reaction except the ego remains more intact. The common component of depression is a fixation upon oral-aggessive techniques which interfere with development of the super-ego. Aggressive impulses of the child pull harsh, punitive responses from the parents, and these parental behaviors are incorporated into the developing super-ego. Later when the individual's aggressive impulses are aroused by loss of a loved one, the climacteric, or insults to the ego, the harsh super-ego is mobilized and the inwardly-turned counterattack that marks depressive episodes may result. In mania the pattern is the same, except here the warped super-ego permits periods of unrestricted satiation of infantile demands which must be followed by a phase of self-punishment (Munroe, 1955).

Horney (1945), Fromm (1947), and other neo-Freudians have written extensively and originally about types or groups of more or less neurotic individuals. Except for Sullivan, few of them have suggested revisions of the conventional categories of psychoses. Sullivan, however, has had a marked influence on modern views of schizophrenia. He regarded simple schizophrenia as a distinct insidiously developing, organic, degenerative disease with a poor prognosis. Hebephrenic, catatonic, and paranoid syndromes were seen as separate phases in the course of the same functional disorder. The "process" and "reactive" schizophrenias represent similar differentiations.

For Sullivan (1947, pp. 72–82), catatonia is part of the more or less acute onset of schizophrenia. The catatonic finds it essential yet impossible to understand what is happening and alternatingly reacts to his bewilderment with complete inaction or violent excitement. From the catatonic phase, the patient may remit, develop a paranoid syndrome, or become hebephrenic. Paranoid developments represent a resolution of chaos by adopting inadequate rationalizations and delusional beliefs to account for experiences. The hebephrenic phase may follow either the catatonic or the paranoid phases. It represents a giving up of the attempt to evaluate experience, a further withdrawal from attempts at maintaining interpersonal relations, and a further regression into the infantile state. In hebephrenia, normal human needs are repressed. Infantile behavior becomes characteristic and any situation which calls for normal, organized behavior evokes anxiety.

AMERICAN STANDARD NOMENCLATURES

By the late 1920's Kraepelin's nomenclature had been widely adopted in the United States. But there remained enormous variations among the teaching centers in the degree to which they adhered to his system and the extent to which they modified it or substituted their own systems. The nomenclature in most general use was contained in the *Statistical Manual for the Use of Hospitals for Mental Diseases*. The *Manual* was based on a schema adopted by the American Psychiatric Association in 1917 and published by the National Committee for Mental Hygiene. In 1933 the *Manual* was revised in line with the first edition of the *Standard Nomenclature of Disease* which appeared the same year. Two other editions of the *Manual* appeared prior to World War II, but changes were slight. The nomenclature remained largely Kraepelinian and aimed at meeting the needs of public psychiatric hospitals.

It has been estimated that only about 10 per cent of the psychiatric casualties of World War II could be accurately classified by means of the existent system. The problem was most obvious with the "minor" disorders. Personality disturbances and psychosomatic reactions, for example, had to be diagnosed as psychopathic personalities and as organ diseases. The Navy partially revised the standard nomenclature in 1944. The Army discarded the nomenclature entirely in 1945 for a system of new categories or new labels for old categories. The Army's nomenclature emphasized Meyer's concept of psychiatric conditions as reaction patterns to life events. The Veterans Administration (VA) endorsed a system much like the Army's in 1946.

In 1950 the American Psychiatric Association adopted its current nosology by a modified majority vote procedure. The next year it was published as part of the *Fourth Edition of the Standard Nomenclature of Diseases and Operations* (American Medical Association, 1952). The system is a slight modification of the Army and VA schemas. Most of the changes concern disorders associated with brain impairment. Work on a fifth edition of the nomenclature is currently in progress.

SUMMARY

The historical events leading to the present psychiatric nomenclature have been briefly sketched. It has been shown how each of the currently accepted syndromes came to be recognized and organized into a diagnostic system. Also evident is the fact that psychiatric nosologies are based on potpourris of differential criteria. The common recipe for a system seems to call for pinches dashes, dabs or gobs of manifest behavior, life history episodes, prognostic guesses, and etiological assumptions. Recognition of the logical priority of syndrome identification to etiology has waxed and waned. In recent years, largely as a consequence of interest in dynamics, etiology has again usurped the role of systematic description in the molding of psychiatric diagnostic categories. Throughout, there is the failure to differentiate and consequent confusion of syndrome and patient type. Diseases are not readily catalogued into hierarchical classes like zoological or botanical specimens. However, patient types do lend themselves to such categorization. This may be one reason for the use of these two basically different approaches.

CHAPTER 11

A REVIEW OF TYPING STUDIES

SOME of the concepts basic to the measurement of similarity have now been sketched. The notion of a type or class of persons has been formulated and a number of proposed statistical procedures for evaluating types have been examined. In the last chapter, the history of the isolation of types by clinical method was presented in some detail. In the present chapter, the handful of statistical typing studies based on behavior observations are examined, compared, and evaluated. Typing studies based on social history, psychological tests or self-report inventories are specifically excluded. Since the domains of similarity are different, such types are simply not comparable to those evolved from observational and interview data. The review will be guided by the criteria outlined in Chapter 9 and by several questions. Do the types isolated agree from one experiment to the next? What correspondence is there between the types generated by statistical means and the types evolved clinically

TYPES THROUGH FACTOR ANALYSIS

Factor analysis has often been proposed as the method of choic for locating types within a heterogeneous population. In such a analysis, the correlations among a sample of individuals are factored As indicated in an earlier chapter, the procedure is inappropriat for the task which is to locate clusters and not dimensions Nevertheless, application of the method has been fairly wide spread.

Interpretation of the type-factors is not easy. Each type facto is defined by those patients who exhibit high positive or hig negative correlations with the factor. Typically most patients ar "mixtures" of the type-factors. In order to interpret the resul it is necessary to have some persons who are relatively "pure" f each factor, that is, who correlate highly with one and only one of the factors. Next it is necessary to examine the profiles of those persons who are most "pure" in each of the type-factors. Inspection of their symptoms or of their mean ratings indicate what "pure" members of a type have in common as well as what distinguishes one type from another. Another more rigorous approach is to correlate each descriptive variable with each of the type-factors, treating the type-correlations as if they were scores. Those variables significantly correlated with each type-factor characterize it. Still other procedures are possible but the typical approach has been to examine those cases most characteristic of the type.

One early study was by Guertin (1952), who reported a factor analysis based on twenty schizophrenics (twelve white females and eight white males) on the admission ward of one state hospital. Of these subjects nine were diagnosed mixed type, five paranoid, five catatonic, and one hebephrenic. Fifty-two symptoms of a previously factored set were employed to describe these patients after several mental status interviews. Similarity was expressed in terms of tetrachoric correlations between patients across the fifty-two symptoms. Guertin extracted three monopolar factors which were interpreted as Paranoid, Confused-withdrawn, and Hebephrenic. Ten patients defined one type-factor while the other patients defined one or both of the remaining factors. Since the findings are dimensions, an individual may define several dimensions. The factors were interpreted by inspection of the symptoms of the three most typical individuals and by correlating the symptom factor scores with the type-factors. The Paranoid type was characterized by paranoid delusions and relatively intact thought processes. The second type, called Confused-withdrawn, was described as apathetic, disoriented, and indifferent as to personal appearance or needs. The third type, called Hebephrenic, displayed conceptual disorganization and inappropriate affect.

The study is based on a factored schedule of symptoms but some areas of behavior are unrepresented and others are marginally represented. The correlations are based on items rather than clusters and thus are less meaningful. No bounds are set for inclusion in a type nor are the types replicated. Correspondence of the types to conventional diagnosis is suggested but no data are offered to confirm these inferences. However, the study does represent an interesting pioneering effort.

In a later analysis, Guertin and Jenkins (1956) factored a thirty by thirty matrix of tetrachoric correlations among twenty-nine schizophrenic patients and one hypothetical normal. The hypothetical normal was introduced as an aid in the interpretation of the factors isolated. The rating instrument consisted of fifty-five Multidimensional Scales for Rating Psychiatric Patients. The series included first admissions and readmissions unselected except for the diagnosis of schizophrenia and accessibility to interview. The diagnoses represented were ten paranoid types, four catatonic types, and fourteen chronic undifferentiated types. Four factors were extracted, of which the first was bipolar. The factors were interpreted by inspecting the ratings of the patients correlating most highly with the type-factor. The first factor was interpreted in terms of level of pathology. But since it is bipolar, it represents two groups; a normal-appearing group and a disorganized, disoriented, withdrawn group. The second type-factor patients appear to be mainly withdrawn without disorganization, while the third appear to be disorganized but not tense. The fourth type-factor patients are characterized by perplexity, morbid fears, anxiety and self-depreciation. This last symptom picture corresponds to the Involutional psychotic.

The study illustrates the difficulties that arise in using items rather than homogeneous, independent syndromes, and in applying factor analysis to typing problems. The correlations are inflated spuriously to an unknown extent because the "dimensions" of similarity are often highly correlated. The first factor represents two groupings, while inspection of the second type-factor suggests that it might have disappeared if clustering procedures had been applied. On the positive side, it can be said that the range of behaviors represented is quite adequate. The authors, however, provide no modal profiles and establish no limits to the classes evolved. Finally, no data on replicability of the types are provided.

An analysis of some interest has been reported by Stammeyer (1958). He used as a similarity index the common elements coefficient (McNemar, 1955). First, ten clear-cut cases of hebephrenia, catatonia, paranoid schizophrenia, and agitated depression were selected independently by hospital staff members. Then Stammeyer, without knowledge of patient diagnosis, interviewed the forty patients selected and consulted ward personnel. Subsequently, he rated each patient on a 115-item checklist of symptoms and behaviors. Four type-factors were then extracted. To identify the symptoms significantly characterizing each type factor, each symptom was correlated with each factor. One type was defined by nine hebephrenics and four catatonics; another by six catatonics and two agitated depressives; a third by eight agitated depressives and one hebephrenic. The fourth type was defined entirely by paranoids. The symptoms descriptive of the four types corresponded well with clinical descriptions of these diagnostic classes. The study thus tended to support the Kraepelinian classification scheme.

One shortcoming of the study lies in the use of items instead of dimensions, although the checklist did tap the domain of psychopathology rather well. Other doubts relate to the degree of dependence of the findings on the patients selected for the investigation and the interviewer. What would have happened if, instead, an unselected sample of patients rated by an independent interviewer had been typed? Stammeyer gives no upper or lower bounds to his types and provides no modal profiles. However, from the viewpoint of conventional diagnostic categories, the extent of confirmation is relatively good.

In another primarily methodological study, Guertin (1961) sought to identify the salient characteristics of type-factors through use of DuMas' method of manifest structure analysis (1956). The forty-nine chronic schizophrenic patients in the analysis were described by means of interview ratings made during the first week after admission. The computed tetrachoric correlations among patients were then factored. The DuMas procedure was next applied to identify the symptoms characterizing each type factor. Since the method is complex and not easily described, the interested reader is referred to the DuMas monograph. The types isolated were interpreted as Normal, Catatonic-Withdrawn versus Over-Expressive, Paranoid, Resistive Isolation, and Anxious Dysphoric.

Guertin's purpose was to illustrate the use of manifest structure analysis (MSA). For this reason, he provides no cross-validation of the type-factors or of the MSA scales developed. For the same reason, the restriction of the sample to chronic schizophrenics must be overlooked. As for the use of MSA to establish scales of symptoms, several observations may be made. It is evident from the presence of high negative and high positive values that at least one of the type factors is bipolar and thus defines two separate groups. Catatonic-Withdrawn patients and Over-Expressive patients, from this point of view, are actually distinctive groups and not two ends of a continuum. Use of factor analysis in this context encourages the representation of patient groups as continua. In a multivariate setting, a type is a class of individuals defined by a complex pattern of scores and not by high or low scores on a single dimension. Another point is that DuMas defines a "manifest variable" as a continuous variable or "magnitudinal continuum". The type-factor correlations play the role of measures of the manifest variable. It is difficult to conceive of ranked individuals as representing a continuous interval manifest variable scale like time or length.

TYPES BY AGREEMENT ANALYSIS

A procedure developed by Jenkins and Ackerson (1933), which resembles the agreement analysis process proposed by Zubin (1938) and McQuitty (1954), served as the basis of an investigation by Jenkins and Lorr (1954). The basic data consisted of ratings on 423 hospitalized male psychotics on fifty-four short descriptive scales previously factored. *A priori* rating patterns were prepared for types labeled ambulatory schizophrenic, paranoid, schizophrenic disorganization, catatonic withdrawal, manic, depressed and agitated depression. A pattern consisted of one or more scale values (rating like two, three, and four) on each of the fifty-four scales. By means of a card punch scorer, each patient's ratings were scored on each of the key patterns. A score consisted of the total number of agreements between a patient's rating pattern and the key or master pattern. The distribution of scores on each of the patterns was obtained and cutting points were so selected as to minimize the number of cases falling into more than one group. Cases falling above the cutting point on one and only one pattern were utilized for the preparation of a second set of patterns

All cases were rescored on the second set and a third set of patterns derived, and so on.

The final patterns derived were named Normality, Resistive Isolation, Schizophrenic Disorganization, Paranoid Stabilization, Manic Excitement, Mournful Depression, and Panicky Agitation. As the investigators point out, the solution achieved by the method is not wholly independent of the points of origin. Another difficulty is that agreement (similarity) is dependent on specific and relatively unreliable single scales. The results, on the other hand, support the notion that relatively independent psychotic types do exist.

ANALYSIS OF DIAGNOSTIC GROUPS

How homogeneous are groups of patients with identical diagnoses? This question has often been raised. What follows is a summary of several attempts to answer this question in a limited way. Shortly following the development of the Wittenborn Psychiatric Rating Scale (PRS), Wittenborn and Bailey (1952) conducted a study of the symptomatic similarities and dissimilarities among a sample of twenty consecutively admitted patients with a diagnosis of Involutional psychosis. The twenty patients were intercorrelated on the basis of their ratings on the fifty-five scales of the PRS. A factor analysis yielded six possible type-factors. The authors concluded that the patients so diagnosed were symptomatically heterogeneous; some were practically asymptomatic, others were without important symptoms of depression, while still others were characterized by all combinations of symptoms other than depression. Instead of one important general type factor, as one might expect, there were six group factors.

In a subsequent study Wittenborn and Weiss (1952) secured PRS descriptions of twenty newly admitted patients staff diagnosed Manic depressive psychosis, manic state. The correlation coefficient was again used as the index of similarity between patients. It was agreed that if the diagnosis was descriptively efficient, one would expect that all patients would form one conspicuous general factor. A factor analysis of the correlations among the twenty patients revealed six type-factors. Again it was concluded that patients diagnosed manic (at least in the sample studied) differ symptomatically from each other. In addition, some sex-related factors were found.

A group of twenty-nine male patients diagnosed paranoid schizophrenia was analyzed by Guertin (1958) with a somewhat different purpose in mind. Guertin argued that paranoid schizophrenia seemed to be the most clearly defined schizophrenic category. Nevertheless, symptomatology varies sufficiently among these patients as to suggest further subclassification. Each patient's ward and interview behavior was described on the MSRPP. Tetrachoric correlation coefficients were employed as indices of similarity. The resulting table of correlations among patients was then factored and transformed to attain simple structure. Type-factors were named on the basis of symptoms shown by individuals with the highest correlation with a given factor. The four factors isolated were named Normalcy, Withdrawal and Deterioration, Tense and Labile, and Encapsulated Schizophrenic.

The first or Normalcy factor, reported to be the largest, may represent a possible common type-factor but lack of data makes inferences doubtful. The second type-factor was descriptive of seven patients who in addition to being delusional were also deteriorated and withdrawn. The last two factors were quite small and Guertin reports difficulty in interpretation. One limitation to the analysis is that the patients included were nearly all chronic. Moreover, the large first factor reported may be a general factor and thus supports the hypothesis that the diagnostic category is homogeneous. Information in the report does not permit further judgment.

What might be concluded from these three studies? The investigators acknowledge certain limitations to their samples. Further, from the viewpoint of method, procedures other than factor analysis might have resulted in fewer acceptable patient classes. However, Wittenborn's profiles leave little doubt that the groups he studied were mixed symptomatically. Thus, the evidence tends to support the contention that conventional diagnostic categories as ordinarily applied are heterogeneous. The basis for this condition is not obscure. The diagnostician does not have available precise definitions of symptoms nor does he have a guide as to how many symptoms must be present and to what degree of severity. It is left to his clinical acumen to decide in what class a patient belongs.

SUMMARY

An effort was made here to review critically the available statistical typing studies based on behavioral data. Investigations based on inventories, tests and social history were ignored. The four investigations utilizing factor analysis as a technique for isolating types appear to have suggestive findings. Types resembling Paranoid reaction, Involutional psychosis, and hebephrenic reaction appear repeatedly in the analyses. However, the samples analyzed have been far too small and unrepresentative of psychotic types to yield definitive results. The statistical method applied is regarded as inappropriate and in no instance was replication of findings on comparable samples attempted. At best, these and related studies support the contention of many psychiatrists that conventional groupings are heterogeneous.

A more hopeful picture emerges in the next chapter. A typing process reveals six sharply distinguishable syndrome-based psychotic types. Each of these is replicated in four independent samples.

CHAPTER 12

SYNDROME-BASED TYPES

A NUMBER of published studies in typing were reviewed in the previous chapter. In general, there was little consistency in the findings. Judged in terms of the suggested criteria for an adequate typing study, delineated in Chapter 9, nearly every investigation was defective in several respects. The present chapter consists of a description of a series of analyses based on IMPS data that resulted in six replicated syndrome-based types. The term type is defined here to mean a group of individuals, all of whom may be characterized in the same way. The domain of similarity is that defined by the psychotic syndromes derived by factor analysis from behavior observable in a psychiatric interview.

PROBLEM AND SAMPLE

The major goal set for the study was to isolate and to replicate some of the more frequently occurring psychotic types. The descriptive measures used were the ten syndromes defined by IMPS. The approach assumed that some types exist as, needless to say perhaps, most clinicians would agree. However, the attitude taken was as if there were no Kraepelinian or Bleulerian diagnostic categories. The problem was simply to determine what types statistical procedure could reveal. Suppose, despite the differences in methods of observation, identification, and confirmation, there are similarities. Then the congruence will be supportive of common findings. If agreement is slight or non-existent, there are several explanations possible. It could be that either or both procedures (clinical and statistical) are defective, or it is possible that the qualitative, medical disease-type of categories are simply different from the multivariate classes isolated here. In brief, whatever types emerge should be judged on their own merits regardless of the currently recognized psychiatric categories.

The sample consisted of 556 psychotic patients previously described as the norm group for the standardization of IMPS. One subsample consisted of 207 patients selected to assure representation of all likely sources of syndrome variation. Another subsample was comprised of 359 newly admitted schizophrenics. In all, forty-four private, state, and federal hospitals were represented in the sample. Each patient had been rated by two independent observers on IMPS following a one-hour interview. The two ratings on each syndrome were combined into a single raw score. To make the ten syndrome scores comparable in metric, each was converted into a standard score with an arbitrary mean of five and a standard deviation of one. The ten standardized syndrome scores received by each patient were the basic criteria for classification.

THE SIMILARITY INDICES

The typing problem was to isolate and then to replicate if possible each of the major types existing in the data. To make replication possible, the total sample was randomized and partitioned into five sets or subsamples. Three samples consisted of one hundred cases each, and two samples were made up of 133 cases each.

Three indices of similarity were employed in evolving the types (see Chapter 9). One index was the distance squared measure (D^2) between each case and every other case within each of the five sets. The covariance or the mean of the cross-products of the standard scores of the two individuals compared was also available. The third similarity index was the between-person correlations among all cases included within a set. It will be recalled (Chapter 9) that D^2_{GH} includes all information concerning differences in mean level, scatter of scores, and profile shape. The covariance measure, $Q_{GH}\sigma_G\sigma_H$, loses information concerning the level of scores but retains other bases of difference. The third index Q_{GH}, the person–person correlation loses information concerning level and scatter but retains profile shape and direction.

THE TYPING PROCESS

The procedure followed for identifying types was essentially a method of clustering indices of similarity. Cattell (1944) has described a variety of methods for determining the clusters in a correlation matrix. Sawrey, Keller, and Conger (1960) have outlined procedures for objectively clustering D^2s.

The process was begun by focusing on the inter-person correlations. A lower limit for inclusion within a cluster was initially set at 0.60 which is roughly twice the standard error of a correlation coefficient based on an N of ten. Each case in the subsample was listed in a table by code number. The code numbers of all other cases correlating 0.60 or higher with each individual were then listed. To form a cluster the individual with the longest associated list was chosen as a pivot. Several individuals most highly correlated with the pivot were chosen to form the nucleus of the first cluster. Each case in the matrix was examined in turn and added to the initial cluster if his average correlation with the nucleus was 0.55 or better. When a case was added to the nucleus it was eliminated from the table of code numbers.

To identify additional clusters the reduced table of code numbers was again systematically examined. The nucleus was based on several individuals with the longest associated lists who were simultaneously (a) highly similar in profile (Q above 0.60) to each other and (b) dissimilar (Q either negative or below 0.35) to persons in the first cluster. Other individuals satisfying both the upper and the lower limits were added until no others could be found in the table. No limit was set on the size of the negative correlation between members of two clusters. Negatively correlated individuals have profiles that tend to be mirror images of each other and thus are by definition dissimilar. Cases correlating highly with two clusters were excluded from both.

Additional clusters were identified and generated in the same fashion. For the third cluster, for example, the reduced table was examined to find a set of individuals highly similar to each other (Q above 0.60) but dissimilar (Q less than 0.35) from members of other clusters. Unless a cluster comprised four or more individuals it was rejected. Without some practical limitation on size, an indefinite number of tiny unstable clusters consisting of two or three individuals could emerge. While it was recognized that relatively rare types could thus escape detection, the task of isolating such types was seen as one to be approached at a later stage of research.

REPLICATION OF THE TYPES

An essential but neglected step in establishing types is to obtain confirmatory evidence by applying the same criteria of type membership to additional samples. If the same relatively independent classes of patients emerge then they may be regarded with some degree of confidence; otherwise they must be rejected. Thus there is a problem of defining group membership. The similarity index is not adequate for this purpose because it is global in nature. It indicates how similar two sets of scores are when considered simultaneously. To define type membership some bounds must be set for each syndrome. To make the problem more concrete consider each of the ten syndromes to be separate dimensions or coordinate axes. Then each person may be represented as a point in multi-dimensional space. Thus viewed geometrically the members of each type represent a swarm of points in ten-dimensional space. If there are a half-dozen overlapping swarms of points, then some limits must be established if these are to be defined as mutually exclusive.

As a first step, the standard scores of each member of a type were plotted in conventional fashion on a two-dimensional graph, as illustrated by the figures. The vertical axis represents the standard scores and the base line represents the ten syndromes. Then by inspecting the range of scores and the means, the characteristic bounds of a type could be fixed. Typically the syndrome scores that distinguished a type were elevated above the norm mean (5.0) while all other scores were below the mean. However, in two instances one syndrome (CNP) failed to discriminate as there were as many scores above as below the norm mean. (See Appendix D.)

To replicate the six types found in the first subsample, the profiles of each member of remaining subsamples was examined to see to which type it belonged. To be a type member each and every syndrome score had to fall within the bounds established for that syndrome. Each profile was checked against the criteria of each type. As a final step the correlations among the cases unassigned to any of the six groups were systematically examined. The purpose was to determine whether any additional correlational clusters of appropriate size could be detected. Only small groupings of three to six members that could not be confirmed in other samples were generated.

ISOLATION OF TYPES BY D^2

The squares of the distances (D^2) between individuals within each of the subsamples were also searched for types. This index of similarity has probably been the most popular in recent analyses. Its major advantage is that information concerning level and scatter of scores in a profile are not lost. To explore the utility of D^2 for isolating psychotic types one of the authors applied the typing procedure to several subsamples. The analyses were conducted without knowledge of the groupings obtained on the basis of person–person correlations by procedures similar to those already described. The lower limit for admission to a group was initially set at six-tenths of the sum of the variances of the ten syndromes (a measure of distance).

The typing process generated one large group of cases and numerous small groups of two to five cases. Repetition of the process on a second subsample of one hundred produced similar results. Next an attempt was made to use the groups identified in the correlations as a possible base. D^2s were substituted for the correlations in the matrix defining the six types in the first subsample. Although some clusters hung together, the correlation-defined types tended to merge when D^2s were substituted. At this point the use of D^2s was abandoned. One likely reason for the failure of the typing process when applied to D^2s is that the syndrome scores are all strongly skewed (see Table 12.14) i.e., most patients receive relatively low scores and the remainder receive intermediate or high scores. Experience with use of D^2s on other data suggests that the index is more useful when the score distributions are symmetric.

TYPING WITH COVARIANCES

The third set of indices of similarity available were the covariances. The covariance index has the advantage of taking into account the extent of variation in scores in a profile which the person–person correlation coefficient does not. Unlike the distance measure, it also reflects the direction of differences. Since covariances may be positive or negative, they also indicate whether two profiles are dissimilar in shape and not simply how distant. The person–person covariances were substituted for the correlations among individuals defining the six types evolved in the

TABLE 12.1

SYNDROME MEANS BY TYPE AND SAMPLE SET

		Syndrome										
	Set	EXC	HOS	PAR	GRN	PCP	INP	RTD	DIS	MTR	CNP	N
EXC-GRN	1	69	48	47	59	44	46	41	51	52	56	6
	2	69	51	45	64	48	46	47	46	50	52	5
	3	68	50	48	64	51	46	43	47	48	53	5
	4	--	--	--	--	--	--	--	--	--	--	-
	5	70	46	48	64	45	44	40	50	54	59	5
EXC-HOS	1	66	67	48	48	45	42	42	46	45	50	4
	2	--	--	--	--	--	--	--	--	--	--	-
	3	61	63	49	50	46	45	46	45	47	59	3
	4	66	62	44	50	44	45	41	50	46	49	4
	5	62	68	46	48	44	42	41	50	46	48	6
RTD	1	44	42	40	44	48	45	60	48	46	45	7
	2	42	45	41	44	43	49	61	50	46	45	5
	3	42	42	43	45	46	46	62	46	48	48	5
	4	42	43	41	44	44	45	62	50	44	45	11
	5	41	44	42	44	45	44	60	51	44	44	4

13

TABLE 12.1 (CONTINUED)

	SET	EXC	HOS	PAR	GRN	PCP	INP	RTD	DIS	MTR	CNP	N
INP	1	48	48	45	47	43	68	48	47	47	44	10
	2	44	45	43	44	45	62	47	46	44	43	18
	3	43	46	41	46	48	64	46	46	44	44	4
	4	44	43	44	44	46	65	48	50	43	43	9
	5	46	47	47	44	45	60	46	50	45	44	8
HOS-PAR	1	44	59	63	47	48	48	46	46	45	45	7
	2	53	62	69	47	54	48	43	48	49	47	7
	3	47	61	56	47	44	46	45	47	43	44	6
	4	48	64	60	46	44	44	45	50	45	44	7
	5	45	60	60	44	46	42	40	50	40	42	2
DIS	1	53	49	49	48	50	45	63	87	77	68	6
	2	46	43	44	46	47	44	65	80	65	62	8
	3	52	46	42	44	45	42	60	71	70	70	3
	4	47	43	41	45	46	40	68	75	70	64	3
	5	46	46	40	44	45	45	65	72	71	58	3

first subsample. The clusters were found to retain their independence and internal consistency fairly well. However, a small number of individuals with jagged profiles (diverse and extreme scores) tended to relate very highly with each other and across several clusters. The reason for this may be seen from the arithmetic of the covariance index. The index consists of the person–person correlation multiplied by the measures of scatter of the two individuals involved. If one or both dispersion measures are large the covariance increases rapidly in size. In as much as the covariances did not appear to lead to strikingly different groups than those determined by the correlations in the manner described, further trials to evolve types were discontinued.

TABLE 12.2
MEAN AND MEDIAN STANDARD SYNDROME SCORES FOR SIX PATIENT TYPES
(ALL SAMPLES COMBINED)

SYNDROMES	EXC-GRN		EXC-HOS		RTD		INP		PAR		DIS	
	MEAN	MEDIAN	MEAN	MEDIAN	MEAN	MEDIAN	MEAN	MEDIAN	MEAN	MEDIAN	MEAN	MEDIAN
EXCITEMENT	69	69	64	65	42	42	45	44	48	48	49	47
HOSTILE BELLIGERENCE	49	48	68	64	43	42	46	45	61	62	45	42
PARANOID PROJECTION	47	48	47	46	41	40	44	44	62	63	44	43
GRANDIOSE EXPANSIVENESS	63	62	48	50	44	44	45	44	46	46	46	44
PERCEPTUAL DISTORTION	47	44	45	43	45	44	45	44	48	45	47	46
ANXIOUS INTROPUNITIVENESS	46	45	43	44	46	45	64	62	46	46	43	42
RETARDATION AND APATHY	46	42	42	42	61	59	47	45	44	45	64	64
DISORIENTATION	49	51	46	46	46	45	45	45	45	45	70	71
MOTOR DISTURBANCE	49	46	48	49	49	49	48	46	48	46	79	85
CONCEPTUAL DISORGANIZATION	55	54	51	48	45	44	43	42	45	43	64	64

EVIDENCE FOR THE SIX TYPES

The mean syndrome scores for each of the six psychotic types isolated in the five sample sets are presented in Table 12.1. The members of each type from each of the five sample sets were combined. The mean and median syndrome scores for the total sample are given in Table 12.2. As may be seen from inspection, the profiles within and across sample sets are quite consistent. One type of estimate of consistency among profiles is the median correlation obtaining within the samples of each type as shown below.

Excited-Grandiose	0.88	Intropunitive	0.94
Excited-Hostile	0.91	Hostile-Paranoid	0.90
Retarded	0.93	Disorganized	0.93

These values indicate considerable consistency among profile shapes within each patient type.

The types should preferably be independent of each other. Evidence of the degree of independence among clusters within each sample set is given in Tables 12.3 through 12.7. The coefficients represent correlations among sums of variables (Gulliksen, 1950, p. 74). The correlations, with but few exceptions, are either negative or negligible. The two excited types as well as the paranoid and the excited-hostile types tend to be related. Likewise the Disorganized and the Retarded groups show some positive correlation. In each such instance one syndrome is above the norm mean for both types. Further evidence of the independence of the six patient classes is reported in the next chapter. A discriminant function analysis indicated that all types were significantly distant from each other.

To what extent are the six types confirmed in the replication of sample sets? It may be seen by examining Table 12.1 that there were no Excited-Grandiose patients who fitted the criteria in sample set 4. No Excited-Hostile type was found in sample set 2. With these exceptions confirmation is good as judged by consistency within profiles and independence of types within each of the samples. In addition no other types could be established that could be confirmed in other samples. In general the study satisfies the criterion (Chapter 9) that a type should be invariant under changes in the sample of people studied.

Table 12.3 Correlations Among Clusters Within Set 1 (Decimal points omitted)

	EXC-GRN	EXC-HOS	RTD	INP	PAR
Excited-Grandiose					
Excited-Hostile	49				
Retarded	-31	-29			
Intropunitive	-10	-08	13		
Hostile-Paranoid	-34	29	-30	-06	
Disorganized	00	-27	-18	-41	-47

Table 12.4 Correlations Among Clusters Within Set 2* (Decimal points omitted)

	EXC-GRN	RTD	INP	PAR
Excited-Grandiose				
Retarded	-30			
Intropunitive	-28	32		
Hostile-Paranoid	-20	-49	-22	
Disorganized	-14	14	-50	-45

* No EXC-HOS patients represented in this set.

Table 12.5 Correlations Among Clusters Within Set 3 (Decimal points omitted)

	EXC-GRN	EXC-HOS	RTD	INP	PAR
Excited-Grandiose					
Excited-Hostile	36				
Retarded	-39	-43			
Intropunitive	-24	-33	16		
Hostile-Paranoid	-11	47	-28	01	
Disorganized	-24	04	22	-48	-56

TABLE 12.6
CORRELATIONS AMONG CLUSTERS WITHIN SET 4*
(DECIMAL POINTS OMITTED)

	EXC-HOS	RTD	INP	PAR
EXCITED-HOSTILE				
RETARDED	-43			
INTROPUNITIVE	-30	16		
HOSTILE-PARANOID	33	-30	-30	
DISORGANIZED	-26	59	-24	-33

* No EXC-GRN patients represented in this set.

TABLE 12.7
CORRELATIONS AMONG CLUSTERS WITHIN SET 5
(DECIMAL POINTS OMITTED)

	EXC-GRN	EXC-HOS	RTD	INP	PAR
EXCITED-GRANDIOSE					
EXCITED-HOSTILE	38				
RETARDED	-52	-36			
INTROPUNITIVE	-31	-04	00		
HOSTILE-PARANOID	-21	54	-28	-09	
DISORGANIZED	-04	-26	63	-12	-48

A practical question one might ask concerns the proportion of the sample accounted for by the six types. A count shows that the percentages are forty, forty-three, twenty-five, twenty-six and twenty-five for the successive sample sets. It is difficult to compare these percentages with those achieved by conventional diagnostic categories. For an adequate contrast a stratified random sample of patients would be required. Then the two typing procedures could be applied independently and the resulting data compared. A rigorous test must thus be left for a future study.

TABLE 12.8

T SCORE DISTRIBUTIONS OF EXC-GRN PATIENTS

T	SYNDROMES									
	EXC	HOS	PAR	GRN	PCP	INP	RTD	DIS	MTR	CNP
37-38						1	3			
39-40			1			5	3			
41-42		2	5			1	7		2	1
43-44		3	2		12	3	2	*	2	2
45-46		2	0		2	2	2	13	0	0
47-48		5	4	1	1	3	1	*	3	4
49-50		4	5	0	2	2	2	6	3	0
51-52		0	2	2	2	1	0	*	4	2
53-54	1	2	0	1	0	2	1	0	4	2
55-56	0	2	0	1	0	0		*	2	2
57-58	1	0	1	2	0	0		0	0	0
59-60	1	0	0	2	1	1		*	0	1
61-62	2	0	1	2	0			2	0	2
63-64	0	1		1	0			*	0	1
65-66	1			1	1				0	0
67-68	2			2					0	1
69-70	6			0					1	0
71-72	2			2						1
73-74	1			2						0
75-76	2			2						0
77-78	0									1
79-80	1									0
81-82	0									1
83-84	0									
85-86	0									
87-88	0									
89-90	1									

* *T* scores do not appear in these intervals.

INTERPRETATION OF THE PATIENT TYPES

Two slightly related but distinctive excited types emerged (see Figures 12.1 and 12.2). The Excited-Grandiose type is defined by scores elevated above the norm mean on Excitement and Grandiose Expansiveness. All other scores except CNP are well below the mean. Conceptual Disorganization appears not to be a

TABLE 12.9
T SCORE DISTRIBUTIONS OF EXC-HOS PATIENTS

T	SYNDROMES									
	EXC	HOS	PAR	GRN	PCP	INP	RTD	DIS	MTR	CNP
37–38						1	2			
39–40			3			4	6	*	2	
41–42			2			3	1	1	5	
43–44			0	3	11	1	4	*	1	6
45–46			4	2	3	6	1	7	1	0
47–48			1	1	0	1	3	*	4	3
49–50			4	5	2	0		9	1	0
51–52	2		1	5	1	0		*	1	1
53–54	1	2	0	1		1			1	1
55–56	1	0	1						0	2
57–58	2	0	1						1	1
59–60	1	1								2
61–62	1	2								0
63–64	0	4								0
65–66	3	4								1
67–68	1	0								
69–70	1	0								
71–72	1	2								
73–74	0	0								
75–76	2	0								
77–78	1	0								
79–80		0								
81–82		1								
83–84		1								

* *T* scores do not appear in these intervals.

differentiating variable. The Excited-Hostile type is defined by the possession of scores elevated in Excitement and Hostility. Other syndromes are below the norm mean although CNP scores are just about as frequent above as below the mean. The Excited-Grandiose type appears to correspond to the traditional euphoric manic. The Excited-Hostile patient seems not to be recognized in the literature except possibly by Moore (1933, pp. 65–66). Moore calls the state paranoia irritabilitis and observes that it is often confused with manic excitement. He goes on to say that the two may be separated on the basis of the presence or absence of

TABLE 12.10

T SCORE DISTRIBUTIONS OF INP PATIENTS

T	Syndromes									
	EXC	HOS	PAR	GRN	PCP	INP	RTD	DIS	MTR	CNP
37–38							2			
39–40		6	16				7	*	7	
41–42	13	9	7				2	0	11	30
43–44	17	5	4	40	35		5	*	6	10
45–46	4	14	8	3	2		11	31	13	6
47–48	4	5	4	3	6		2	*	5	1
49–50	7	3	6	0	2		4	18	4	1
51–52	1	3	1	1	0	1	6	*	2	1
53–54	0	1	0	1	1	5	5	0	0	
55–56	2	1	2	0	1	4	2	*	1	
57–58	1	1	0	0	1	4	3			
59–60		1	1	0	0	9				
61–62				0	0	4				
63–64				0	0	3				
65–66				1	1	1				
67–68						4				
69–70						2				
71–72						4				
73–74						4				
75–76						2				
77–78						0				
79–80						1				
81–82						0				
83–84						0				
85–86						1				

* *T* scores do not appear in these intervals.

euphoria. The type defined here, however, does not exhibit paranoid delusions. Another possibility is that excitement may be associated either with hostile irritability or with euphoria. The data described in the chapter on the syndrome circle provides some support for this hypothesis.

The class of patients called Intropunitive are defined principally by elevated scores on Intropunitiveness. All other scores except Retardation are below the norm mean. Conceptual Disorganization,

TABLE 12.11
T SCORE DISTRIBUTIONS OF RTD PATIENTS

T	Syndromes									
	EXC	HOS	PAR	GRN	PCP	INP	RTD	DIS	MTR	CNP
37–38										
39–40		8	17			2			3	
41–42	21	13	7	1		5			4	11
43–44	7	4	1	28	22	7		*	8	6
45–46	2	1	6	2	2	8		14	4	5
47–48	0	2	0	0	1	6		*	6	5
49–50	1	3	1	1	0	2		15	4	3
51–52	1	1			5	0	1	*	1	1
53–54					1	0	3	1	1	1
55–56					0	0	5	*	1	
57–58					1	1	7	1		
59–60						0	3	*		
61–62						0	3	1		
63–64						0	2	*		
65–66						1	2			
67–68							2			
69–70							0			
71–72							1			
73–74							0			
75–76							1			
77–78							1			
79–80							1			

* *T* scores do not appear in these intervals.

Motor Disturbances and Grandiosity are exceptionally low. The Retardation score discriminates the Intropunitives from the Retarded (yet to be described) although one-third of the Intropunitives exhibit Retardation scores above the general mean. The type bears closest resemblance to the pattern of the Involutional psychotic reaction. However, there is no evidence that the pattern is restricted to patients in the involutional period. Briefly characterized, this is a group of agitated depressives who often exhibit psychomotor slowing but who rarely show thinking disorganization or motor disturbances.

Table 12.12
T Score Distributions of PAR Patients

T	Syndromes									
	EXC	HOS	PAR	GRN	PCP	INP	RTD	DIS	MTR	CNP
37–38						1	2			
39–40						2	3		5	
41–42	2					3	6		3	12
43–44	6			9	14	3	3	*	6	8
45–46	3			8	5	7	4	19	5	1
47–48	8			6	1	3	8	*	4	4
49–50	5		1	2	2	5	1	9	2	1
51–52	1	5	0	2	2	3	1	*	3	2
53–54	1	2	4	2	3	1	1	0	0	0
55–56	1	2	4		0	1		*	1	1
57–58	1	3	2		0			1		
59–60	0	3	2		1					
61–62	0	2	1		0					
63–64	0	1	6		0					
65–66	0	4	2		0					
67–68	1	3	2		0					
69–70		0	1		0					
71–72		1	2		0					
73–74		0	0		0					
75–76		1	2		0					
77–78		1			0					
79–80		1			1					

* *T* scores do not appear in these intervals.

The scores of the Retarded type are all below the norm mean except on Retardation and Apathy. Inspection of Table 12.2 shows exceptionally low scores on Excitement, Paranoid Projection, Grandiosity, and Hostility. The Retarded type patients are most similar to the Intropunitives probably because both tend to exhibit psychomotor slowing. Comparison with conventional psychiatric diagnoses suggests that the Retarded correspond most closely to the Manic-Depressive reaction, depressed type. However, this correspondence may be relatively superficial. A high percentage of members of this type are diagnosed schizophrenic. Other relevant data that bear on this issue came to light

TABLE 12.13

T SCORE DISTRIBUTIONS OF DIS PATIENTS

T	Syndromes									
	EXC	HOS	PAR	GRN	PCP	INP	RTD	DIS	MTR	CNP
37–38						3				
39–40		8	8			5				
41–42	3	4	3			4				1
43–44	5	0	5	17	11	3				1
45–46	3	4	2	1	1	3				1
47–48	3	0	0	1	5	2	1			1
49–50	2	3	2	1	1	1	0			0
51–52	0	1	0	1	2	1	0	*	1	1
53–54	1	1	0	1	1	0	2	3	2	2
55–56	2	1	0	0	1	0	0	*	1	1
57–58	2	0	3	1	0	0	3	0	0	1
59–60	0	0			0	1	2	*	1	1
61–62	1	1			0		2	2	2	1
63–64	0				0		2	*	1	1
65–66	0				0		1	1	1	1
67–68	1				0		3	*	0	1
69–70					0		3	2	2	0
71–72					1		1	*	2	1
73–74							0	1	3	2
75–76							0	*	0	0
77–78							2	1	1	2
79–80							1	*	2	0
81–82								0	0	1
83–84								*	1	1
85–86								4	1	1
87–88								*	1	0
89–90								4	0	1
91–92								*	0	
93–94								5	0	
95–96								*	1	

* *T* scores do not appear in these intervals.

in studies by Payne and Hewlett (1960) on thought disorders in psychotics. They identified a factor of Retardation that differentiated between psychotics as a group and all other subjects, but which did not differentiate between schizophrenics and depressives. All tests correlated with this factor were speed tests.

TABLE 12.14
T SCORE DISTRIBUTIONS OF ALL 171 PATIENTS TYPED

T	Syndromes									
	EXC	HOS	PAR	GRN	PCP	INP	RTD	DIS	MTR	CNP
37–38						6	9			
39–40		22	45			18	19		17	
41–42	39	28	24	1		16	16		25	55
43–44	35	12	12	98	105	17	14		23	33
45–46	12	21	20	16	15	26	18	84	23	13
47–48	15	12	9	12	14	15	15	*	22	18
49–50	15	13	19	9	9	10	7	57	14	5
51–52	5	10	4	11	12	6	8	*	12	8
53–54	4	8	4	6	6	9	12	4	8	6
55–56	6	6	7	1	2	5	7	*	6	6
57–58	7	4	7	3	2	5	13	3	1	2
59–60	2	5	3	2	2	11	5	*	1	4
61–62	4	5	2	2	0	4	5	5	2	3
63–64	0	6	6	1	0	3	4	*	1	2
65–66	4	8	2	2	2	2	3	1	1	2
67–68	5	3	2	2	0	4	5	*	0	2
69–70	7	0	1	0	0	2	3	2	3	0
71–72	3	3	2	2	1	4	2	*	2	2
73–74	1	0	0	2	0	4	0	1	3	2
75–76	4	1	2	2	0	2	1	*	0	0
77–78	1	1			0	0	3	1	1	3
79–80	1	1			1	1	2	*	2	0
81–82	0	1				0		0	0	2
83–84	0	1				0		*	1	1
85–86	0					1		4	1	1
87–88	0							*	1	0
89–90	1							4	0	1
91–92								*	0	
93–94								5	0	
95–96								*	1	

* *T* scores do not appear in these intervals.

Thus abnormal slowness in psychological function does not uniquely define the depressed patient. Analogously, the RTD syndrome may be defining a type not distinguishable as depressives but rather as withdrawn, apathetic, and slowed-up. In support of this notion is the clinical fact that retarded depressives are often confused diagnostically with apathetic schizophrenics.

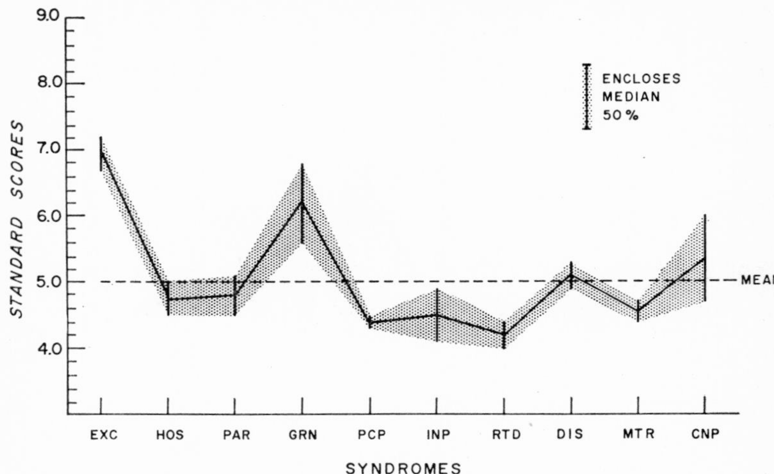

FIG. 12.1. Median profile for *EXC-GRN* patients.

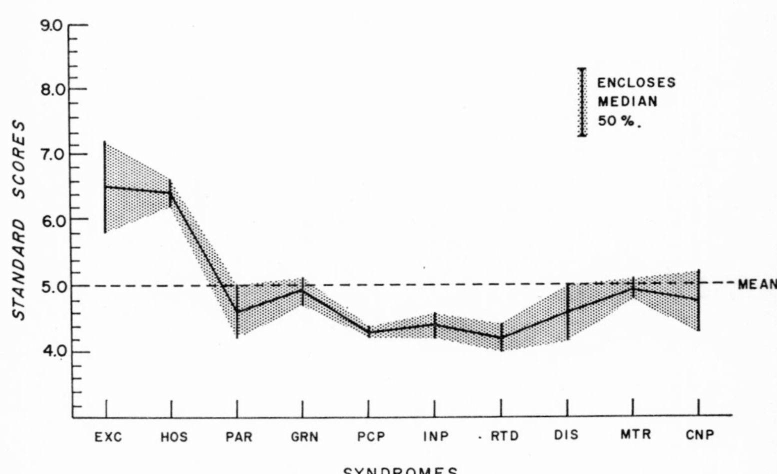

FIG. 12.2. Median profile for *EXC-HOS* patients.

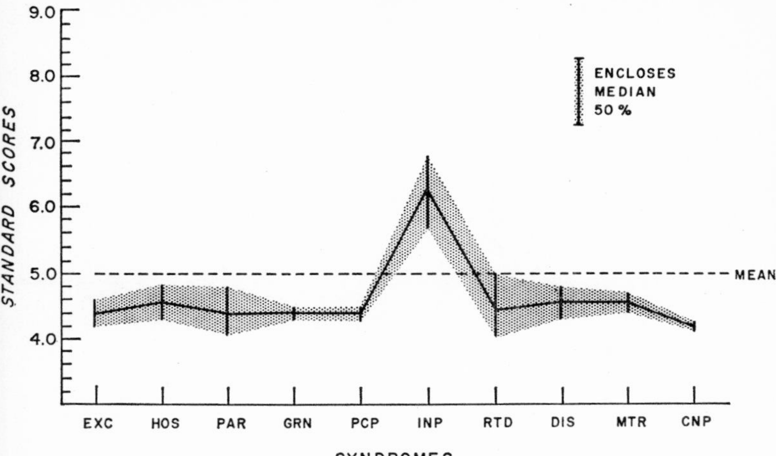

FIG. 12.3. Median profile for *INP* patients.

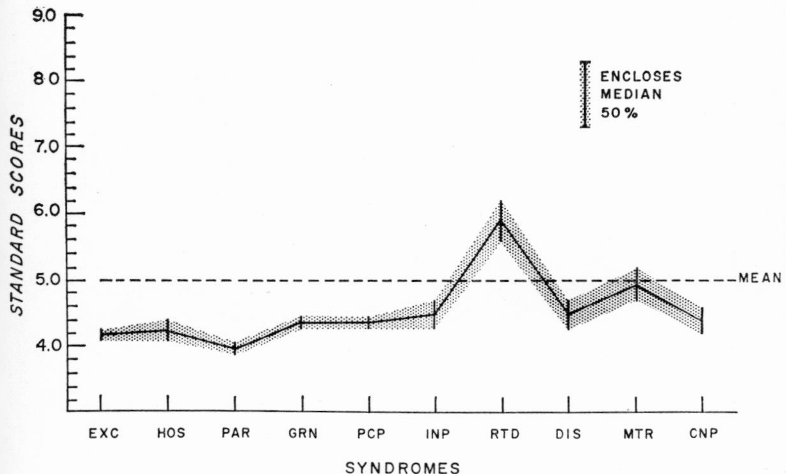

FIG. 12.4. Median profile for *RTD* patients.

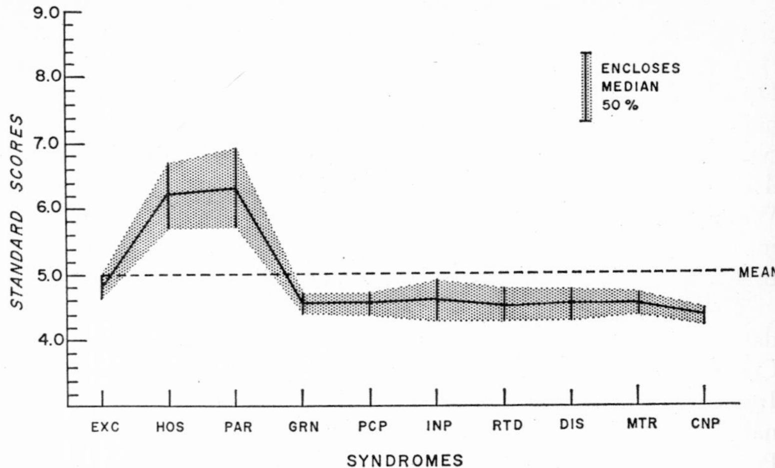

FIG 12.5. Median profile for *PAR* patients.

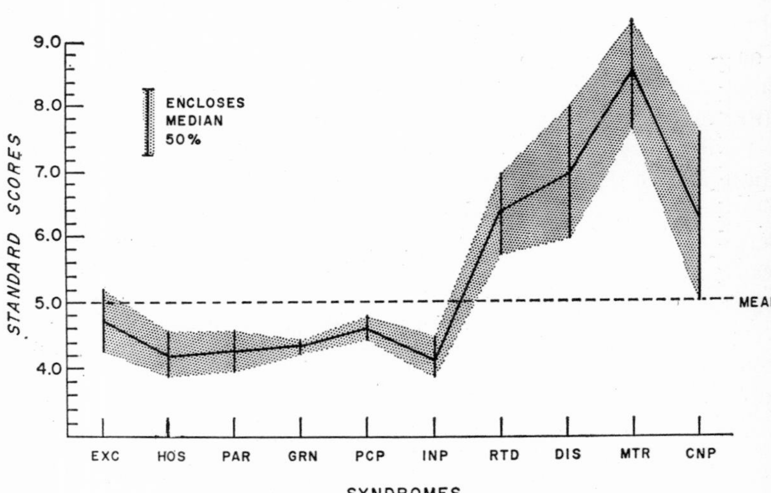

FIG. 12.6. Median profile for *DIS* patients.

The type here labeled Hostile Paranoid is characterized by elevated scores on Paranoid Projection and Hostility (Figure 12.5). At the same time scores on Motor Disturbances and Conceptual Disorganization are quite low. It is also interesting to note that hallucinations (PCP) occur only infrequently in patients of this type. No diagnostic category in the 1952 diagnostic manual of *Mental Disorders* corresponds closely to the type isolated here. While Paranoid state is characterized by paranoid delusions no mention is made of hostility. Perhaps the hostile component in this type has been minimized in current descriptions.

The sixth patient type is defined by elevated scores on Retardation and Apathy, Motor Disturbances, Disorientation, and Conceptual Disorganization (see Figure 12.6). Grandiosity and Intropunitive scores are exceptionally low. The fact that hallucinations play no role is also of interest. As was indicated earlier, Perceptual Distortion may be evidence of a tendency to reorganize perceptual input and not an indication of disintegration. No single schizophrenic reaction described in *Mental Disorders* resembles this class of patients which is called Disorganized. Since all of the defining syndromes are characteristic of schizophrenics, this type perhaps should also be labeled schizophrenic. The four syndromes jointly also define the second-order factor called Schizophrenic Disorganization. Some validity data on the latter are presented in the chapter on validity.

While the six types are viewed with considerable confidence, the limitations of the study out of which they evolved should be noted. The ratings were not collected with a typing study in mind and hence the sample is far from ideal. The sample is lacking with respect to representativeness; mute catatonics and some depressive types are missing. Certain other controls are lacking and supportive validity data are not yet available. For these reasons the types isolated are offered primarily as an illustration of what the philosophy of approach and the method can produce.

SUMMARY

A process for typing patients was sketched and discussed in relation to several indices of similarity. The typing process was then applied to a sample set of one hundred psychotics and six patient types were isolated. Application of the type criteria to four additional samples served to replicate the types evolved. The type-profiles were shown to be consistent across samples and relatively independent of each other. Several of the types, subjectively judged, seemed to correspond to conventionally accepted psychiatric diagnoses. Because of lack of data no rigorous objective comparisons could be made.

The reader interested in applying the types to data will find two procedures outlined in the Appendix. To provide the clinician with some concrete examples, independent clinical case histories were obtained. These as well as IMPS profiles are presented in the Appendix.

CHAPTER 13

DIMENSIONS OF TYPE DIFFERENCES

IN AN earlier chapter, the problems of classifying patients into classes or types were described. Next, a bird's-eye view of the history of psychiatric classification was provided. Recent statistical typing studies were critically reviewed in the chapter that followed. Then, in Chapter 12, the results of an experiment in isolating types were presented as a possible beginning of a system for classifying psychotics in our culture. The present chapter offers data concerning the dimensions that separate the six patient groups. Such between-group dimensions will not ordinarily correspond to the higher order factors which describe the elements common to the syndromes. Their value lies in the light they can shed on the nature of the patient groups isolated.

STUDY PURPOSES

In the previous chapter some evidence was presented for the existence of at least six psychotic types or classes. Each individual was classified on the basis of his ten syndrome standard scores. The major goals here are (1) to determine the number of dimensions necessary to account for the differences between individuals belonging to the six different psychotic classes, and (2) to specify the nature of the between-group differences in terms of these dimensions. A third purpose is to test whether the differences among the means of the six types are significantly different, although it is fairly clear from the method of isolating types that significant between-type differences will be found.

Perhaps it is not immediately obvious that neither the first- nor the second-order syndromes need correspond to the dimensions required to describe differences between *G* groups. The statistical method to be used, multivariate linear discriminant analysis, may be likened to a form of factor analysis which extracts only those dimensions that distinguish between groups. Each dimension is defined in terms of groups of homogeneous individuals. Suppose, for example, a discriminant function analysis had been made on three groups differing in body type: ectomorphs, endomorphs, and mesomorphs. Assume that two dimensions were found to distinguish between the three groups. The basic variables used to describe the types are such measures as height, weight, length of limbs, chest depth, chest width, width of hips, ratings of muscularity of the body appendages, and ratios of some of these measures. Now suppose the first dimensions separated the endomorphs (rounded, wide hips, long torso) and the ectomorphs (slender, narrow hips, long legs relative to torso). Then the nature of the dimension of difference could be inferred from this contrast and by studying how the various measures are ranked on the first dimension (called canonical variate). The inference would probably be that the two groups differed on a bipolar dimension of slenderness and underweight versus rotundity and overweight.

Assume now that the second dimension was defined by the mesomorphs (wide shoulders, muscular build, narrow hips) against the other two body types. Then the dimension of difference would be inferred to be muscularity. In this illustration the defining anthropomorphic factors are limb length, chest width, trunk size, body weight, body girth, and chest depth (Thurstone, 1946). The dimensions of differences between the body types would appear to be of a different nature. They are likely to be broader more complex patterns than the first-order factors (Lorr and Fields, 1953). In brief, contrasts between homogeneous groups can be of interest if they serve to broaden one's understanding of their nature.

THE MULTIPLE DISCRIMINANT ANALYSIS

This section presents a description of the technical aspects of the statistical procedure followed. The general reader may want to skip over this portion and continue in the next section.

Samples of either equal size or proportional to population sizes may be desirable in discriminant analysis, depending on whether the purpose is to characterize populations or to assign subjects to groups with minimum error (Jones and Bock, 1958). Since our purpose was to characterize the patient types, giving equal attention to each type, equal size groups seemed more appropriate for analysis. However, the smallest group (Excited-Hostile patients) comprised only seventeen patients, and there was some risk of distortion if all groups were reduced to this rather small size. Accordingly, two discriminant analyses were run. The first was based on six groups of seventeen patients each. Patients were randomly eliminated from the five groups assigned more than seventeen patients in the earlier typing analyses. As a check, a second analysis was performed on all cases assigned to the six type-groups (*N*s ranged from seventeen to forty-nine). Since no appreciable differences between the two analyses were found, only the equal size group analysis is reported.

Mean standardized IMPS syndrome scores for six types of psychotics are presented in Table 13.1. The multiple discriminant analysis (Rao, 1952) was run on an IBM 7090 computer by

TABLE 13.1
SYNDROME MEANS OF SIX PATIENT TYPES
($N = 17$ PER PATIENT GROUP)

IMPS SYNDROME	PATIENT TYPE					
	EXCITED-GRANDIOSE	EXCITED-HOSTILE	RETARDED	INTRO-PUNITIVE	PARANOID	DISOR-GANIZED
EXCITEMENT	6.86	6.35	4.21	4.40	4.82	4.86
HOSTILE BELLIGERENCE	4.85	6.56	4.36	4.53	6.41	4.44
PARANOID PROJECTION	4.67	4.67	4.18	4.32	6.19	4.36
GRANDIOSE EXPANSIVENESS	6.18	4.85	4.43	4.53	4.61	4.54
PERCEPTUAL DISTORTION	4.66	4.46	4.53	4.50	4.80	4.84
ANXIOUS INTROPUNITIVENESS	4.48	4.34	4.69	6.42	4.61	4.38
RETARDATION AND APATHY	4.25	4.21	6.01	4.73	4.54	6.49
DISORIENTATION	4.91	4.79	4.88	4.65	4.79	7.92
MOTOR DISTURBANCE	5.14	4.58	4.54	4.49	4.47	7.06
CONCEPTUAL DISORGANIZATION	5.68	5.06	4.52	4.26	4.47	6.44

procedures described by Jones and Bock. For the interested reader, between groups (B) and within groups (W) dispersion matrices are given in the Appendix. The five non-vanishing latent roots (λ) of the determinantal equation $B - \lambda W = 0$ are given in Table 13.2.

The number of groups (k) is six, the number of persons per group (n) is seventeen and the number of variables (p) is ten. Then the total between-group variation, $k(n - 1)(\Sigma\lambda p)$, is approximately distributed as χ^2 with $p(k - 1)$ degrees of freedom and is an appropriate test for the hypothesis of equal means. The obtained χ^2 of 1945.45 (Table 13.3) resulted in rejection of the hypothesis of equal group means beyond the 0.001 point.

TABLE 13.2

PER CENT OF BETWEEN-GROUP VARIANCE ACCOUNTED FOR BY EACH LATENT ROOT

CANONICAL VARIATE	LATENT ROOT	% VARIANCE
I	9.5647	47.2
II	5.1842	25.6
III	3.3631	16.6
IV	1.2237	6.0
V	.9294	4.6

Next, significance tests were made to determine the number of independent dimensions required to account for between-group variation. Table 13.3 presents successive latent roots extracted and the tests for significance of the residual variation. Because the χ^2 test employed is relatively crude, a stringent 0.001 significance level was adopted. By this criterion, all five roots are significant, indicating that five independent dimensions are required to account for the between-group variation. However, almost ninety per cent of the total between-group variance is concentrated in the first three canonical variates, and the interpretation of the kind and pattern of between-group differences will be based principally on these three variates.

Finally, the six groups were compared with respect to differences in mean score on each of the canonical variates. The results of the significance tests are summarized in Table 13.7 (Rao, 1952). The squared distances, D^2, of each group from every other group, also computed, are given in Table 13.6.

A few words of explanation concerning the dimensions of difference are called for. The canonical variate procedure is a way of determining the minimum number of dimensions needed to describe the differences between G groups on K quantitative variables. The first canonical variate is that linear combination of the K variables (here the ten syndromes) that gives the largest F ratio between the group means. The second canonical variate is that combination of the variables that gives the largest F ratio

TABLE 13.3

CHI-SQUARE TEST OF DIMENSIONALITY

SOURCE OF VARIANCE	DF	$\chi^2 = K(N-1)\Sigma\lambda_i$	P
CANONICAL VARIATES I–V	$P(K-1) = 50$	1945.45	$< .001$
CANONICAL VARIATES II–V	$(P-1)(K-2) = 36$	1027.49	$< .001$
CANONICAL VARIATES III–V	$(P-2)(K-3) = 24$	529.81	$< .001$
CANONICAL VARIATES IV–V	$(P-3)(K-4) = 14$	206.95	$< .001$
CANONICAL VARIATE V	$(P-4)(K-5) = 6$	89.48	$< .001$

for the residual variance, and so on. Thus the successive functions provide optimal discrimination among the means of the groups. As a consequence each variate is complex rather than unitary as in the case of an ordinary factor analysis.

Another way to view the problem is to consider the statistical procedure followed in predicting a dependent variable, as for example length of hospital stay, from a set of independent variables, say Wechsler–Bellevue Test scores. The weight given each independent variable in the linear equation is its "regression coefficient". The weights are so determined as to minimize the residual errors and do not ordinarily have any direct psychological meaning. This is because they depend on the number of given variables, their dispersions and their intercorrelations with each other and the dependent variable. In factor analysis all given variables are treated as independent and coordinate. The goal is to account for the correlations among the tests in terms of a smaller number of derived variables. The weights given the derived variables do have meaning and are stable if simple structure has been achieved. It is for these reasons that the type difference dimensions must be interpreted with caution. The weights of the syndromes in each column representing a discriminant function are regression weights. The equations implied represent regressions of the discriminant functions on the syndromes. Thus they may be arbitrary and unstable. The major reason for some confidence in the interpretation is that a very high proportion of all possible behavior deviation in the domain of psychosis is already included. Thus the weights are not likely to change much with the introduction of new variables.

THE DIMENSIONS OF TYPE DIFFERENCE

The first four dimensions of type differences (canonical variates) will be interpreted with the aid of Tables 13.4, 13.5, 13.6, and the four figures. First the syndromes which serve to define each dimension will be examined. Syndromes with high coefficients and syndromes with low coefficients will be contrasted with a view to inferring the nature of the variable separating the types. Next the mean scaled canonical scores of the six types will be inspected. This time the groups with high and low scores will be compared in order to infer what characteristics separate them. The two approaches should, of course, yield the same explanatory hypotheses. Figures 13.1 to 13.3 are two-dimensional plots of the first three canonical scores of the individual patients in the six groups. Figure 13.4 is a three-dimensional diagram of the group means on the first three dimensions (Table 13.5). The figures are designed to assist in visualizing the relations among and distances between the groups.

The first column of Table 13.4 represents the most influential dimension, accounting for forty-seven per cent of the between-group variance. Syndromes HOS, GRN, and INP have the highest positive coefficients, while RTD, MTR, and DIS have the highest negative coefficients. This first artificial variate appears to contrast behavior marked by non-responsiveness to surroundings, withdrawal, retardation, and uncommunicativeness, against accessibility and communicativeness regarding preoccupations and symptomatology. The dimension appears to represent a continuum of degree of contact with reality. The ordering of the four syndromes with low coefficients also appears consistent with this interpretation.

TABLE 13.4

SCALED CANONICAL VARIATES

SYNDROME	I	II	III	IV
EXCITEMENT	.021	-.086	.018	.007
HOSTILE BELLIGERENCE	.078	.060	.097	-.079
PARANOID PROJECTION	-.032	.027	.083	.067
GRANDIOSE EXPANSIVENESS	.072	-.196	-.045	.044
PERCEPTUAL DISTORTION	-.001	.020	.011	.016
ANXIOUS INTROPUNITIVENESS	.062	.074	-.122	-.107
RETARDATION AND APATHY	-.142	-.004	.030	.117
DISORIENTATION	-.051	-.042	.049	-.086
MOTOR DISTURBANCE	-.086	.016	-.014	-.031
CONCEPTUAL DISORGANIZATION	.005	-.016	-.030	-.038

TABLE 13.5

MEAN SCALED CANONICAL SCORES OF SIX PATIENT TYPES
SIGNS OF I, II, AND IV ARE REFLECTED

PATIENT TYPE	CANONICAL VARIATE			
	I	II	III	IV
EXCITED-GRANDIOSE	1.75	11.91	3.36	4.50
EXCITED-HOSTILE	.98	7.92	5.85	5.90
RETARDED	5.67	6.44	3.45	2.96
INTROPUNITIVE	2.44	5.21	1.20	5.97
PARANOID	2.33	5.46	6.80	4.55
DISORGANIZED	9.94	8.50	4.87	5.98

TABLE 13.6
SQUARED DISTANCES, D^2, BETWEEN PSYCHOTIC TYPES

PATIENT TYPE	EXCITED-GRANDIOSE	EXCITED-HOSTILE	RETARDED	INTRO-PUNITIVE	PARANOID
EXCITED-GRANDIOSE					
EXCITED-HOSTILE	24.71				
RETARDED	47.72	38.65			
INTROPUNITIVE	52.23	31.10	26.18		
PARANOID	53.73	10.56	25.89	33.47	
DISORGANIZED	83.20	81.64	33.57	80.54	72.89

The alignment of the groups in Figures 13.1 and 13.4 and the tests of group differences (Table 13.7) supports this interpretation. The Disorganized and Retarded groups were significantly different from the other four groups on the first variate. The Disorganized patients were significantly higher on the first dimension than the Retarded cases. There are no significant

TABLE 13.7
CANONICAL VARIATES ON WHICH SIX IMPS GROUPS DIFFER SIGNIFICANTLY*

PATIENT TYPE	EXCITED-GRANDIOSE	EXCITED-HOSTILE	RETARDED	INTRO-PUNITIVE	PARANOID
EXCITED-GRANDIOSE					
EXCITED-HOSTILE	II				
RETARDED	I, II	I, IV			
INTROPUNITIVE	II	II, III	I, IV		
PARANOID	II, III		I, III	III	
DISORGANIZED	I, II	I	I, IV	I, II, III	I, II

* $p < .001$ for all differences.

differences among the other four types on Variate 1, although the Excited-Hostile patients appear to be most in contact and accessible.

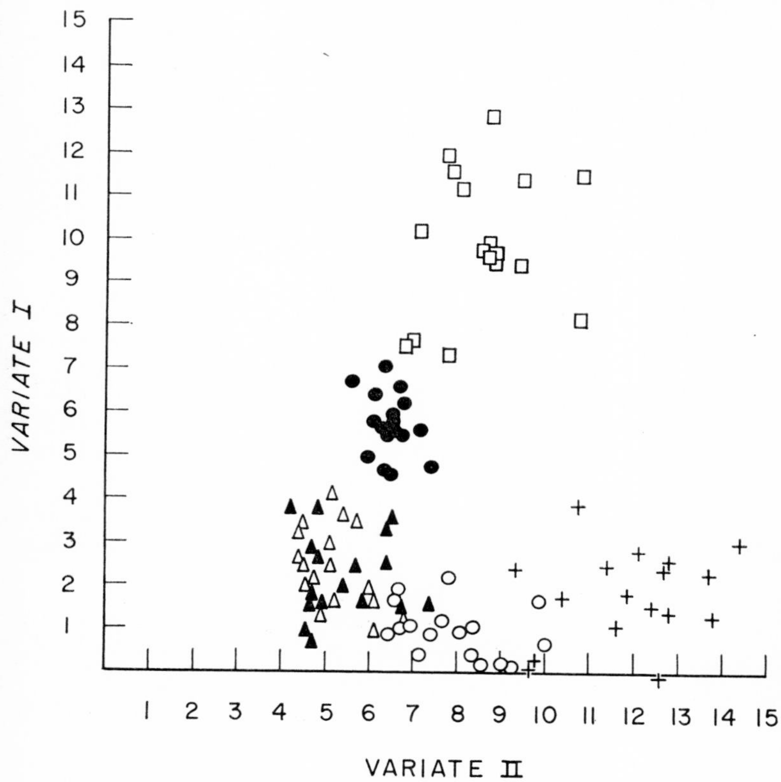

FIG. 13.1. Location of patients of six types in two dimensions determined by two canonical variates.
+ Excited-grandiose, ○ Excited-hostile, ▲ Paranoid, △ Intropunitive, ● Retarded, □ Disorganized.

The second dimension accounts for 26 per cent of the between-patient type variance. It is defined principally by GRN and EXC at one end, and INP at the other end. GRN and EXC have in common an inflated self-evaluation, whereas self-devaluation is a prominent feature of the Intropunitive syndrome. The function appears to assess degree of self-expansiveness. To check this inference the group scores can be examined. Mean canonical scores of the Grandiose type are significantly higher than all other groups (Figures 13.2 and 13.4, and Table 13.7). The Intropuni-

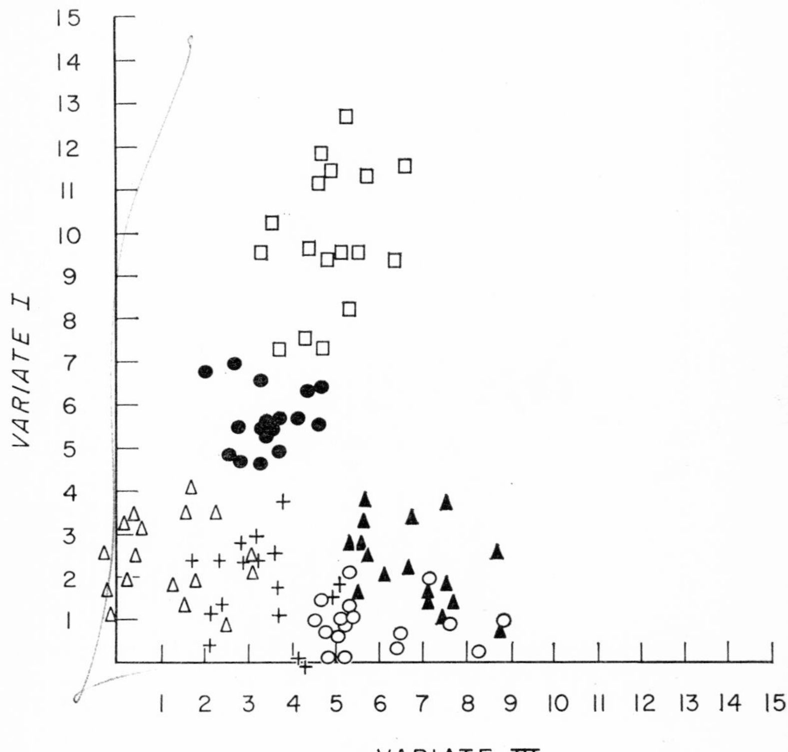

FIG. 13.2. Location of patients of six types in two dimensions determined by two canonical variates.
+ Excited-grandiose, ○ Excited-hostile, ▲ Paranoid,
△ Intropunitive, ● Retarded, □ Disorganized.

tive group has the lowest mean canonical score, and is significantly lower than the Hostile and Disorganized groups. Paranoid type patients also have significantly smaller scores than the Disorganized patients. A plausible hypothesis, then, is that the second dimension of type difference relates to degree of self-expansiveness.

The third canonical variate accounts for 17 per cent of the between-type variance. INP defines one end, and HOS and PAR the other. The function contrasts syndromes characterized by self-directed blame and hostility with syndromes in which

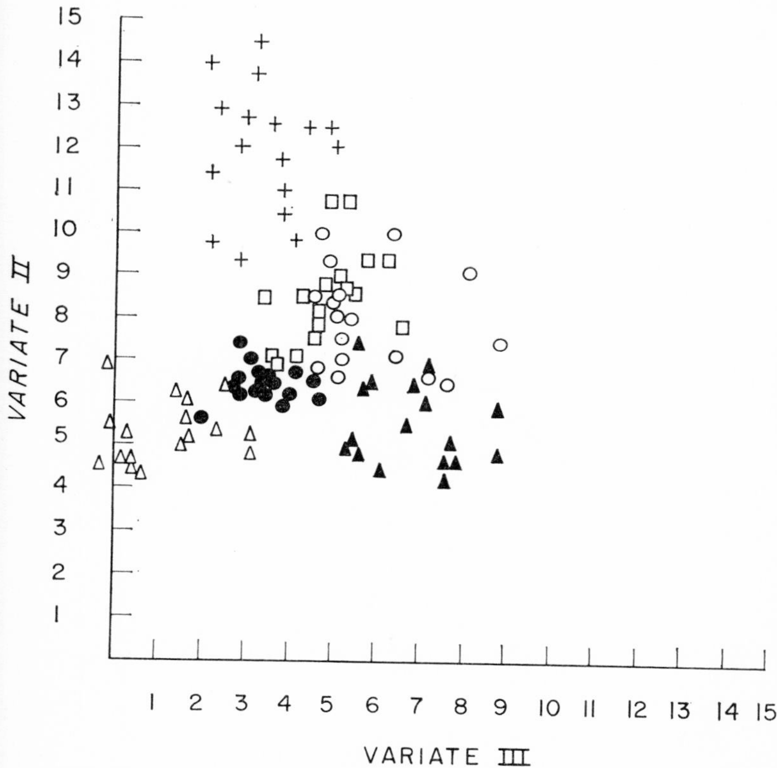

FIG. 13.3. Location of patients of six types in two dimensions determined by two canonical variates.
+ Excited-grandiose, ○ Excited-hostile, ▲ Paranoid, △ Intropunitive, ● Retarded, □ Disorganized.

externally or other-directed hostility is most prominent. The Paranoid and the Excited-Hostile types have the highest mean scores. Both groups have significantly higher scores than the Intropunitive type cases. The Paranoids also have significantly higher scores than the retarded and the Excited-Grandiose; both tend to deny or inhibit hostile behavior. The third dimension, therefore, may represent a bipolar inner-directed versus outer-directed blame and hostility.

The fourth canonical variate accounts for 6 per cent of the between-type variance. The RTD syndrome defines one end of this dimension while DIS and HOS define the lower end. As far

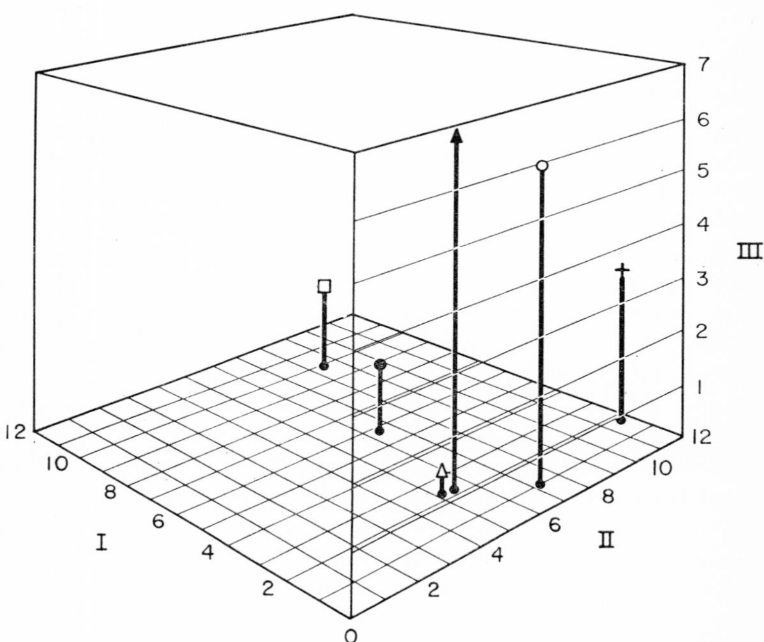

FIG. 13.4. Location of patients of six types in three dimensions determined by three canonical variates.
+ Excited-grandiose, ○ Excited-hostile, ▲ Paranoid, △ Intropunitive, ● Retarded, □ Disorganized.

as the types are concerned the Retarded type stands out at one pole while at the opposite pole are the Intropunitive, the Hostile, and the Disorganized groups. These relations suggest that the dimension represented may be one of degree of affect or emotionality manifested. The Retarded patients exhibit apathy while the hostile, the anxious, and the disorganized exhibit various types of affective responses.

COMPARISON WITH SECOND-ORDER FACTORS

At the beginning of the chapter, mention was made that the between-group dimensions may or may not correspond to the second-order dimensions of psychotic behavior. The similarities and differences between the findings of the two approaches may now be examined.

Three second-order factors are measured in IMPS syndrome data. These were Excitement versus Retardation, Paranoid Process, and Schizophrenic Disorganization. Anxious Intropunitiveness represents a possible fourth dimension found in other data. The between-type dimensions are: Accessibility (Responsiveness), Self-Expansiveness, Self- versus Externally-Directed Hostility, and Affect. It is immediately apparent that the correspondence is not close.

The Schizophrenic Disorganization pattern, it will be recalled, is defined by RTD, DIS, MTR, and CNP. Each of these variables is also consistent with a hypothesis of loss of reality contact and inaccessibility, as well as of behavior disorganization. If this inference is valid, then the first dimension of type-difference is similar to the second-order factor just described. It should be possible to test this hypothesis by comparing the groups on their mean second-order factors. A check reveals that the Disorganized group mean is highest, but the Retarded and the Excited-Grandiose means are about the same. Thus, there is fair agreement between the two types of inferred dimensions. The dimension should, however, be reinterpreted as representing both disorganization and loss of reality contact.

The third dimension of type difference, Self- versus Externally-Directed Hostility, may represent a contrast between the second-order factors of Intropunitiveness and Paranoid Process. If this inference is correct, then the scores of the two contrasted groups (Paranoid versus Intropunitive) on the two second-order factors should be related negatively. Inspection of scores in Table 13.1 that define the Intropunitive and the Paranoid Types reveals that the two types are indeed negatively related on the PAR, HOS, and INP syndromes as expected.

The second-order Excitement versus Retardation appears not to have any single corresponding between-type dimension. The grandiosity of type-factor Self-Expansiveness is not prominent in the second-order factor. The factor of Loss of Affect (4th type factor) may correspond to the apathetic end of Excitement versus Retardation.

Thus, exploration of the type differences has revealed some interesting dimensions worthy of further examination and confirmation. The dimension of Schizophrenic Disorganization and Loss of Reality Contact is quite similar to the corresponding second-order factor. In addition, there is a type dimension of Expansiveness, a bipolar dimension of Self-Directed versus Other-Directed Hostility. One possible implication of the latter is that the defense mechanisms implied are in opposition. Attribution of blame and hostile feeling to the self and to others are not simply independent, but the presence of one precludes the presence of the other at any given time. How these mechanisms operate over time is another matter. As with excitement and depression, these defensive alternatives may be cyclical.

CLASSIFYING PATIENTS

The major use of discriminant functions is to classify individuals into one of six mutually exclusive groups on the basis of their scores. These functions provide an answer to the question, "To what class does the patient belong?" Such classification can be done according to various criteria such as minimizing the number of misclassifications or minimizing the costs of misclassifications. Suppose the goal is to minimize the number of misclassifications in assigning N persons to one of two mutally exclusive groups on the basis of a single quantitative predictor. For example, a psychiatrist wants to classify a newly admitted patient as psychotic or neurotic on the basis of a single test. The solution (Guttman, 1941) is to assign each individual to that group where the likelihood of his score is at a maximum. Concretely, if the score frequency distributions of the two groups are available, their point of intersection will provide the best cutoff. All persons with scores above the cutoff point are assigned to the group with the higher mean; persons below the cutoff are assigned to the group with the lower mean.

The principle is essentially the same in the case of two or more quantitative predictors and any number of groups. The chief difference is that the frequency distribution within each group is now multivariate rather than univariate. Also, the correlations among the predictors must be taken into consideration. Lubin (1950) offers a lucid exposition of the mathematics involved, while Rao and Slater (1949) provide a clear example of an application of the method to differentiate between neurotic groups.

The number of misclassifications involved in assigning all patients to one of the six patient types could have been determined. However, as the groups are regarded as tentative and a fresh sample is needed, such a determination would have been a mere exercise. Figures 13.1 to 13.4 provide a basis for judging the degree of separation of the various groups. The Disorganized type is sharply separated from all others in each of the two-dimensional figures. The retarded type also shows no overlap. Inspection of the Intropunitive group cases indicates very little overlap on two of the figures. The Excited-Grandiose sample is well distinguished by dimensions I vs. II and II vs. III. The Excited-Hostile overlap somewhat with the Paranoids. Thus, as judged by the figures, the number of misclassifications is small for the members of the six types. The extent of overlap and the number of misclassifications will obviously be much greater if another sample is assigned on the basis of the four discriminant functions determined.

SUMMARY

The chapter focused on the possible dimensions of type differences. Exploration of this problem by the method of multiple discriminant analysis revealed four interpretable dimensions of difference. The three major dimensions were interpreted as Disorganization and Loss of Reality Contact, Self-Expansiveness, and Self-Directed versus Other-Directed Hostility. Only one factor of type difference corresponds well to a second-order dimension common to the syndromes. The chapter concludes with a discussion of the problem of assigning patients to the type to which they belong.

APPENDIX A

INPATIENT MULTIDIMENSIONAL PSYCHIATRIC SCALE

BOOKLET

PROFILE SHEET

ANSWER SHEET

SCORING SHEET

INPATIENT MULTIDIMENSIONAL PSYCHIATRIC SCALE (IMPS)

(A) *Type of Patient:* IMPS is designed for use with functional psychotics or severe psychoneurotics who can be interviewed. The very inaccessible or mute patient can better be described on a ward rating form.

(B) *Observation Period:* Ordinarily IMPS can be completed following a 45 minute interview of the patient. However, some interviews are as brief as 30 minutes or as long as several hours.

(C) *Behavior Rated:* Only behavior observable in the interview or reported by the patient is to be rated or checked. Ward observations or clinical notes should not be used in making ratings.

(D) *Type of Interview:* Observations required to complete IMPS may be obtained nondirectively or by means of a more conventional semi-structured interview.

MAURICE LORR AND DOUGLAS M. MCNAIR
Outpatient Psychiatric Research Laboratory, Washington, D. C.
and
C. JAMES KLETT and JULIAN J. LASKY
Central NP Research Laboratory, VAH, Perry Point, Md.

January, 1962

PLEASE RETAIN THIS REUSABLE QUESTION BOOKLET

Rating Guide

1. Base rating on your interview only.	Consider only what the patient does and what he reports or admits. Disregard prior ward or interview data or social history descriptions.
2. Compare the patient with normal individuals.	The standard of comparison should be the typical behavior of a normal individual of comparable age, sex, and social class.
3. Rate what is most typical or characteristic.	Behavior manifested during the interview may vary. Try to indicate what is most characteristic.
4. Consider each question independently.	Make no effort to describe a consistent personality or diagnostic picture. It is well known that patients may manifest seemingly contradictory behavior for dynamic reasons.
5. Avoid dynamic interpretations.	As much as possible, base your ratings on manifest behavior content and first order inferences. If, for example, a patient is overly polite and deferent, don't rate him as (unconsciously) hostile.
6. Consider the patient's reactions to you.	In judging traits such as hostility, dominance, or emotional responsiveness, consider the patient's attitudes and reactions to *you* along with his self-reports.
7. Use extreme ratings whenever warranted.	Avoid tending to rate near the bottom or middle on all scales.
8. Rate each item quickly.	If you are unable to reach a decision, go on to the next item and come back later to those you skipped.
9. Rate every question.	If information needed to answer a question could not be obtained, rate "Not at all".
10. Record your ratings only on the separate answer sheet.	Instructions appear on the Answer Sheet.

Compared to the normal person to what degree does he . . .

*1. Manifest speech that is slowed, deliberate, or labored?

*2. Give answers that are irrelevant or unrelated in any immediately conceivable way to the question asked or topic discussed?

Cues: Do not rate here wandering or rambling conversation which veers away from the topic at issue (see item 4). Also, do not rate the coherence of the answer.

* Items scored in Brief Scale (see Manual)

*3. Give answers that are grammatically disconnected, incoherent, or scattered, i.e., not sensible or not understandable?

CUES: Judge the grammatical structure of his speech, not the content which may or may not be bizarre.

4. Tend to ramble, wander, or drift off the subject or away from the point at issue in responding to questions or topics discussed?

CUES: Do not rate here responses that are obviously unrelated to the question asked (see item 2).

*5. Verbally express feelings of hostility, ill will, or dislike of others?

CUES: Makes hostile comments regarding others such as attendants, other patients, his family, or persons in authority. Reports conflicts on the ward.

*6. Exhibit postures that are peculiar, unnatural, rigid, or bizarre?

CUES: Head twisted to one side; or arm and hand held oddly. Judge the degree of peculiarity of the posture.

7. Express or exhibit feelings and emotions openly, impulsively, or without apparent restraint or control?

CUES: Shows temper outbursts; weeps or wrings hands in loud complaint; jokes or talks boisterously; gestures excitedly.

8. Exhibit indifference or apathy towards such matters as his treatment, his release from the hospital, or plans for the future?

CUES: Content to stay. Willing to "leave it to the doctor". Sees no need for treatment. Seems to have no goals or expectations.

*9. Manifest speech that is hurried, accelerated, or pushed?

CUE: Pressure of speech.

10. Manifest overt signs of tension?

CUES: Moves or shifts restlessly; body musculature appears taut, strained or tense; fingers clothing; scratches, drums or fiddles with objects; face or neck muscles twitch; exhibits startle reactions; palms feel sweaty.

* Items scored in Brief Scale (see Manual)

11. Express a feeling or attitude of contempt, disdain, or scorn towards other people as unworthy or beneath him?

    CUES: Derogatory or snide comments about others; sarcasm or ridicule of others; condescending.

12. Exhibit an elevation in mood, a sense of well-being or euphoria, or an optimistic and hopeful attitude towards himself and others?

    CUES: Everything is wonderful and this is the best of all possible worlds.

13. Exhibit a facial expression that is fixed, immobile, and without discernible play of feeling or expression?

*14. Tend to blame, criticize, condemn, or otherwise hold himself responsible for past or present, real or fancied, thought or actions?

    CUES: Blames self for failure, difficulties, and frustrations in family relations, work, or finances.

15. Exhibit in demeanor and-or in verbalizations an attitude of self-importance, superiority, or conceit?

    CUES: Speech is pompous or stilted; boasts of his accomplishments; demands and expects special privileges.

*16. Manifest movements or gestures that are slowed, deliberate, labored, or delayed?

    CUES: Acts as if he is fatigued; walking and moving seem to require special effort.

17. Dramatize or seek to attract the attention of others to himself or his symptoms?

    CUES: Seems to enjoy being observed by others; histrionic in his gestures; affected or artificial; a "show-off".

18. Manifest a hostile, sullen, or morose attitude towards others, by tone of voice, demeanor, or facial expression?

    CUES: Seems to have a chip on his shoulder; slams door or bangs chair; sarcastic tone. Try not to judge on the basis of content of remarks.

* Items scored in Brief Scale (see Manual)

19. Exhibit a deficit in his memory for events of the last week?

    CUES: Does not know what he had for supper last night, what he did yesterday, or what treatments he received the past week.

20. Manifest speech that is loud, boisterous, and-or intense in tone?

*21. Report or admit being uneasy or anxious in anticipation of specific future difficulties or problems?

    CUES: Worried about his symptoms, his family, or his finances.

22. Manifest blocking, halting, or irregular interruptions in his speech?

    CUES: Stuttering or stammering should not be rated here.

23. Exhibit apathy, indifference, or lack of response in feeling to a discussion of his own problems, of his family, or to his surroundings?

    CUES: Doesn't laugh, smile, or react when kidded; neither sad nor angry; doesn't seem to care what goes on; discusses emotional matters in a flat, detached manner.

24. Report or admit feeling anxious, apprehensive, or worried in anticipation of vague indefinable future misfortunes or outcomes?

    CUES: Feels worried about coming events but doesn't know why.

*25. Manifest irritability, grouchiness, annoyance, or anger?

    CUES: Tone of voice; sharpness of response; explosiveness of retorts; use of profane or obscene language resulting from irritation.

26. Exhibit overactivity, restlessness, and-or acceleration in body movements?

    CUES: Paces or shifts about restlessly. Bearing, posture and gestures suggest excitement or agitation.

27. Exhibit in his general demeanor or in his verbalizations an attitude of self-depreciation, inadequacy, or inferiority?

    CUES: Talks about faults, failures, or his uselessness to others.

* Items scored in Brief Scale (see Manual)

28. Tend to blame, criticize, or hold other people, objects or circumstances responsible for his difficulties, failures, or frustrations?

29. Manifest verbally or in demeanor a dejection or depression in mood and a despondent or despairing attitude?

    CUES: Says he doesn't want to talk; complains of loss of interest and enjoyment; lack of energy; discouraged about being helped; expresses lack of hope; may wish he were dead; reports crying spells or tearfulness; expects the worst; everything seems flat and stale.

30. Exhibit a slovenly, unkempt, or disordered appearance and-or asocial manners?

31. Express feelings of guilt, sorrow or remorse for having done wrong, that are accompanied by a desire to make amends?

    CUES: Says he has been a terrible father or husband; claims sexual misdeeds; recounts past "sins"; says he hates himself for what he did; concerned with atoning for his "guilt"; has let people down.

32. Express feelings of bitterness and resentment because he feels others have wronged, cheated, injured, or slighted him?

33. Manifest speech that is low, weak, whispered, or difficult to hear?

34. Complain, criticize, gripe, or find fault with people and conditions in or out of the hospital?

    CUES: Complains about everything and anything: The medical care, the food, the aides, fellow patients, the routine, the hospital, people in general.

*35. Exhibit an excess of speech?

    CUES: Difficult to stop flow of speech once started or to get a word in edgewise. Judge the amount of speech and not its rate or relevance.

* Items scored in Brief Scale (see Manual)

36. Express suspicion of people or their motives?

    CUES: Expresses lack of trust in others; feels or suspects others are hostile towards him; questions motives of examiner; questions fidelity of wife.

37. Try to dominate, control, or direct the conduct of the interview?

    CUES: Number of times he interrupts, or "talks down" the interviewer. Tries to control or dominate the conversation.

38. Fail to respond to questions, answer in monosyllables, or give only minimal responses?

    CUES: Answers "yes" or "no"; stares blankly; has to be pushed to get an answer. Judge amount, not rate or relevance of speech.

39. Show a lack of insight regarding himself or an inability to recognize that he has problems?

    CUES: Offers physical illness as an explanation. Believes he is in a rest home or prison. Asks to be sent home immediately. Denies illness or need for treatment.

Answer the following on the basis of the patient's reports or admissions. If a symptom is not present, rate "not at all".

TO WHAT EXTENT DOES HE APPEAR PREOCCUPIED WITH . . .

40. Suicidal thoughts or impulses?
41. Unwanted ideas or impulses that recur persistently and which he recognizes as irrational?
42. One or more specific irrational morbid fears (phobias) of objects, persons, or situations? (Avoid confusing phobias with anxieties.)
43. Compulsive acts which he regards as irrational? (Touching, counting, etc.)
44. Delusional beliefs or convictions?
45. Hallucinatory voices?

HOW OFTEN DURING THE INTERVIEW DID HE . . .

46. Grin or giggle inappropriately? (Exclude reactions resulting from embarrassment.)

*47. Grimace peculiarly or otherwise exhibit unusual or bizarre frowns or other facial expressions?

48. Exhibit peculiar, inappropriate, or bizarre repetitive gestures and-or manneristic body movements (e.g., rhythmic neck twisting, lip smacking, odd gestures)?

49. Use phrases or coin words not found in the ordinary language or the dictionary (neologisms)?

50. Mechanically repeat certain words or fixed phrases in a seemingly meaningless way (stereotypy)?

51. Talk, mutter, or mumble to himself without an apparent provoking stimulus?

52. Glance around at and-or appear to be startled as if hearing voices?

Answer on the basis of evidence obtained in the interview that the patient had hallucinatory experiences during the past week or during the interview.

HOW OFTEN DID HE . . .

*53. Hear voices that accused, blamed, or said "bad" things about him (e.g., he is a spy, homosexual, murderer)?

54. Hear voices that praised, extolled, or spoke to him about divine missions?

55. Hear voices that threatened punishment, torture, or death?

*56. Hear voices that ordered him to carry out or perform certain tasks?

57. See actual visions? (Note: check carefully as this is infrequent except in organic cases.)

58. Have other hallucinatory experiences: Tactual, gustatory, olfactory? (e.g., sensations of crawling on the skin, smells queer or foul odors, food or drink tastes peculiar or "bad".)

Answer on the basis of evidence obtained in the interview that the patient NOW has or during the past week had delusional beliefs.

* Items scored in Brief Scale (see Manual)

DOES HE BELIEVE THAT . . .

*59. Some people talk about, refer to, or watch him?

60. He is being blocked, cheated, deprived, discriminated against, or persecuted?

*61. Certain people are plotting or conspiring against him (e.g., secret police, criminals, international spies)?

62. Certain people are trying to or now do control his actions or thinking?

63. Certain external forces (e.g., machines, electronic devices) are influencing or controlling his behavior and thinking?

*64. He has unusual or extraordinary abilities, powers, or knowledge (e.g., scientific or religious)?

65. He is a well-known present day or historical personality (e.g., president, Christ)?

66. He is unworthy, sinful, evil, and-or guilty of unpardonable sins and crimes?

67. Familiar things, people, or surroundings have changed and are unreal?

68. His body is diseased, distorted, or that his internal organs are rotted or missing?

*69. He has a distinct divine mission, that he received commands from God, or that he has other religious "calls"?

DOES HE KNOW . . .

70. That he is in a hospital?

*71. In what state the hospital is located or the nearest large city?

72. The name of at least one person in the hospital?

73. The season of the year (allow for transitional periods)?

74. The calendar year?

*75. His own age?

* Items scored in Brief Scale (see Manual)

PROFILE SHEET

IMPS

Standard Score	Exc	Hos	Par	Grn	Pcp	Inp	Rtd	Dis	Mtr	Cnp	Standard Score
				Raw Scores (Two raters)							
8.0	104	115		55	68	130	122		81	56	8.0
—	101	112		53	67	127	119		79	55	—
—	98	109		52	65	124	116	8	77	53	—
—	96	106		50	63	121	113		75	52	—
—	93	103	110	49	61	118	110		73	50	—
7.5	90	100	107	47	59	114	107		71	49	7.5
—	88	98	104	46	57	111	104	7	69	47	—
—	85	95	101	44	55	108	101		67	46	—
—	82	92	98	43	53	105	98		66	44	—
—	80	89	94	41	52	102	95		64	43	—
7.0	77	86	91	40	50	99	93	6	62	41	7.0
—	74	83	88	38	48	96	90		60	40	—
—	72	80	85	37	46	92	87		58	38	—
—	69	77	82	35	44	89	84		56	37	—
—	66	75	79	33	42	86	81	5	54	35	—
6.5	63	72	76	32	40	83	78		52	34	6.5
—	61	69	73	30	38	80	75		50	33	—
—	58	66	70	29	37	77	72		48	31	—
—	55	63	67	27	35	74	69	4	46	30	—
—	53	60	64	26	33	71	66		44	28	—
6.0	50	57	61	24	31	67	63		42	27	6.0

	—	47	55	58	23	29	64	61		40	25	—
	—	45	52	55	21	27	61	57	3	38	24	—
	—	42	49	52	20	25	58	55		36	22	—
	—	39	46	49	18	24	55	52		34	21	—
	5.5	37	43	46	17	22	52	49		32	19	5.5
	—	34	40	43	15	20	49	46	2	30	18	—
	—	31	37	40	14	18	45	43		28	16	—
	—	29	34	37	12	16	42	40		26	15	—
	—	26	32	34	10	14	39	37		24	13	—
M	5.0	23	29	31	9	12	36	34	1	22	12	5.0 M
	—	20	26	28	7	10	33	32		20	11	—
	—	18	23	25	6	9	30	29		18	9	—
	—	15	20	22	4	7	27	26		16	8	—
	—	12	17	19	3	5	24	23	0	14	6	—
	4.5	10	14	16	1	3	20	20		12	5	4.5
	—	7	12	13	0	1	17	17		10	3	—
	—	4	9	10		0	14	14		8	2	—
	—	2	6	7			11	11		6	0	—
	—	0	3	4			8	8		4		—
	4.0		0	1			5	5		2		4.0
	—			0			2	2		0		—
	—						0	0				—

* Only the bottom score of each class interval is given. Each interval extends from the given score up to but not including the next higher score. To profile, circle the patient's score in each column and connect circles with straight lines.

INPATIENT MULTIDIMENSIONAL PSYCHIATRIC SCALE

ANSWER SHEET

PATIENT'S NAME.. CODE # ....

HOSPITAL.. WARD NO................. TYPE OF WARD..............................

SEX................ AGE.............. DIAGNOSTIC IMPRESSION...

RATER'S NAME.. POSITION OF RATER................

DATE OF RATING..RATING PERIOD...

....

....

DIRECTIONS

CIRCLE ONE POINT ON EACH NUMBERED VERTICAL SCALE AS ILLUSTRATED BELOW. ASTERISKED ITEMS APPEAR IN BRIEF SCALE.

EXTREMELY	8	⑧	8	8	8
MARKEDLY	7	7	7	⑦	7
DISTINCTLY	6	6	6	6	6
QUITE A BIT	5	5	5	5	5
MODERATELY	④	4	4	4	4
MILDLY	3	3	3	3	3
A LITTLE	2	2	2	2	2
VERY SLIGHTLY	1	1	1	1	①
NOT AT ALL	0	0	⓪	0	0
SCALE NO.	(1)	(2)	(3)	(4)	(5)

EXAMPLE: On the characteristic assessed by Scale 1 the patient is rated "moderately" compared with the normal person. On Scale 2 he is rated "extremely", and on Scale 3 he is rated "not at all". On Scale 4 he is rated "markedly". On scale 5 he is rated "very slightly".

Extremely	8	8	8	8	8	8	8	8	8
Markedly	7	7	7	7	7	7	7	7	7
Distinctly	6	6	6	6	6	6	6	6	6
Quite a bit	5	5	5	5	5	5	5	5	5
Moderately	4	4	4	4	4	4	4	4	4
Mildly	3	3	3	3	3	3	3	3	3
A little	2	2	2	2	2	2	2	2	2
Very slightly	1	1	1	1	1	1	1	1	1
Not at all	0	0	0	0	0	0	0	0	0
Scale No.	*(1)	*(2)	*(3)	(4)	*(5)	*(6)	(7)	(8)	*(9)

Extremely	8	8	8	8	8	8	8	8	8
Markedly	7	7	7	7	7	7	7	7	7
Distinctly	6	6	6	6	6	6	6	6	6
Quite a bit	5	5	5	5	5	5	5	5	5
Moderately	4	4	4	4	4	4	4	4	4
Mildly	3	3	3	3	3	3	3	3	3
A little	2	2	2	2	2	2	2	2	2
Very slightly	1	1	1	1	1	1	1	1	1
Not at all	0	0	0	0	0	0	0	0	0
Scale No.	(10)	(11)	(12)	(13)	*(14)	(15)	*(16)	(17)	(18)

Extremely	8	8	8	8	8	8	8	8	8
Markedly	7	7	7	7	7	7	7	7	7
Distinctly	6	6	6	6	6	6	6	6	6
Quite a bit	5	5	5	5	5	5	5	5	5
Moderately	4	4	4	4	4	4	4	4	4
Mildly	3	3	3	3	3	3	3	3	3
A little	2	2	2	2	2	2	2	2	2
Very slightly	1	1	1	1	1	1	1	1	1
Not at all	0	0	0	0	0	0	0	0	0
Scale No.	(19)	(20)	*(21)	(22)	(23)	(24)	*(25)	(26)	(27)

Extremely	8	8	8	8	8	8	8	8	8
Markedly	7	7	7	7	7	7	7	7	7
Distinctly	6	6	6	6	6	6	6	6	6
Quite a bit	5	5	5	5	5	5	5	5	5
Moderately	4	4	4	4	4	4	4	4	4
Mildly	3	3	3	3	3	3	3	3	3
A little	2	2	2	2	2	2	2	2	2
Very slightly	1	1	1	1	1	1	1	1	1
Not at all	0	0	0	0	0	0	0	0	0
Scale No.	(28)	(29)	(30)	(31)	(32)	(33)	(34)	*(35)	(36)

EXTREMELY	8	8	8	8	8	8	8	8	8
MARKEDLY	7	7	7	7	7	7	7	7	7
DISTINCTLY	6	6	6	6	6	6	6	6	6
QUITE A BIT	5	5	5	5	5	5	5	5	5
MODERATELY	4	4	4	4	4	4	4	4	4
MILDLY	3	3	3	3	3	3	3	3	3
A LITTLE	2	2	2	2	2	2	2	2	2
VERY SLIGHTLY	1	1	1	1	1	1	1	1	1
NOT AT ALL	0	0	0	0	0	0	0	0	0
SCALE NO.	(37)	(38)	(39)	(40)	(41)	(42)	(43)	(44)	(45)

VERY OFTEN	4	4	4	4	4	4	4	4	4
FAIRLY OFTEN	3	3	3	3	3	3	3	3	3
A FEW TIMES	2	2	2	2	2	2	2	2	2
ONCE OR TWICE	1	1	1	1	1	1	1	1	1
NOT AT ALL	0	0	0	0	0	0	0	0	0
SCALE NO.	(46)	*(47)	(48)	(49)	(50)	(51)	(52)	*(53)	(54)

VERY OFTEN	4	4	4	4
FAIRLY OFTEN	3	3	3	3
A FEW TIMES	2	2	2	2
ONCE OR TWICE	1	1	1	1
NOT AT ALL	0	0	0	0
SCALE NO.	(55)	*(56)	(57)	(58)

YES	1	1	1	1	1	1	1	1	1
NO	0	0	0	0	0	0	0	0	0
ITEM NO.	*(59)	(60)	*(61)	(62)	(63)	*(64)	(65)	(66)	(67)

YES	1	1	1	1	1	1	1	1
NO	0	0	0	0	0	0	0	0
ITEM NO.	(68)	*(69)	(70)	*(71)	(72)	(73)	(74)	*(75)

INPATIENT MULTIDIMENSIONAL PSYCHIATRIC SCALE

SCORING SHEET

............EXCITEMENT (EXC)

7............		Unrestrained
* 9............		Hurried speech
12............		Elevated mood
15............		Superiority
17............		Dramatization
20............		Loud
26............		Overactive
*35............		Excess speech
37............		Dominates

............HOSTILE BELLIGERENCE (HOS)

* 5............		Verbal
11............		Contempt
18............		Attitude
*25............		Irritability
28............		Blames others
32............		Bitter
34............		Complaints
36............		Suspicious

............PARANOID PROJECTION (PAR)

44............		Delusional
*59............	×8	Reference
60............	×8	Persecution
*61............	×8	Conspiracy
62............	×8	People controlling
63............	×8	External controlling
68............	×8	Body destruction

............GRANDIOSE EXPANSIVENESS (GRN)

15............		Superiority
54............	×2	Voices extoll
*64............	×8	Unusual powers
65............	×8	Great personality
*69............	×8	Divine mission

............PERCEPTUAL DISTORTION (PCP)

45............		Hears voices
*53............	×2	Voices accuse
55............	×2	Voices threaten
*56............	×2	Voices order
57............	×2	Visions
58............	×2	Other hallucination
67............	×8	Ideas of change

............ANXIOUS INTROPUNITIVENESS (INP)

*14............		Blames self
*21............		Anxiety (specific)
24............		Apprehensive
27............		Self depreciating
29............		Depressed
31............		Guilt
39............	× −1	Insight
40............		Suicidal
41............		Obsessive
42............		Fears
66............	×8	Sinfulness
8		scoring constant

............RETARDATION AND APATHY (RTD)

* 1............		Slowed speech
8............		Lack of goals
13............		Fixed facies
*16............		Slowed movements
19............		Memory deficit
22............		Speech blocking
23............		Apathy
33............		Whispered speech
38............		Failure to answer

............Disorientation (DIS)

70............ × −1 Hospital
*71............ × −1 State
72............ × −1 Knows no one
73............ × −1 Season
74............ × −1 Year
*75............ × ......1 Age

6 scoring constant

............Motor Disturbances (MTR)

* 6............ Posturing
10............ Tension
30............ Slovenly
46............ ×2 Giggling
*47............ ×2 Grimacing
48............ ×2 Repet. movements
51............ ×2 Talks to self
52............ ×2 Startled glances

............Conceptual Disorganization (C

* 2............ Irrelevant
* 3............ Incoherent
4............ Rambling
49............ ×2 Neologisms
50............ ×2 Stereotypy

APPENDIX B

INPATIENT MULTIDIMENSIONAL PSYCHIATRIC SCALE

FIRST-ORDER FACTORS

Table B1

Orthogonal Factor Matrix F
(Decimal points omitted)

Scale number		Syndromes										
		EXC	HOS	PAR	GRN	PCP	INP	RTD	DIS	MTR	CNP	h_j^2
	7	73	15	−10	−01	03	12	06	−09	12	−02	61
	9	85	−07	05	−11	00	−01	−07	−02	−11	09	77
	12	54	−30	02	13	03	−18	−05	03	−07	−16	47
E	15	70	18	07	30	−04	−10	00	04	−07	−01	64
X	17	74	−01	−05	02	−01	09	−08	02	04	−14	59
C	20	81	14	−07	−04	05	00	05	−02	−01	01	69
	26	65	−06	03	−02	−01	10	11	−03	28	02	53
	35	86	−12	03	−08	−05	−02	−04	05	−09	13	79
	37	82	06	04	−08	−06	−01	03	02	−11	04	70
	5	40	75	01	06	01	09	−06	03	01	07	74
	11	64	39	−08	10	−01	−04	08	04	−03	−06	59
H	18	37	69	−22	01	−02	−02	16	−03	11	05	70
O	25	50	63	−20	−02	−01	05	13	−06	06	−01	71
S	28	36	64	29	−07	00	01	−16	06	−08	−03	65
	32	37	76	18	−03	06	11	−10	01	−03	−04	77
	34	51	62	03	−03	−04	09	−04	−02	−05	−01	66
	36	29	66	41	−01	−06	16	−02	04	−02	04	72

TABLE B1 (CONTINUED)

Scale Number		Syndromes										
		EXC	HOS	PAR	GRN	PCP	INP	RTD	DIS	MTR	CNP	h_j^2
	44	26	29	59	13	04	28	09	−05	−07	11	62
	59	07	24	63	00	−05	23	−12	01	06	00	53
P	60	29	58	45	00	−09	08	−06	02	03	−04	64
A	61	22	41	61	00	−02	13	−04	−04	−02	−04	61
R	62	16	19	65	02	03	14	−04	01	00	−02	51
	63	15	04	54	00	18	11	01	−04	−05	03	37
	68	09	16	17	05	08	22	−03	−01	08	12	14
	15	70	18	07	30	−04	−10	00	04	−07	−01	64
G	54	08	04	22	49	49	−02	09	05	−06	05	55
R	64	42	02	31	56	02	02	01	−06	−13	−04	61
N	65	13	−04	25	42	13	12	07	−03	−12	11	32
	69	20	−09	25	68	19	09	07	03	−04	09	63
	45	00	06	43	02	55	19	13	07	08	13	57
	53	−01	05	37	−13	62	26	01	−06	−02	−06	62
P	55	−01	09	35	−06	69	24	−02	02	04	−08	68
C	56	00	−01	36	13	54	08	10	04	01	02	46
P	57	06	05	31	11	44	18	07	−01	−07	02	35
	58	02	04	26	−07	44	11	01	−07	−04	−03	29
	67	−02	−04	32	12	24	30	03	01	05	06	27

TABLE B1 (CONTINUED)

Scale number		Syndromes										
		EXC	HOS	PAR	GRN	PCP	INP	RTD	DIS	MTR	CNP	h_j^2
	70	01	04	−03	00	−13	09	−13	60	−01	−20	44
D	71	01	05	06	02	−09	10	−30	67	−11	−21	62
I	72	05	01	02	−02	−06	01	−29	55	−06	−14	42
S	73	03	01	05	00	−01	06	−32	56	−16	−21	49
	74	02	01	−02	01	−09	08	−31	67	−14	−16	61
	75	06	06	03	−01	−04	15	−25	67	−11	−26	62
	6	15	−07	09	−02	01	01	51	−05	60	−04	66
	10	34	07	02	−07	01	32	20	00	32	04	37
M	30	19	01	00	01	02	−03	52	−05	15	03	33
T	46	22	−09	12	10	12	−17	15	02	34	04	26
R	47	20	−08	17	−12	01	−03	37	01	70	−01	72
	48	19	−12	12	−04	01	−05	30	02	65	01	58
	51	16	01	11	04	19	02	27	02	28	23	28
	52	12	08	20	−07	19	05	26	−08	34	06	30
	2	38	−13	29	−01	07	−01	38	−03	14	57	74
C	3	31	−12	24	−05	11	−04	31	02	15	62	69
N	4	60	−10	33	−06	−03	−01	22	07	06	38	68
P	49	29	−03	17	06	11	−11	12	06	06	42	34
	50	20	−02	06	06	00	−09	30	−12	07	47	39

TABLE B1 (CONTINUED)

Scale number		Syndromes										
		EXC	HOS	PAR	GRN	PCP	INP	RTD	DIS	MTR	CNP	h_j^2
	14	-09	-07	-08	05	-08	75	-06	03	-03	00	60
	21	01	11	00	-09	-05	68	-16	01	07	-10	53
	24	-07	05	06	01	00	73	-01	01	03	-04	55
	27	-15	-13	-06	00	-11	79	00	-05	01	03	68
I	29	-26	07	-14	-05	-05	68	29	-03	-03	-03	58
N	31	-11	-07	00	13	-05	74	01	00	-05	02	59
P	39	21	22	17	09	02	-40	35	04	00	11	43
	40	-09	05	-08	-06	10	65	-01	02	02	-01	45
	41	00	04	13	-01	21	56	-15	01	00	-02	40
	42	02	08	15	-05	01	45	-02	-04	02	10	25
	66	-07	-12	02	06	02	66	09	03	-02	08	48
	1	-38	-02	-08	00	-09	24	71	03	01	-06	73
	8	-14	-10	05	02	10	-17	52	04	03	03	35
	13	-38	04	05	-01	-04	06	60	04	-15	05	54
R	16	-40	-08	-13	-07	-04	28	66	02	-07	-08	72
T	19	-11	-06	05	-03	09	05	46	-24	-03	10	31
D	22	-16	-06	07	02	02	26	64	-06	15	01	54
	23	-39	-05	13	02	08	-12	61	06	-01	06	57
	33	-32	-06	-01	-01	01	22	63	01	-05	01	55
	38	-29	05	-08	03	-01	-01	72	-14	10	-01	64

TABLE B2

OBLIQUE FACTOR MATRIX V
CORRELATIONS OF SCALES WITH TEN SYNDROMES
(DECIMAL POINTS OMITTED)

SCALE NUMBER		SYNDROMES									
		EXC	HOS	PAR	GRN	PCP	INP	RTD	DIS	MTR	CNP
EXC	7	40	25	−10	07	04	13	00	−09	16	−04
	9	58	00	06	−03	00	00	−06	−02	−07	08
	12	50	−28	03	18	02	−17	02	03	02	−15
	15	34	23	02	36	−08	−15	05	04	02	00
	17	50	05	−02	10	02	09	−03	02	13	−15
	20	49	22	−07	04	05	00	05	−02	05	00
	26	38	04	−01	07	00	10	−03	−03	31	01
	35	58	−03	04	00	−05	00	−04	05	−05	15
	37	55	11	08	−01	−05	01	06	02	−05	04
HOS	5	−10	76	−03	10	01	01	−01	03	04	08
	11	29	42	−06	16	−02	−07	14	04	05	−05
	18	−06	74	−20	06	−03	−04	12	−03	12	04
	25	09	68	−16	03	−01	04	13	−06	09	−03
	28	−02	54	27	−04	02	−10	−03	06	−04	−01
	32	−05	70	14	00	08	−01	01	01	01	−04
	34	10	61	06	02	−03	04	04	−02	−01	−02
	36	−08	58	36	02	−04	02	04	04	00	05

Table B2 (Continued)

Scale number		Syndromes									
		EXC	HOS	PAR	GRN	PCP	INP	RTD	DIS	MTR	CNP
	14	02	03	-04	04	00	74	-04	03	-03	01
	21	01	15	04	-08	05	65	-11	01	08	-09
	24	00	10	05	01	08	68	00	01	03	-04
	27	01	-02	-02	-01	-03	80	-04	-05	-01	02
I	29	-02	13	-05	-08	03	68	26	-03	-07	-04
N	31	01	02	00	11	01	71	01	00	-05	02
P	39	05	18	11	11	-04	-44	29	04	01	12
	40	-01	12	-10	-07	18	61	00	02	01	00
	41	00	07	02	-01	27	46	-11	01	00	-02
	42	-02	12	10	-05	05	40	-06	-04	-01	09
	66	05	-02	-02	05	08	62	05	03	-03	09
	1	08	-02	03	-04	-05	26	61	03	06	-05
	8	06	-12	02	01	08	-19	41	04	02	04
	13	-15	-01	11	-06	-03	05	55	04	-18	06
R	16	06	-09	00	-11	01	31	60	02	-08	-07
T	19	08	-05	02	-04	06	06	30	-24	-10	03
D	22	07	-03	06	02	04	24	45	-06	12	-01
	23	-13	-11	10	-02	06	-16	50	06	-04	07
	33	04	-06	04	-05	04	21	54	01	-07	01
	38	-03	05	-04	01	-03	02	54	-14	06	-05

TABLE B2 (CONTINUED)

Scale number		Syndromes									
		EXC	HOS	PAR	GRN	PCP	INP	RTD	DIS	MTR	CNP
	70	06	00	01	00	−02	04	10	60	13	−03
D	71	01	−01	06	01	02	01	01	67	04	−02
I	72	01	−03	01	−02	03	−05	−05	55	06	01
S	73	05	−06	05	−01	09	−02	−01	56	−02	−05
	74	02	−03	00	00	02	02	00	67	00	03
	75	08	00	04	−01	09	06	07	67	06	−07
	6	08	−01	−01	04	01	02	20	−05	59	−05
	10	16	16	−02	−01	05	30	04	00	32	04
M	30	20	05	−01	04	00	−03	36	−05	14	02
T	46	05	−05	−05	15	08	−18	−02	02	34	04
R	47	04	−03	03	−04	02	−04	04	01	68	−01
	48	02	−05	−03	03	01	−04	00	02	64	02
	51	−02	09	−08	08	15	−05	04	02	24	23
	52	−01	09	05	−03	18	−02	06	−08	30	04
	2	13	01	07	04	−01	01	05	−03	04	54
C	3	04	02	00	−01	03	−03	−02	02	04	60
N	4	32	−02	20	00	−06	−02	04	07	03	38
P	49	02	07	−03	09	04	−11	−06	06	00	42
	50	−12	10	−08	08	−09	−02	03	−12	−03	42

TABLE B2 (CONTINUED)

Scale number		Syndromes									
		EXC	HOS	PAR	GRN	PCP	INP	RTD	DIS	MTR	CNP
	44	06	24	44	15	03	11	08	−05	−07	09
	59	−09	13	52	01	−03	09	−10	01	06	00
P	60	−05	47	41	03	−07	−05	00	02	06	−03
A	61	00	28	53	02	00	−02	01	−04	00	−05
R	62	03	07	53	04	04	−02	−01	01	02	−02
	63	10	−05	38	01	18	−02	01	−04	−05	02
	68	−08	19	05	06	08	14	−08	−01	06	11
	15	34	23	02	36	−08	−15	05	04	02	00
G	54	04	06	−12	49	41	−15	03	05	−02	06
R	64	22	03	16	59	−06	−03	−01	−06	−05	−05
N	65	05	00	06	42	06	07	00	−03	−10	10
	69	03	−01	−03	69	09	04	−04	03	02	09
	45	−06	03	05	03	54	−03	05	07	06	14
	53	06	−03	08	−13	65	07	03	−06	−03	−07
P	55	00	02	00	−06	72	04	01	02	05	−07
C	56	00	−05	02	13	52	−12	08	04	02	03
P	57	05	02	05	11	42	01	08	−01	−06	02
	58	05	−02	05	−07	44	−02	02	−07	−05	−05
	67	−06	−04	12	12	24	17	−02	01	04	06

TABLE B3
OBLIQUE TRANSFORMATION MATRIX
(DECIMAL POINTS OMITTED)

Orthogonal Axes	Final Oblique Axes									
	EXC	HOS	PAR	GRN	PCP	INP	RTD	DIS	MTR	CNP
Excitement	642	093		099					077	
Hostile Belligerence	−399	925				−085	082			
Paranoid Projection		−204	798			−188				
Grandiose Expansiveness	−197	111	−207	992	−136	035	−119		077	
Perceptual Distortion			−438		970	−198				
Anxious Intropunitiveness	094	111			107	942				
Retardation and Apathy	294		064				823			
Disorientation	−026		−115		116	−122	213	1.000	154	270
Motor Disturbance	−363	111	−215	078		030	−370		959	
Conceptual Disorganization	−403	240	−255		−126	119	−345		−211	963

APPENDIX C

INPATIENT MULTIDIMENSIONAL PSYCHIATRIC SCALE

HIGHER ORDER FACTORS

Table C1

Arbitrary Orthogonal Second-Order Factor Matrix
(Decimal points omitted)

First-Order Factors	Second-Order Factors I	II	III	H_J^2
Excitement	70	-05	38	64
Hostile Belligerence	63	06	00	40
Paranoid Projection	16	68	06	49
Grandiose Expansiveness	-02	43	-06	19
Perceptual Distortion	03	68	00	46
Anxious Intropunitiveness	-23	17	-23	13
Retardation and Apathy	-58	01	38	48
Disorientation	-26	10	57	41
Motor Disturbance	-06	11	61	39
Conceptual Disorganization	-03	34	60	47

Table C2

Transformation ψ_{pq} for Relating Scales to Second-Order Factors (Decimal points omitted)

First-Order Factors	Second-Order Factors		
	X	Y	Z
Excitement	996	-073	548
Hostile Belligerence	761	075	-001
Paranoid Projection	210	873	076
Grandiose Expansiveness	-017	460	-060
Perceptual Distortion	031	806	-004
Anxious Intropunitiveness	-238	182	-239
Retardation and Apathy	-773	015	512
Disorientation	306	-122	-683
Motor Disturbance	-075	127	725
Conceptual Disorganization	-041	453	797

TABLE C3

TRANSFORMATION FOR RELATING ORTHOGONAL AND OBLIQUE SECOND-ORDER FACTORS (DECIMAL POINTS OMITTED)

ORTHOGONAL	OBLIQUE		
	X	Y	Z
I	946	065	-410
II	-029	980	000
III	324	-186	912

TABLE C4

CORRELATIONS AMONG SECOND-ORDER FACTORS (DECIMAL POINTS OMITTED)

	X	Y	Z
X	1000		
Y	046	1000	
Z	099	200	1000

TABLE C5

THIRD-ORDER FACTOR MATRIX (DECIMAL POINTS OMITTED)

SECOND-ORDER FACTORS	TAU
X	152
Y	310
Z	672

APPENDIX D

TWO METHODS OF CLASSIFYING PSYCHOTICS

I. A Method for Categorizing Psychotics

The procedure is designed to determine whether or not a patient is a member of a type. Membership requirements are given in the section that follows.

The sequence of steps for allocating a patient to a type are:

(A) Record the IMPS raw scores on the syndromes. Then record the corresponding standard scores, e.g.:

Score	EXC	HOS	PAR	GRN	PCP	INP	RTD	DIS	MTR	CNP
Raw	68	30	13	30	12	12	13	38	20	21
Standard	6.6	5.0	4.4	6.4	5.0	4.2	4.2	5.1	4.9	5.6

(B) Inspect the syndrome standard scores which are most prominent and above the norm mean of 5.0. Select a type most similar to the patient in profile.

(C) Compare the patient's scores with the criteria defining the type. If he satisfies all criteria, he is assigned to that type. In the example above, the patient's scores are elevated on EXC and GRN, and below 5.4 on all other scores except CNP. Thus he is an EXC-GRN type.

Suppose a patient is "similar" to two types but does not clearly satisfy all of the criteria of either. An anxious and retarded patient is an example. Then count the number of instances that the patient is above (or below) the bounds established for the two classes considered. Assign him to the class where the number of errors is least. Of course, some patients will have scores that are all below the norm mean. Other patients will have highly irregular profiles. At present, no procedure has been developed for assigning such patients.

The criteria set for the six types are regarded as tentative and should be so considered.

CRITERIA FOR TYPE MEMBERSHIP

Excited-Grandiose

(a) 5.3 or higher on EXC and GRN
(b) Any score on CNP
(c) 5.4 or lower on all other syndromes

EXCITED-HOSTILE

(a) 5.1 or higher on EXC and HOS
(b) Any score on CNP
(c) 5.2 or lower on GRN
(d) 5.0 or lower on all other syndromes

INTROPUNITIVE

(a) 5.1 or higher on INP
(b) 5.8 or lower on RTD
(c) 5.4 or lower on all other syndromes

RETARDED

(a) 5.1 or higher on RTD
(b) 5.2 or lower on all other syndromes

HOSTILE-PARANOID

(a) 5.1 or higher on PAR and HOS
(b) 5.4 or lower on all other syndromes

DISORGANIZED

(a) 5.1 or higher on RTD, MTR, DIS, and CNP
(b) Any score on EXC
(c) 5.2 or lower on all other syndromes

II. A second tentative method of classifying psychotic patients into one of the six patient types is outlined below. Some investigators may wish to utilize the approach to classify patients in their research projects. The user should remember that the method is a preliminary procedure based on research findings to date. He should weigh carefully the cautions and limitations noted in Chapters 12 and 13 in any use of the scheme. The steps in the method are outlined and then an example is presented.

(A) Use the table of norms in the IMPS Manual (Lorr, Klett, McNair, and Lasky, 1962) to convert the patients' raw scores on IMPS to standardized syndrome scores.

(B) Multiply the patients' standardized syndrome scores by each of the following four rows of weights to obtain four canonical scores (R, S, T, U) for each patient. The syndrome weights are the coefficients (rounded and multiplied by 10) of the discriminant functions in Table 13.4. To simplify computations, a number of the smaller coefficients in Table 13.4 were dropped. When computer facilities are available, the investigator is advised to use all the coefficients in Table 13.4.

Canonical Score	Syndrome Weights									
	EXC	HOS	PAR	GRN	PCP	INP	RTD	DIS	MTR	CNP
R		−0.8		−0.7		−0.7	1.4	0.5	0.9	
S	0.9	−0.6		2.0		−0.7				
T		1.0	0.8			−1.2		0.5		−0.3
U		0.8	−0.7			1.1	−1.2	0.9		

(Signs of weights for R, S, and U are reflected.)

(C) Obtain D^2 between the patients' four canonical scores and the mean canonical scores of each of the six types. Thus six D^2s are computed for each patient by summing the squares of the differences between the patient's scores and the type means. The table below presents adjusted canonical means for the six types. The means below differ from those in Table 13.5 because only the rounded coefficients above were used to compute them from Table 13.1.

Patient Type	Adjusted Mean Canonical Score[1] R	S	T	U
Excited-Grandiose	1.69	12.49	3.96	5.59
Excited-Hostile	0.73	8.44	5.97	5.49
Retarded	5.07	6.75	3.16	3.74
Intropunitive	1.70	5.81	1.33	6.81
Paranoid	1.19	6.48	6.88	5.22
Disorganized	9.60	7.72	4.70	7.04

[1] The means are not always in the same rank order as in Table 13.5, but this occurs only for groups that were not discriminated by the variate.

(D) The patient may be assigned to the type to which he is most similar (minimum D^2) according to the following guides:

(1) If $D^2 \lesssim 10.0$ with any type he may be assigned to that type;
(2) If $D^2 \lesssim 15.0$ with the Disorganized type he may be assigned to that type;
(3) If $D^2 > 15.0$, he is probably not a member of any of the six types.

Note: Steps C and D can be eliminated for most cases, as the type classification will be obvious from comparing the patient's canonical scores with the group means.

Example:

A. The IMPS raw scores below were obtained for a patient and converted to standardized scores:

Score	EXC	HOS	PAR	GRN	PCP	INP	RTD	DIS	MTR	CNP
Raw	68	30	13	30	12	12	13	38	20	21
Standardized	6.6	5.0	4.4	6.4	5.0	4.2	4.2	5.1	4.9	5.6

B. The standardized scores were next multiplied by the four sets of weights and the following canonical scores were obtained:

$$R = 1.42 \qquad T = 4.35$$
$$S = 12.80 \qquad U = 5.09$$

C. The distances squared between the patient's canonical scores and the group mean canonical scores are next obtained; e.g., the distance from the Excited-Grandiose type is:

$$D^2 = (1.69 - 1.42)^2 + (12.49 - 12.80)^2 + (3.96 - 4.35)^2 + (5.59 - 5.09)^2$$

The distances squared between the patient and each of the six types are:

	D^2
Excited-Grandiose	0.7
Excited-Hostile	22.3
Retarded	53.2
Intropunitive	61.0
Paranoid	41.5
Disorganized	96.8

The patient should thus be classified as a member of the Excited-Grandiose type.

APPENDIX E

ILLUSTRATIVE CASE HISTORIES OF THE SIX PATIENT TYPES

THE CASE HISTORIES

After the six types were isolated an effort was made to secure independent clinical description of typed cases where they were available. As a consequence these illustrative cases lack uniformity and are far from ideal. At best the cases indicate broadly the social history backgrounds of such types. After each case summary the IMPS profile is given in standard score form.

EXCITED-GRANDIOSE

This 65-year-old white married male has been committed since 1959. He carries the diagnosis of pulmonary tuberculosis and manic-depressive reaction, manic type. The clinical record depicts a verbose, overfriendly, hyperactive, manipulative, expansive, belligerent, and grandiose veteran who ingeniously solicits privileges and promises from patients and personnel. Bizarrely dressed with pockets bulging with trivia, he often disturbs patients, albeit he acts without apparent malicious intent. Though well-oriented and in good contact with his environment, he exhibits marked psychomotor activity and is eccentric, even humorous. One evening he disturbed his entire ward by going through calisthenics, standing erectly on his bed.

He has been quite a management problem and goes on and off privilege status for various reasons. He frequently makes unauthorized phone calls, once to a brother-in-law (a former governor) to intercede for him. On another occasion he called a taxi, left the hospital and was returned by local authorities when he argued with a local tavern owner about the loss of his clothing. Confinement on maximum security and stern talks by the ward physician almost invariably but only temporarily make him docile and inoffensive. On regaining privilege status, he takes flight in overactivity. Distractible and impatient, he is not amenable to occupational therapy assignments.

He neither hallucinates nor exhibits crystallized delusions. But he exaggerates the truth about his material wealth and prestige with influential persons. Insight and judgment are lacking. He writes voluminous letters to the Director of the Hospital, the Chief of Staff, and his Ward Physician. Trial visits with his wife have dwindled for she cannot cope with his hyperkinetic behavior.

EXC	HOS	PAR	GRN	PCP	INP	RTD	DIS	MTR	CNP
8.9	4.2	3.9	5.2	4.3	4.0	3.9	5.6	4.6	6.3

EXCITED-HOSTILE

This is a first admission 38-year-old white male, who is unemployed, married, and has two children. His chief complaint for the previous week is feeling like he's "losing his mind". The patient dates onset of his difficulty to a time of transfer in the Air Force, when he was assigned to running the bar in the Officers' Club. He found the strain terrific because of inability to handle drunken officers. He began drinking heavily and after a year and a half was re-assigned to the Adjutant General's office, where he was dissatisfied with his rating as a typist. He feels he was disliked by the colonel in charge of the office because of difficulty he had had with him in the Officers' Club. Six months later he was broken to staff sergeant for drinking and transferred to Labrador, where he says he had nothing to do but drink. When he returned to the States in 1956, he cut down on drinking and worked nights as a bartender. In 1957 he was transferred to Germany, where he was shifted from one office to another because of excessive drinking. He requested and received an honorable discharge in 1960. He worked at various jobs after discharge and continued to drink heavily. He attended two AA meetings and drank only occasionally during the summer.

Six weeks before admission he decided to come to this city to look for work; he started drinking before getting on the bus, got into card games, and passed checks on an account he knew was closed. In his hotel room he proceeded to get drunker. Then he remembers playing poker and wandering around town writing bad checks. At his hotel room, he thought of jumping out the window but the idea struck him as so ridiculous he became hysterical. One day before admission he awoke in "somebody's boathouse". He felt ill, vomitted frequently and was so frightened by ideas flying through his head that he came to this hospital for help.

Following admission the patient acted anxious to please, making all kinds of promises never to get in trouble. He was a commendable worker at hospital jobs and had good memory and orientation. On the ward and in groups he was continuously boisterous and jocular because, he said, he would rather do that than cry. In spite of his promises and his anxiousness to please, he refused group or individual therapy because he felt he had only two problems—financial difficulties and fear of his wife's leaving him. One week before discharge, he received legal papers for his wife's divorce, which upset him considerably. His acting out became more marked. He became destructive and disturbing to other patients on his ward and was discharged. He was rated on IMPS one week prior to discharge. On MMPI shortly after admission he showed elevated scores on the Depression, Psychopathic Deviate, Paranoia, Psychasthenia, and Manic scales. He was diagnosed as a sociopathic personality with alcoholism.

EXC	HOS	PAR	GRN	PCP	INP	RTD	DIS	MTR	CNP
7.1	6.6	4.2	5.1	4.3	5.3	4.4	5.4	5.0	4.4

PARANOID

On admission the patient stated he heard voices. Sometimes they directed him to smother his wife as he stood over her with a pillow. For some years he had heard male voices talking to him, directing him to do things he didn't want, upsetting him so he could not sleep. His third wife stated he felt people were peeping in the window at him and someone was squeezing his chest. He had extremely poor insight. Commitment proceedings were begun by his wife after he tried to choke her with a pillow. She had also been up with him several nights and was exceedingly afraid of him. He did not want to remain hospitalized.

The patient has never associated with others, even as a child. He was not interested in activities around him and disliked being in groups. He quit school during the second grade. Recently, he has begun constant wandering about his home town in the early mornings. Sometimes he would be reported by townspeople and sometimes he called his wife to come after him. When he insisted on leaving home, she would call the police to restrain him and he would become angry with her for "putting the officers on me."

While hospitalized during February and March, he was inordinately hostile. At first, he would not attend entertainment or industrial and occupational therapy. A psychological report showed he did not take part in group therapy discussions. He objected that he was in the hospital against his will and wanted to go home. Phenothiazines partly alleviated his symptoms. He became pleasant, agreeable, and cooperative, participating in industrial and occupational therapy. During the last three weeks of hospitalization he became more relevant in his statements, expressed less hostility, and occasionally showed a sense of humor. He was diagnosed as a paranoid schizophrenic reaction.

EXC	HOS	PAR	GRN	PCP	INP	RTD	DIS	MTR	CNP
5.3	6.2	6.4	4.7	6.0	5.1	4.3	5.0	5.8	4.8

INTROPUNITIVE

This 64-year-old married, male patient complained of insomnia the last seven days before admission. Previous bouts of insomnia were noted in 1919, 1925, and 1945. Concurrent with the insomnia there was a seven pound weight loss over the last three or four months, decreased appetite and somatic complaints. He claims perfect health until 1919, when he was hospitalized for severe influenza and insomnia. In 1925 he again was hospitalized for insomnia. He did well until two weeks before the current admission, when he developed a flu syndrome. He reported agitation and frequent urination at night (up to fifteen times), eye irritation, tachycardia, and a warm, flushed feeling in his body. He felt no one could help him and life wasn't worth living. One week before admission he burned a cigarette into his leg; he felt he didn't have the courage to kill himself though he would like to. His wife felt he had been ill the last two or three months, increasingly withdrawn, not wanting to visit friends. The last two weeks he sat and stared.

Family history is almost noncontributory, due to the patient's vagueness and inability to talk effectively about his parents. He had previously exhibited an obsessive-compulsive personality. His childhood was marred by fear of being alone and rather high goals and standards were set for him. His mother ran the home and seemingly sacrificed for the children. He has gradually retired from work at the shipyards to manufacturing a tool in his basement from which he derives his total income.

The patient was assigned to a study in which various antidepressant drugs were compared but he began to sleep poorly, became agitated and quite uncomfortable. It was necessary to break the drug code and he was found to have been on dextroamphetamine. Subsequently he had various somatic complaints and believed the doctor was trying to kill him. He was placed on electroshock therapy for three weeks and became confused and "organic" in behavior. Following discontinuation of EST, he gradually changed for the better. He continued to give the definite clinical impression of being depressed yet began to eat and sleep well and socialize with other patients. He experienced a feeling of being "too alert" which on closer examination appeared to be mild agitation. The agitation was controlled quite well with Thorazine. Later he was given a work pass and did well. It was felt he could be managed on trial visit, although a moderate degree of depression remained. He made an excellent adjustment but re-established some of his compulsive defenses.

EXC	HOS	PAR	GRN	PCP	INP	RTD	DIS	MTR	CNP
4.1	4.3	4.2	4.4	4.3	7.4	5.7	4.0	4.6	4.2

RETARDED

The patient is an obese, 39-year-old, World War II veteran with brown hair and hazel eyes. Physical and neurological tests are negative, except for very dry lips. He has unusual somatic complaints, e.g., his stomach is "full of salt". He sits quietly, appears withdrawn and depressed, with markedly flattened affect. His speech is relatively slow, hesitant, monotonous, and very soft. He is oriented for time, place, and person and has good memory for past events. He denies hallucinations and ideas of reference. He states he is worthless and a drag to his family, although he claims his family is his only thing of value. He denies ideas of suicide or harming anyone. He avoids speaking about himself by asking questions or turning to irrelevant material.

In 1955 the patient was admitted to this hospital, but eloped after a year. His wife describes an unusual identification with his domineering older brother, whom he idolizes. He and the brother "fight like mad" when together, yet the patient seems strongly attached to him when separated. A suicide attempt by the brother in a mental hospital greatly affected the patient, leaving him feeling extremely guilty. Three of four siblings have emotional difficulties; his father was alcoholic and abusive, his mother passive-dependent. The patient presents a discouraged, disillusioned picture of himself, continually stating his family would be better off without him. He feels he deceived his wife into marrying him when he was twenty and she seventeen. He feels he kept her to himself rather than taking her around friends who might have pointed out his difficulties to her. His son is finishing high school and asked for career advice; the patient refuses to answer, saying he must make up his own mind.

During the interim between hospitalizations his work production was sparse and unstable, the longest work being eight months on a farm. He feels he is unable to work and support his family. He dropped out of his first year of high school to work. Several years ago he purchased a farm and during the past year spent eight months living alone and trying to work. He felt it would be better if he was completely removed from his family, but became so nervous and distraught he returned to the city. His wife states that before admission he was not working, was a chronic eloper, and, though previously abusive, became quite docile. His running around occasioned her calling the police and having him committed.

He is diagnosed a schizophrenic reaction, undifferentiated type, chronic.

EXC	HOS	PAR	GRN	PCP	INP	RTD	DIS	MTR	CNP
4.2	4.3	3.9	4.4	4.3	4.1	6.4	9.0	4.8	4.4

DISORGANIZED

This was the first admission for a 64-year-old white male. The patient's marked psychotic predisposition was shown by lifelong peculiarity of habits. He had not worked since discharge from service after World War I. He preferred staying at home with his sister and busying himself with household tasks. One month before admission, he began to complain of chest pains and was preoccupied with an inguinal hernia he had had for thirty years. He stated everything seemed hopeless and he would die. He became more withdrawn, refused to speak, ate little. He saw his local physician but didn't respond to the tranquilizers which were prescribed.

On admission he seemed confused and unable to talk, except for repetition of a few sentence fragments. He would answer questions with "yes" or "no" and appeared frightened and suspicious, with flattened affect and waxy flexibility. He was agitated, possibly hallucinating, but able to comply with simple commands. On the hospital's closed ward, he continued his depressed, mute, withdrawn behavior, with periodic motor retardation. He ate and slept poorly. At night he was particularly agitated, picking at his clothes, getting out of bed frequently, and behaving in a generally confused manner. He was diagnosed a chronic catatonic schizophrenic.

Three days after admission an IMPS rating was made and nurses described a probable Jacksonian seizure. It began with twitching of the left side of the mouth, spread to the left side of the body, and became generalized. An abnormal EEG and history of withdrawal of tranquilizers suggested metabolic encephalopathy. Repeat EEG's returned to normal limits, accompanied by improvement in the patient's psychotic state. He showed striking initial improvement in coherence of speech and interest in ward activities. He remained seclusive, confused at times, but cooperative regarding ward routine. The patient's niece stated that the seclusive, confused behavior was typical of him over the forty years she had known him.

EXC	HOS	PAR	GRN	PCP	INP	RTD	DIS	MTR	CNP
6.2	4.9	5.8	5.8	5.1	4.9	6.5	7.0	7.4	6.7

APPENDIX F

SYNDROME-BASED TYPES

DISCRIMINANT ANALYSIS

TABLE F1

IMPS: DISCRIMINANT ANALYSIS
BETWEEN GROUPS VARIANCE–COVARIANCE MATRIX

	EXC	HOS	PAR	GRN	PCP	INP	RTD	DIS	MTR	CNP
EXCITEMENT	99.2142									
HOSTILE BELLIGERENCE	35.8362	85.9604								
PARANOID PROJECTION	4.5623	45.2937	45.6870							
GRANDIOSE EXPANSIVENESS	51.4201	.7884	.7330	36.8878						
PERCEPTUAL DISTORTION	- 1.2546	- .3016	4.7716	.2310	2.1439					
ANXIOUS INTROPUNITIVENESS	-34.1482	-23.6745	-11.5171	-12.1396	- 4.2768	52.9500				
RETARDATION AND APATHY	-54.6531	-52.7561	-26.2122	-28.2362	4.6479	- 8.1021	78.3700			
DISORIENTATION	-16.5790	-39.4887	-19.4379	-14.0208	11.0934	-27.7562	76.3414	135.4860		
MOTOR DISTURBANCE	1.6897	-34.8526	-17.6057	.2728	8.8426	-23.2678	53.3091	105.7030	86.2730	
CONCEPTUAL DISORGANIZATION	32.8945	-16.2893	-13.0396	17.0484	6.0859	-31.7801	25.2018	73.3026	64.6117	59.1980

TABLE F2

IMPS: DISCRIMINANT ANALYSIS

WITHIN GROUPS VARIANCE–COVARIANCE MATRIX

	EXC	HOS	PAR	GRN	PCP	INP	RTD	DIS	MTR	CNP
Excitement	40.9573									
Hostile Belligerence	9.2814	34.2849								
Paranoid Projection	4.6142	11.8449	30.6851							
Grandiose Expansiveness	3.4181	5.6096	6.2093	16.3783						
Perceptual Distortion	5.5928	- 1.2745	11.3426	3.8922	33.5456					
Anxious Intropunitiveness	- 2.1557	.0663	7.7693	6.8535	6.0565	35.7370				
Retardation and Apathy	- 8.5381	3.2543	- .5156	4.3558	- 1.5559	11.4585	26.9250			
Disorientation	- .1269	- 1.8039	.7820	- .1292	5.3956	5.9885	4.9781	40.5259		
Motor Disturbance	14.9573	9.1713	2.4937	5.6026	5.9527	- .5854	- 2.2561	9.1995	43.2687	
Conceptual Disorganization	17.5663	6.3604	3.8904	- .7382	5.0225	-10.5288	.2168	5.3449	16.8160	61.0796

REFERENCES

ACKERKNECHT, E. H., *A short history of psychiatry*, Hafner, New York, 1959.

ALLPORT, G. W., and ODBERT, H. S., "Trait names: Psycho-lexical study", *Psychol. Monogr.*, 1936, 47, No. 211.

AMERICAN MEDICAL ASSOCIATION, *Fourth edition of the standard nomenclature of diseases and operations*, Commonwealth Fund, New York, 1952.

AMERICAN PSYCHIATRIC ASSOCIATION, *Diagnostic and statistical manual for mental disorders*, Mental Hospital Service, Washington, 1952.

AMERICAN PSYCHOLOGICAL ASSOCIATION, "Technical recommendations for psychological tests and diagnostic techniques", *Psychol. Bull. Supplement*, 1954, 51, 1–38.

ARIETI, S., "Manic-depressive psychosis", In S. Arieti (Ed.), *American handbook of psychiatry*, Basic Books, New York, 1959, pp. 419–454.

ASH, P., "The reliability of psychiatric diagnoses", *J. abnorm. soc. Psychol.*, 1949, 44, 272.

AZIMA, H., DUROST, H., and ARTHURS, DOROTHY, "The effects of thioridazine (Mellaril) on mental syndromes. Comparison with chlorpromazine and promazine", *Canad. M. A. J.*, 1959, 31, 549–553.

BECHTOLDT, H. P., "Statistical tests of hypotheses in confirmatory factor analysis", *Amer. Psychol.*, 1958, 13, 380 (Abstract).

BECHTOLDT, H. P., "Factor analysis and the investigation of hypotheses", *Perc. & Motor Skills*, 1962, 14, 319–342.

BECK, A. T., "Reliability of psychiatric diagnoses: 1. A critique of systematic studies", *Amer. J. Psychiat.*, 1962, 119, 210–216.

BECK, A. T., WARD, C. H., MENDELSON, M., MOCK, J. E., and ERBAUGH, J. K., "Reliability of psychiatric diagnoses: 2. A study of consistency of clinical judgments and ratings", *Amer. J. Psychiat.*, 1962, 119, 351–357.

BLAIR, H. W., *A factor analytic study of the social behavior of schizophrenics*, Ann Arbor: Univ. of Michigan, 1952.

BLEULER, E., *Dementia praecox*, International Univ. Press, New York, 1950.

BLEWETT, D. B., and STEFANIUK, W. B., "Weyburn assessment scale", *J. ment. Sci.*, 1958, 104, 359–371.

BOISEN, A., "Types of dementia praecox", *Psychiat.*, 1938, 1, 233.

BOSTIAN, D. W., SMITH, P. A., LASKY, J. J., HOVER, R. J., and GING, ROSALIE J., "Empirical observations on mental-status examination", *Archives gen. Psychiat.*, 1959, 1. 253–262.

Braceland, F. J., "Kraepelin, his system and his influence", *Amer. J. Psychiat.*, 1957, 113, 871–876.

Burt, C., *The factors of the mind*, Univ. of London Press, London, 1940.

Burt, C., "Group factor analyses", *Brit. J. Psychol., Stat. Sect.*, 1950, 3, 40–75.

Cameron, N., "The functional psychoses", in J. McV. Hunt (Ed.), *Personality and the behaviour disorders*, Vol. 2. Ronald Press, New York, 1944, pp. 861–921.

Cameron, N., *The psychology of behavior disorders*, Houghton Mifflin, Boston, 1947.

Cameron, N., "Paranoid conditions and paranoia", in S. Arieti (Ed.), *American handbook of psychiatry*. Basic Books, New York, 1959, pp. 508–539.

Campbell, D. T., and Fiske, D. M., "Convergent and discriminant validation by the multitrait–multimethod matrix", *Psychol. Bull.*, 1959, 56, 81–105.

Casey, J. F., Hollister, L. E., Klett, C. J., Lasky, J. J., and Caffey, E. M., Jr., "Combined drug therapy of chronic schizophrenics: A controlled evaluation of placebo, dextroamphetamine, imipramine, isocarboxazid and trifluoperazine added to maintenance doses of chlorpromazine", *Amer. J. Psychiat.*, 1961, 117, 997–1003.

Cattell, R. B., "The description of personality. 1. Foundations of trait measurement", *Psychol. Rev.*, 1940, 50, 559–594.

Cattell, R. B., "A note on correlation clusters and cluster search methods", *Psychometrika*, 1944, 9, 169–185.

Cattell, R. B., "r_p and other coefficients of pattern similarity", *Psychometrika*, 1949, 14, 279–298.

Cattell, R. B., "The three basic factor-analytic research designs—their inter-relations and derivatives", *Psychol. Bull.*, 1952, 49, 499–520.

Cattell, R. B., *Personality and motivation structure and measurement*, World Book, New York, 1957.

Cattell, R. B., and Dickman, K., "A dynamic model of physical influences demonstrating the necessity of oblique simple structure", *Psych. Bull.*, 1962, 59, 389–400.

Cattell, R. B., and Scheier, I., *Neuroticism and anxiety*, Ronald Press, New York, 1961.

Cavenny, E. L., Wittson, C., Hunt, W. A., and Herrman, R. F., "Psychiatric diagnosis, its nature and function", *J. nerv. ment. Dis.*, 1955, 121, 367.

Chodoff, P., "The problem of psychiatric diagnosis: Can biochemistry and neurophysiology help?", *Psychiatry*, 1960, 23, 185–191.

Cliff, N., "Adverbs as multipliers", *Psychol. Rev.*, 1959, 66, 27–43.

Cronbach, L. J., and Gleser, G. C., "Assessing similarity between profiles", *Psychol. Bull.*, 1953, 50, 456–476.

Dahlstrom, W. G., "An exploration of mental status syndromes by a factor analytic technique", Unpubl. doctor's thesis: Univ. of Minnesota, 1949.

DEGAN, J. W., "Dimensions of functional psychosis", *Psychometric Monogr.*, 1952, No. 6.

DU MAS, F. M., "The coefficient of profile similarity", *J. Clin. Psychol.*, 1949, 5, 123–131.

DU MAS, F. M., *Manifest structure analysis*, Montana State Univ. Press, Missoula, 1955.

EBEL, R., "Estimation of the reliability of ratings", *Psychometrika*, 1951, 16, 407–424.

EKMAN, G., "On typological and dimensional systems of reference in describing personality", *Acta. Psychol.*, 1951, 8, 1–24.

ELLSWORTH, R. B., *The MACC behaviour adjustment scale*, Western Psychological Services, Los Angeles, 1957.

EYSENCK, H. J., *Dimensions of personality*, Kegan Paul, London, 1947.

EYSENCK, H. J., *The Structure of human personality*, Wiley & Sons, New York, 1953.

EYSENCK, H. J., "Classification and the problem of diagnosis", in H. J. EYSENCK (Ed.), *Handbook of abnormal psychology*, Basic Books, New York, 1960, pp. 1–31.

FENICHEL, O., *The psychoanalytic theory of neurosis*, Norton, New York, 1945.

FINNEY, B. C., *Palo Alto group psychotherapy scale*, Veterans Admin. Hosp., Palo Alto, 1957.

FOULDS, G. A., "Reliability of psychiatric and validity of psychological diagnoses", *J. ment. Sci.*, 1955, 101, 851.

FREUDENBERG, R. K., and ROBERTSON, J. P. S., "Symptoms in relation to psychiatric diagnosis and treatment", *Arch. Neurol. Psychiat.*, 1956, 76, 14–22.

FROMM, E., *Man for himself*, Rinehart, New York, 1947.

GLESER, G., "Logical constructs underlying various methods of grouping persons", in Lindley, C. J. (Ed.), *Transactions, annual research conference, VA cooperative studies in psychiatry*, Vol. 6. Washington: Dept. Med. Surg., 1961, pp. 130–133.

GRINKER, R. R. JR., MILLER, J., SABSHIN, M., NUNN, R., and NUNNALLY, J. C., *The phenomena of depressions*, Hoeber, New York, 1961.

GUERTIN, W. H., "A factor-analytic study of schizophrenic symptoms", *J. consult. Psychol.*, 1952, 16, 308–312.

GUERTIN, W. H., "An inverted factor analytic study of schizophrenics", *J. consult. Psychol.*, 1952, 16, 371–375.

GUERTIN, W. H., "A factor analysis of schizophrenic ratings on the hospital adjustment scale", *J. clin. Psychol.*, 1955, 10, 70–73.

GUERTIN, W. H., "A transposed analysis of paranoid schizophrenics", *Psychol. Reports*, 1958, 4, 591–594.

GUERTIN, W. H., "Empirical syndrome groupings of schizophrenic hospital admissions", *J. clin. Psychol.*, 1961, 17, 268–275.

GUERTIN, W. H., and JENKINS, R. L., "A transposed factor analysis of a group of schizophrenic patients", *J. clin. Psychol.*, 1956, 12, 64–68.

GUERTIN, W. H., and KRUGMAN, A. D., "A factor analytically derived scale for rating activities of psychiatric patients", *J. clin. Psychol.*, 1959, 15, 32–35.

GUILFORD, J. P., "When not to factor analyze", *Psychol. Bull.*, 1952, 49, 26–37.

GUILFORD, J. P., "Dimensions of intellect", *International colloquium on factor analysis*, Paris, 1955.

GULLIKSEN, H., *Theory of mental tests*, Wiley, New York, 1950.

GUTTMAN, L., "The quantification of a class of attributes. Suppl. Study B-3", *The prediction of personal adjustment*, Soc. Sci. Res. Council, New York, 1941.

GUTTMAN, L., "Multiple group methods for common-factor analysis: their bases, computation and interpretation", *Psychometrika*, 1952, 17, 209–222.

GUTTMAN, L., "A new approach to factor analysis: the radex", in P. F. Lazarsfeld, (Ed.), *Mathematical thinking in the social sciences*, Free Press, Glencoe, Ill., 1954.

HAGGARD, E. A., *Intraclass correlation and the analysis of variance*, Dryden Press, New York, 1958.

HAMILTON, M., "A rating scale for depression", *J. Neurol. Neurosurg. & Psychiat.*, 1960, 23, 56–62.

HAMILTON, M., and WHITE, J. M., "Clinical syndromes in depressive states", *J. ment. Sci.*, 1959, 105, 987–998.

HARMAN, H. H., *Modern factor analysis*, Univ. of Chicago Press, Chicago, 1960.

HOLZINGER, K. J., and HARMAN, H. H., *Factor analysis*, Univ. of Chicago Press, Chicago, 1941.

HORNEY, KAREN., *Our inner conflicts*, Norton, New York, 1945.

HUMPHRIES, L. G., "Characteristics of type concepts with special reference to Sheldon's typology", *Psychol. Bull.*, 1957, 54, 218–228.

JENKINS, R. L., "Symptomatology and dynamics in diagnosis: A medical perspective," *J. clin. Psychol.*, 1953, 9, 149–150.

JENKINS, R. L., and ACKERSON, L., "The study of types as a statistical method", *J. juv. Res.*, 1933, 17, 1–9.

JENKINS, R. L., BEMISS, E. L. JR., and LORR, M., "Duration of hospitalization, readmission rate and stability of diagnoses in veterans hospitalized with neuropsychiatric diagnosis", *Psychiat. Quart.*, 1953, 27, 59–72.

JENKINS, R. L., and LORR, M., "Type-tracking among psychotic patients", *J. clin. Psychol.*, 1954, 10, 114–119.

JONES, L. V., and BOCK, R. D., *Multiple discriminant analysis applied to "ways to live" ratings of six cultural groups*, Psychometric Lab., Univ. of N. Carolina, Chapel Hill, 1958.

JONES, M. B., *Molar correlational analysis*, U. S. Naval School of Aviation Medicine, Pensacola, 1960.

KAISER, H. F., "The varimax criterion for analytic rotation in factor analysis", *Psychometrika*, 1958, 23, 187–200.

KEMPF, E. J., "The behavior chart in mental disease", *Amer. J. Insanity*, 1914–15, 71, 761–772.

KENDALL, M. G., *Rank correlation methods*, Griffin, London, 1948.

KRAEPELIN, E., *Lehrbuch der psychiatrie*. (A. R. Diependorf, Tr.), MacMillan, New York, 1923.

KREITMAN, N., "The reliability of psychiatric diagnosis", *J. ment. Sci.*, 1961, 107, 876–886.

KREITMAN, N., SAINSBURY, P., MORRISSEY, J., TOWERS, J., and SCRIVNER, J., "The reliability of psychiatric assessment: an analysis", *J. ment. Sci.*, 1961, 107, 887–908.

LASKY, J. J., KLETT, C. J., CAFFEY, E. M. JR., BENNETT, J. L., ROSENBLUM, M. P., and HOLLISTER, L. E., "Drug treatment of schizophrenic patients: a comparative evaluation of chlorpromazine, chlorprothixene, fluphenazine, reserpine, thioridazine, and triflupromazine", *Dis. nerv. System*, 1962, 23, 698–706.

LEWIS, N. D. C., *A short history of psychiatric achievement*, Chapman & Hall, London, 1942.

LOEVINGER, JANE., "Objective tests as instruments of psychological theory", *Psychol. Reports*, 1957, 3, 635–694.

LOEVINGER, JANE, GLESER, G. C., and DUBOIS, P. H., "Maximizing the discriminating power of a multiple-choice test", *Psychometrika*, 1953, 18, 309–317.

LORR, M., "Multidimensional scale for rating psychiatric patients", *Vet. Adm. Tech. Bull.*, 10–507, 1953.

LORR, M., "Rating scales and check lists for the evaluation of psychopathology", *Psychol. Bull.*, 1954, 51, 119–127.

LORR, M., "The Wittenborn psychiatric syndromes: an oblique rotation", *J. consult. Psychol.*, 1957, 21, 439–444.

LORR, M., "Rating scales, behavior inventories, and drugs", in L. Uhr, and J. G. Miller (Ed.), *Drugs and behavior*, Wiley, New York, 1960, pp. 519–539.

LORR, M., and FIELDS, V., "A factorial study of body types", *J. clin. Psychol.*, 1954, 10, 182–185.

LORR, M., JENKINS, R. L., and HOLSOPPLE, J. Q., "Factors descriptive of chronic schizophrenics selected for the operation of prefrontal lobotomy", *J. consult. Psychol.*, 1954, 18, 293–296.

LORR, M., JENKINS, R. L., and O'CONNOR, J. P., "Factors descriptive of psychopathology and behavior of hospitalized psychotics", *J. abnorm. soc. Psychol.*, 1955, 50, 78–86.

LORR, M., KLETT, C. J., MCNAIR, D. M., and LASKY, J. J. *Inpatient multidimensional psychiatric scale, manual*, Consult. Psychol. Press, Palo Alto, 1963.

LORR, M., MCNAIR, D. M., KLETT, C. J., and LASKY, J. J., "Evidence of ten psychotic syndromes", *J. consult. Psychol.*, 1962, 26, 185–189.

LORR, M., and O'CONNOR, J. P., "The relation between neurosis and psychosis: a re-analysis", *J. ment. Sci.*, 1957, 103, 375–380.

LORR, M., and O'CONNOR, J. P., "Psychotic symptom patterns in a behavior inventory", *Educ. Psychol. Measmt.*, 1962, 22, 139–146.

LORR, M., O'CONNOR, J. P., and STAFFORD, J. W., "Confirmation of nine psychotic symptom patterns", *J. clin. Psychol.*, 1957, 13, 252–257.

LORR, M., O'CONNOR, J. P., and STAFFORD, J. W., "The psychotic reaction profile", *J. clin. Psychol.*, 1960, 16, 241-245.

LORR, M., WITTMAN, P., and SCHANBERGER, W., "An analysis of the Elgin prognostic scale", *J. clin. Psychol.*, 1951, 7, 260–263.

LUBIN, A., "Linear and non-linear discriminating functions", *Brit. J. Psychol., Statist. Sect.*, 1950, 3, 90–104.

LUBIN, A., and OSBURN, H. G., "A theory of pattern analysis for the prediction of a quantitative criterion", *Psychometrika*, 1957, 22, 63–73.

LUCERO, R. J., and MEYER, B. T., "A behavior rating scale suitable for use in mental hospitals", *J. clin. Psychol.*, 1951, 7, 250–254

LYKKEN, D. T., "A method of actuarial pattern analysis", *Psychol. Bull.*, 1956, 53, 102–108.

MARSCHAK, J., "Probability in the social sciences", in P. F. Lazarsfeld (Ed.), *Mathematical thinking in the social sciences*, Free Press, Glencoe, Ill., 1954.

MCNEMAR, Q., *Psychological Statistics*, (2nd ed.) Wiley, New York, 1955.

MCQUITTY, L. L., "Pattern analyses illustrated in classifying patients and normals", *Educ. Psychol. Measmt.*, 1954, 14, 598–604.

MCREYNOLDS, P., "Delusional thinking and cognitive organization in schizophrenia", Unpublished abstract, 1963.

MCREYNOLDS, P., BALLACHEY, E. L., and FERGUSON, J. T., "Development and evaluation of a behavior scale for appraising the adjustment of hospitalized patients", *Amer. Psychol.*, 1952, 7, 340 (Abstract).

MALAMUD, W., and Sands, S. L., "A revision of the psychiatric rating scale", *Amer. J. Psychiat.*, 1947, 104, 231–237.

MASSERMAN, J., and CARMICHAEL, H., "Diagnosis and prognosis in psychiatry", *J. ment. Sci.*, 1938, 84, 59.

MEEHL, P. E., "Configural scoring", *J. consult. Psychol.*, 1950, 14, 165–171.

MEEHL, P. E., "Some ruminations on the validation of clinical procedures", *Canad. J. Psychol.*, 1959, 13, 102–128.

MEEHL, P. E., "Schizotaxia, schizotypy, schizophrenia", *Amer. Psychol.*, 1962, 17, 827–838.

MEHLMAN, B., "The reliability of psychiatric diagnoses", *J. abnorm. soc. Psychol.*, 1952, 47, 577.

MENNINGER, K., "The practice of psychiatry", *Dig. Neurol. Psychiat,.* 1955, 23, 101.

MONRO, A. B., "Psychiatric types: A Q-technique study of 200 patients", *J. ment. Sci.*, 1955, 101, 330–343.

MOORE, T. V., "The essential psychoses and their fundamental syndromes", *Stud. Psychol. & Psychiat.*, 1933, 3, 1–128.

MUNCIE, W., *Psychobiology and psychiatry*, C. V. Mosley, St. Louis, 1948.

MUNROE, RUTH L., *Schools of psychoanalytic thought*, Dryden Press, New York, 1955.

NORRIS, V., *Mental illness in London*, Maudsley Monogr. No. 6, Chapman & Hall, London, 1959.

ORR, D. B., "A new method for clustering jobs", *J. appl. Psychol.*, 1960, 44, 44–49.

OVERALL, J. E., HOLLISTER, L. E., POKORNY, A. D., CASEY, J. F., and KATZ, G., "Drug therapy in depressions: controlled evaluation of imipramine, isocarboxazid, dextroamphetamine-amobarbital and placebo", *Clin. Pharmacol. & Therapeut.*, 1962, 3, 16–22.

PASAMANICK, B., DINITZ, S., and LEFTON, L., "Psychiatric orientation in relation to diagnosis and treatment", *Amer. J. Psychiat.*, 1959, 116, 127.

PAYNE, R. W., and HEWLETT, J. H. G., "Thought disorder in psychotic patients", in H. J. Eysenck (Ed.), *Experiments in personality*, II, Routledge & Kegan Paul, London, 1960.

PHILLIPS, L., and RABINOVITCH, M. S., "Social role and patterns of symptomatic behaviors", *J. abnorm. soc. Psychol.*, 1958, 57, 181–186.

PLANT, J. S., "Rating scheme for conduct", *Amer. J. Psychiat.*, 1922, 1, 547–572.

POKORNY, A. D., "Psychiatric classification", in C. J. Lindley (Ed.), *Transactions, annual research conference, VA cooperative studies in psychiatry*, Vol. 6, Dept. Med. Surg., Washington, 1961, pp. 110–115.

RAJARATNAM, N., CRONBACH, L. J., and GLESER, G., *Reliability as generalizability*, Bureau Educ. Research, Urbana, Ill., 1960.

RAO, C. R., *Advanced statistical methods in biometric research*, Wiley, New York, 1952.

RAO, C. R., and SLATER, P., "Multivariate analyses applied to differences between neurotic groups", *Brit. J. Psychol., Statist. Sect.*, 1949, 2, 17.

RISS, E., "Are hallucinations illusions? An experimental study of non-veridical perception", *J. Psychol.*, 1959, 48, 367–373.

ROSENZWEIG, S., "The experimental measurement of types of reaction to frustration", in Henry Murray (Ed.), *Explorations in personality*. Oxford Univ. Press, New York, 1938, pp. 585–599.

ROTTER, J., *Social learning and clinical psychology*, Prentice–Hall, New York, 1954.

SAGEBEER, R., "Identifying patterns of ability", in *Educ. Rec. Sup.*, Educational Records Bureau, New York, 1938, p. 19.

SAUNDERS, D. R., and SCHUCMAN, HELEN., "Syndrome analysis: an efficient procedure for isolating meaningful subgroups in a non-random sample of a population", Paper read at 3rd Annual Psychonomic Society Meeting, St. Louis, Mo., Sept., 1962.

SAWREY, W. L., KELLER, L., and CONGER, J. J., "An objective method of grouping profiles by distance functions and its relation to factor analysis", *Educ. & Psychol. Measmt.*, 1960, 20, 651–673.

SCHANBERGER, W. J., "A factorial investigation of some theoretical distinctions between anxiety and guilt feelings", *Stud. Psychol. & Psychiat.*, 1950, 10, 1–65.

SCHMIDT, H. O., and FONDA, C., The reliability of psychiatric diagnoses: a new look, *J. abnorm. soc. Psychol.*, 1956, 52, 262.

SCHNECK, J. M., *A history of psychiatry*, Charles C. Thomas, Springfield, Ill., 1960.

SOMERVILLE, D. M., COHEN, P. H., and GRAVES, GWEN. D., "Phenothiazine side-effects. Comparison of two major tranquilizers", *J. ment. Sci.*, 1960, 106, 1417–1424.

STAMMEYER, E. C., "An isolation of psychiatric symptom pictures applying the common elements approach of statistical analysis", Unpublished master's dissertation, Catholic Univ., Washington, 1958.

STEPHENSON, W., "Some observations on Q-technique", *Psychol. Bull.*, 1952, 49, 483–498.

STEPHENSON, W., *The study of behavior. Q-technique and its methodology*, Univ. of Chicago Press, Chicago, 1953.

STILSON, D. W., "A comparison of pattern and factor analytic results" *Amer. Psychol.*, 1955, 10, 479.

SULLIVAN, C., GRANT, MARGUERITE Q., and GRANT, J. D., "The development of interpersonal maturity: applications to delinquency", *Psychiatry*, 1957, 20, 373–385.

SULLIVAN, H. S., *Conceptions of modern psychiatry*, The William Alanson White Psychiatric Foundation, Washington, 1947.

SZASZ, T. S., "The problem of psychiatric nosology", *Amer. J. Psychiat.*, 1957, 114, 405–413.

SZASZ, T. S., *The myth of mental illness*, Hoeber, New York, 1961.

THOMSON, G. "*The factorial analysis of human ability*", (5th ed.) Houghton Mifflin, New York, 1951.

THORNDIKE, R. L., "Who belongs in the family?" *Psychometrika*, 1953, 18, 267–276.

THURSTONE, L. L., "The vectors of mind", *Psychol. Rev.*, 1933, 41, 1–32.

THURSTONE, L. L., *Analysis of body measurements*, Psychometric Lab., Chicago, 1946.

THURSTONE, L. L., *Multiple-factor analysis*, Univ. of Chicago Press, Chicago, 1947.

TOOPS, H. A., "The use of addends in experimental control, social census, and managerial research", *Psychol. Bull.*, 1948, 45, 41–74.

TORGERSON, W. S., *Theory and methods of scaling*, Wiley, New York, 1958.

TROUTON, D. S., and MAXWELL, A. E., "The relation between neurosis and psychosis", *J. ment. Sci.*, 1956, 102, 1–21.

TUCKER, L., *The role of correlated factors in factor analysis*, Psychometrika, 1940, 5, 141–152.

VIETH, ILZA., "Psychiatric nosology: from Hippocrates to Kraepelin", *Amer. J. Psychiat.*, 1957, 114, 385–391.

WALDROP, F. N., ROBERTSON, R. H., and VAURLEKIS, A., "A comparison of the therapeutic and toxic effects of thioridazine and chlorpromazine in chronic schizophrenic patients", *Comprehensive Psychiatry*, 1961, 2, 96–105.

WARD, C. H., BECK, A. T., MENDELSON, M., MOCK, J. E., and ERBAUGH, J. K., "The psychiatric nomenclature", *Arch. gen. Psychiat.*, 1962, 7, 198–205.

WITTENBORN, J. R., "A new procedure for evaluating mental hospital patients", *J. consult. Psychol.*, 1950, 14, 500–501.

WITTENBORN, J. R., "Symptom patterns in a group of mental hospital patients", *J. consult. Psychol.*, 1951, 15, 290–302.

WITTENBORN, J. R., *Psychiatric rating scales*, Psychological Corp., New York, 1955.

WITTENBORN, J. R., "The dimensions of psychosis", *J. nerv. ment. Dis.*, 1962, 134, 117–128.

WITTENBORN, J. R., and BAILEY, C., "The symptoms of involutional psychosis", *J. consult. Psychol.*, 1952, 16, 13–17.

WITTENBORN, J. R., HERZ, M. I., KURTZ, K. H., MANDELL, W., and TATZ, A., "The effect of rater differences on symptom rating scale clusters", *J. consult. Psychol.*, 1952, 16, 107–109.

WITTENBORN, J. R., and HOLZBERG, J. D., "The generality of psychiatric syndromes", *J. consult. Psychol.*, 1951, 15, 372–380.

WITTENBORN, J. R., and PLANTE, M., "A comparison of physicians and nurses' symptom ratings", Unpublished NIMH Grant Study, 1961.

WITTENBORN, J. R., and WEISS, W., "Patients diagnosed manic depressive psychosis, manic state", *J. consult. Psychol.*, 1952, 16, 193–198.

YOUNG, G., and HOUSEHOLDER, A. S., "Factorial invariance and significance", *Psychometrika*, 1940, 5, 47–56.

ZIGLER, E., and PHILLIPS, L., "Psychiatric diagnoses and symptomatology", *J. abnorm. soc. Psychol.*, 1961, 63, 69–75.

ZILBOORG, G., *A history of medical psychology*, Norton, New York, 1941.

ZUBIN, J., "A technique for measuring likemindedness", *J. abnorm. soc. Psychol.*, 1938, 33, 508–516.

AUTHOR INDEX

SUBJECT INDEX